Selling For Dummies™

Cheat Sheet

1. Prospecting

It's all a matter of numbers.

1. Itch Cycle: People invest in certain products on a regular basis. Learn what that is for your product and find current customers who may be getting ready to "itch."

2. Orphan Adoption: Has anyone left your company recently? Are there old files on past customers? Get permission to adopt these orphan accounts.

3. Technical Advancement: Finding a new feature or having a new product that you can offer your existing clients or those who are currently using the competition's product that doesn't have these features.

The "Thank You" Business Card Technique: Write the words "Thank You" on the front of your business card before you hand it to someone. When they ask you why it's there, you can say, "I'm thanking you in advance for the opportunity to someday serve your ______ needs."

2. Original Contact

My goal is to have my clients like me and trust me.

1. I begin with a smile — almost a grin.

2. I look them in the eyes.

3. I repeat their name to myself at least four times.

4. I'm prepared to shake hands, if offered.

3. Qualification

I am always looking for ways to find my prospect's true N.E.A.D.S.

N What do they have NOW?

E What do they ENJOY most about what they have now?

A What would they ALTER or change about what they have now?

D Who is the final DECISION–MAKER?

S As a professional, it's my responsibility to help them find the best SOLUTION to their needs.

4. Steps to Handling Objections

Hear them out.

Feed the objection back.

Question the objection.

Answer the objection.

Confirm the answer.

Change gears with "By the way . . ."

. . . For Dummies: #1 Book Series for Beginners

Selling For Dummies™

5. Closing

1. To develop my closing instinct, I close too soon and too often.

2. I always radiate empathy during every contact with a prospect or client.

3. I don't tell them things. I ask questions that lead them to the right answers.

4. I am ready to respond with my answer to

   "It costs too much."

   a. "Today, most things do. Can you tell me about how much too much you think it is?"

   b. When I know the amount, I use my calculator to reduce it down to a daily or hourly amount.

   c. "That's fine, Mr. Johnson. Obviously, you wouldn't take your time thinking this thing over if you weren't seriously interested, would you? I mean, I'm sure you're not telling me that just to get rid of me. So, may I assume you will give it very careful consideration? Just to clarify my thinking, what phase of this opportunity is it you want to think over? (Don't pause.) Is it the quality of the service I'll render? Is it something I've forgotten to cover? Please level with me, could it be the money?"

6. The Seven-Step Referral Program

1. Isolate faces for the client to see. (Help the client to bring to mind group(s) of people they know .)

2. Write referral's name on the client's card.

3. Ask qualifying questions.

4. Ask for the address.

5. If the address isn't known, ask for phone book.

6. Ask the client to call and set the appointment.

7. If the client shows nervousness or refuses to call, ask if you can use his or her name when you call the referral.

7. Rejection Words

These are the words to replace in your vocabulary. The word on the left has bad associations for most people. Replace it with the word on the right, which has good associations for most people.

Don't use	Use
Commission	Fee for Service
Cost, Price	Total Amount
Monthly Payment	Monthly Investment
Contract	Agreement, Paperwork
Buy	Own
Sell, Sold	Help Them Acquire, Get Them Involved
Sign	Ok, Endorse, Approve, Authorize

Cheat Sheet $2.95 value. Item 389-5.
For more information about IDG Books, call 1-800-762-2974.

Praise for Tom Hopkins

"For years a motivational expert, Hopkins is renowned as the number one sales trainer in the country, some say the world."

— *Arizona Republic*

"Tom Hopkins is head and shoulders above the rest when it comes to training high-powered sales professionals."

— Harvey Mackay, author of *Swim With the Sharks Without Getting Eaten Alive*

"Tom is terrific. He is number one and the reason is the force of his message — that selling is the essence of every business and every other pursuit in life."

— Scott DeGarmo, Editor-in-Chief, *Success Magazine*

"The reason why most people are still failing to reach their goals is that they are still searching for the exotic without having at least mastered the basics. Tom Hopkins is the master of the basics."

— Jim Rohn

"With over a quarter of a million people attending my SUCCESS seminars each year seeking the path to success, I believe one of the most vital life skills everyone can learn is selling and no one teaches it better than Tom Hopkins."

— Peter Lowe, Founder, Peter Lowe's SUCCESS Seminars

"Tom Hopkins is a dynamic, ethically sound sales trainer with a rich background of personal and business success. His methods and techniques are practical, field tested and effective."

— Zig Ziglar

"After applying Tom's techniques to all our presentations, companywide sales have increased over 40%."

— Adele C. Gorody, Alliance Gas Marketing, Inc.

"After attending one of your seminars, I am happy to report that in spite of a sluggish economy, I have reached my goal of 150% of quota. Thanks for all of the wisdom."

— Thomas G. Ganifin, NCR Corporation

"My first job paid only $10,400 and before I got into sales, I was only up to $25,000. The principles and ideas that Tom teaches changed my life forever and enabled me to start selling right away and have been the basis of my success. Today, I sell at over 400% of quota and earn over $200,000 a year."

— Gerald H. Grossman, The Wheatley Group, Ltd.

"After attending a one day Tom Hopkins seminar, I closed 21 of my next 25 prospects. This stuff works!"

— Robert Black, Meeker Sharkey Financial Services

"The #1 reason for my success has been your teaching of sound basic fundamentals of selling. I've listened to other trainers and no one begins to compare to you."

— Mike Friedman, Vice President, Lon Smith Roofing

"My income increased 100% per year, three years in a row. Thanks for making a difference in my life and so many others."

— Mitchell H. Klipfell, The Franklin

"When I attended your 3-day seminar, I was averaging $259/week gross! The week I returned from the 3-day, I wrote $4,200! The next week $12,000! The following two weeks over $10,000 and after that two weeks just under $10,000!."

— K. F., Health Insurance

"What an investment it turned out to be! We just received a check for $125,000 on a transaction that I know was direct result of your training. Tom Hopkins will be a new standard for our company."

— David Woodling, President, Network Centre

"My first appointment after getting back from your 3-day landed me a $2,000,000 life insurance sale!"

— T.T., Life Insurance

"Like your company symbol, I have raised myself from the ashes of the past and in doing so I have taken my income from $30,000 to $180,000 in three years."

— G. V., Cookware Sales

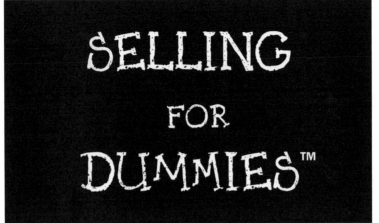

SELLING FOR DUMMIES™

Spirax Sarco Inc.
7760 Olentangy River Road
Suite 120
Columbus, OH 43235
Phone: (614) 436-8055
Fax: (614) 436-8479

spirax sarco

Good Selling!
Paul [illegible]
6-20-96

by Tom Hopkins

IDG Books Worldwide, Inc.
An International Data Group Company

Foster City, CA ♦ Chicago, IL ♦ Indianapolis, IN ♦ Braintree, MA ♦ Dallas, TX

Selling For Dummies™

Published by
IDG Books Worldwide, Inc.
An International Data Group Company
919 E. Hillsdale Blvd.
Suite 400
Foster City, CA 94404

Library of Congress Catalog Card No.: 95-78407

ISBN: 1-56884-389-5

Printed in the United States of America

10 9 8 7 6 5 4 3 2

1E/RT/RQ/ZV

Distributed in the United States by IDG Books Worldwide, Inc.

Distributed by Macmillan Canada for Canada; by Computer and Technical Books for the Caribbean Basin; by Contemporanea de Ediciones for Venezuela; by Distribuidora Cuspide for Argentina; by CITEC for Brazil; by Ediciones ZETA S.C.R. Ltda. for Peru; by Editorial Limusa SA for Mexico; by Transworld Publishers Limited in the United Kingdom and Europe; by Al-Maiman Publishers & Distributors for Saudi Arabia; by Simron Pty. Ltd. for South Africa; by IDG Communications (HK) Ltd. for Hong Kong; by Toppan Company Ltd. for Japan; by Addison Wesley Publishing Company for Korea; by Longman Singapore Publishers Ltd. for Singapore, Malaysia, Thailand, and Indonesia; by Unalis Corporation for Taiwan; by WS Computer Publishing Company, Inc. for the Philippines; by WoodsLane Pty. Ltd. for Australia; by WoodsLane Enterprises Ltd. for New Zealand.

For general information on IDG Books Worldwide's books in the U.S., please call our Consumer Customer Service department at 800-762-2974. For reseller information, including discounts and premium sales, please call our Reseller Customer Service department at 800-434-3422.

For information on where to purchase IDG Books Worldwide's books outside the U.S., contact IDG Books Worldwide at 415-655-3021 or fax 415-655-3295.

For information on translations, contact Marc Jeffrey Mikulich, Director, Foreign & Subsidiary Rights, at IDG Books Worldwide, 415-655-3018 or fax 415-655-3295.

For sales inquiries and special prices for bulk quantities, write to the address above or call IDG Books Worldwide at 415-655-3200.

For information on using IDG Books Worldwide's books in the classroom, or ordering examination copies, contact Jim Kelly at 800-434-2086.

For authorization to photocopy items for corporate, personal, or educational use, please contact Copyright Clearance Center, 222 Rosewood Drive, Danvers, MA 01923, or fax 508-750-4470.

About the Author

Tom Hopkins

Tom Hopkins is the epitome of sales success. A millionaire by the time he reached the age of 27, Hopkins now is president of his own company, and sells selling skills to those who wish to achieve their greatest potential in life.

Thirty years ago, Tom Hopkins considered himself a failure. He had dropped out of college after 90 days and for the next 18 months, he carried steel on construction sites to make a living. Believing that there had to be a better way to earn a living, he went into sales — and ran into the worst period of his life. For six months, Hopkins earned an average of $42 a month and slid deeper into debt and despair. Pulling together his last few dollars, he invested in a five-day sales training seminar that turned his life around. In the next six months, Hopkins sold more than $1 million worth of $25,000 homes.

At age 21, he won the Los Angeles Sales and Marketing Institute's coveted SAMMY Award and began setting records in sales performance that still stand today.

Because of his unique ability to share his enthusiasm for the profession of selling and on successful selling techniques he developed, Hopkins began giving seminars in 1974. Training as many as 10,000 salespeople a month, he quickly became known as the world's leading sales trainer. Today, as president of Tom Hopkins International, he presents approximately 75 seminars a year to approximately 100,000 people throughout the world.

He was a pioneer in producing high-quality audio and videotape programs for those who could not attend the seminars or wanted further reinforcement after the seminars. Recognized as the most effective sales training programs ever produced, they are continually updated and are now being utilized by more than 1 million people.

Tom Hopkins has also written six other books, including the best-selling *How to Master the Art of Selling*, which has sold 1.2 million copies in eight languages and 27 countries.

Hopkins is a member of the National Speakers Association and one of a select few to ever receive its Council of Peers Award for Excellence. He is often the keynote speaker for annual conventions and is a frequent guest on television and radio talk shows.

Welcome to the world of IDG Books Worldwide.

IDG Books Worldwide, Inc., is a subsidiary of International Data Group, the world's largest publisher of computer-related information and the leading global provider of information services on information technology. IDG was founded more than 25 years ago and now employs more than 7,500 people worldwide. IDG publishes more than 235 computer publications in 67 countries (see listing below). More than 70 million people read one or more IDG publications each month.

Launched in 1990, IDG Books Worldwide is today the #1 publisher of best-selling computer books in the United States. We are proud to have received 8 awards from the Computer Press Association in recognition of editorial excellence, and our best-selling *...For Dummies®* series has more than 19 million copies in print with translations in 28 languages. IDG Books Worldwide, through a recent joint venture with IDG's Hi-Tech Beijing, became the first U.S. publisher to publish a computer book in the People's Republic of China. In record time, IDG Books Worldwide has become the first choice for millions of readers around the world who want to learn how to better manage their businesses.

Our mission is simple: Every one of our books is designed to bring extra value and skill-building instructions to the reader. Our books are written by experts who understand and care about our readers. The knowledge base of our editorial staff comes from years of experience in publishing, education, and journalism — experience which we use to produce books for the '90s. In short, we care about books, so we attract the best people. We devote special attention to details such as audience, interior design, use of icons, and illustrations. And because we use an efficient process of authoring, editing, and desktop publishing our books electronically, we can spend more time ensuring superior content and spend less time on the technicalities of making books.

You can count on our commitment to deliver high-quality books at competitive prices on topics consumers want to read about. At IDG Books Worldwide, we value quality, and we have been delivering quality for more than 25 years. You'll find no better book on a subject than an IDG book.

John Kilcullen
President and CEO
IDG Books Worldwide, Inc.

IDG Books Worldwide, Inc., is a subsidiary of International Data Group, the world's largest publisher of computer-related information and the leading global provider of information services on information technology. International Data Group publishes over 235 computer publications in 67 countries. More than seventy million people read one or more International Data Group publications each month. The officers are Patrick J. McGovern, Founder and Board Chairman; Kelly Conlin, President; Jim Casella, Chief Operating Officer. International Data Group's publications include: **ARGENTINA'S** Computerworld Argentina, Infoworld Argentina; **AUSTRALIA'S** Computerworld Australia, Computer Living, Australian PC World, Australian Macworld, Network World, Mobile Business Australia, Publish!, Reseller, IDG Sources; **AUSTRIA'S** Computerwelt Oesterreich, PC Test; **BELGIUM'S** Data News (CW); **BOLIVIA'S** Computerworld; **BRAZIL'S** Computerworld, Connections, Game Power, Mundo Unix, PC World, Publish, Super Game; **BULGARIA'S** Computerworld Bulgaria, PC & Mac World Bulgaria, Network World Bulgaria; **CANADA'S** CIO Canada, Computerworld Canada, InfoCanada, Network World Canada, Reseller; **CHILE'S** Computerworld Chile, Informatica; **COLOMBIA'S** Computerworld Colombia, PC World; **COSTA RICA'S** PC World; **CZECH REPUBLIC'S** Computerworld, Elektronika, PC World; **DENMARK'S** Communications World, Computerworld Denmark, Computerworld Focus, Macintosh Produktkatalog, Macworld Danmark, PC World Danmark, PC Produktguide, Tech World, Windows World; **ECUADOR'S** PC World Ecuador; **EGYPT'S** Computerworld (CW) Middle East, PC World Middle East; **FINLAND'S** MikroPC, Tietoviikko, Tietoverkko; **FRANCE'S** Distributique, GOLDEN MAC, InfoPC, Le Guide du Monde Informatique, Le Monde Informatique, Telecoms & Reseaux; **GERMANY'S** Computerwoche, Computerwoche Focus, Computerwoche Extra, Electronic Entertainment, Gamepro, Information Management, Macwelt, Netzwelt, PC Welt, Publish, Publish; **GREECE'S** Publish & Macworld; **HONG KONG'S** Computerworld Hong Kong, PC World Hong Kong; **HUNGARY'S** Computerworld SZT, PC World; **INDIA'S** Computers & Communications; **INDONESIA'S** Info Komputer; **IRELAND'S** ComputerScope; **ISRAEL'S** Beyond Windows, Computerworld Israel, Multimedia, PC World Israel; **ITALY'S** Computerworld Italia, Lotus Magazine, Macworld Italia, Networking Italia, PC Shopping Italy, PC World Italia; **JAPAN'S** Computerworld Today, Information Systems World, Macworld Japan, Nikkei Personal Computing, SunWorld Japan, Windows World; **KENYA'S** East African Computer News; **KOREA'S** Computerworld Korea, Macworld Korea, PC World Korea; **LATIN AMERICA'S** GamePro; **MALAYSIA'S** Computerworld Malaysia, PC World Malaysia; **MEXICO'S** Compu Edicion, Compu Manufactura, Computacion/Punto de Venta, Computerworld Mexico, MacWorld, Mundo Unix, PC World, Windows; **THE NETHERLANDS'** Computer! Totaal, Computable (CW), LAN Magazine, Lotus Magazine, MacWorld; **NEW ZEALAND'S** Computer Buyer, Computerworld New Zealand, Network World, New Zealand PC World; **NIGERIA'S** PC World Africa; **NORWAY'S** Computerworld Norge, Lotusworld Norge, Macworld Norge, Maxi Data, Networld, PC World Ekspress, PC World Nettverk, PC World Norge, PC World's Produktguide, Publish& Multimedia World, Student Data, Unix World, Windowsworld; **PAKISTAN'S** PC World Pakistan; **PANAMA'S** PC World Panama; **PERU'S** Computerworld Peru, PC World; **PEOPLE'S REPUBLIC OF CHINA'S** China Computerworld, China Infoworld, China PC Info Magazine, Computer Fan, PC World China, Electronics International, Electronics Today/Multimedia World, Electronic Product World, China Network World, Software World Magazine, Telecom Product World; **PHILIPPINES'** Computerworld Philippines, PC Digest (PCW); **POLAND'S** Computerworld Poland, Computerworld Special Report, Networld, PC World/Komputer, Sunworld; **PORTUGAL'S** Cerebro/PC World, Correio Informatico/Computerworld, MacIn; **ROMANIA'S** Computerworld, PC World, Telecom Romania; **RUSSIA'S** Computerworld-Moscow, Mir - PK (PCW), Sety (Networks); **SINGAPORE'S** Computerworld Southeast Asia, PC World Singapore; **SLOVENIA'S** Monitor Magazine; **SOUTH AFRICA'S** Computer Mail (CIO), Computing S.A., Network World S.A., Software World; **SPAIN'S** Advanced Systems, Amiga World, Computerworld Espana, Communicaciones World, Macworld Espana, NeXTWORLD, Super Juegos Magazine (GamePro), PC World Espana, Publish; **SWEDEN'S** Attack, ComputerSweden, Corporate Computing, Macworld, Mikrodatorn, Natverk & Kommunikation, PC World, CAP & Design, Datalngenjoren, Maxi Data,Windows World; **SWITZERLAND'S** Computerworld Schweiz, Macworld Schweiz, PC Tip; **TAIWAN'S** Computerworld Taiwan, PC World Taiwan; **THAILAND'S** Thai Computerworld; **TURKEY'S** Computerworld Monitor, Macworld Turkiye, PC World Turkiye; **UKRAINE'S** Computerworld, Computers+Software Magazine; **UNITED KINGDOM'S** Computing/Computerworld, Connexion/Network World, Lotus Magazine, Macworld, Open Computing/Sunworld; **UNITED STATES'** Advanced Systems, AmigaWorld, Cable in the Classroom, CD Review, CIO, Computerworld, Computerworld Client/Server Journal, Digital Video, DOS World, Electronic Entertainment Magazine (E2), Federal Computer Week, Game Hits, GamePro, IDG Books Worldwide, Infoworld, Laser Event, Macworld, Maximize, Multimedia World, Network World, PC Letter, PC World, Publish, SWATPro, Video Event; **URUGUAY'S** PC World Uruguay; **VENEZUELA'S** Computerworld Venezuela, PC World; **VIETNAM'S** PC World Vietnam.

08/30/95

Dedication

This book is dedicated to all of my teachers and my students. Some of you have been both to me. Thank you for your loyalty and for sharing your successes with me. You are the reason why my life has been so filled with love, laughter, and abundance.

Credits

Vice President and Publisher
Kathleen A. Welton

Executive Editor
Sarah Kennedy

Managing Editor
Stephanie Britt

Brand Manager
Stacy Collins

Executive Assistant
Jamie Klobuchar

Production Director
Beth Jenkins

Supervisor of Project Coordination
Cindy L. Phipps

Supervisor of Page Layout
Kathie S. Schnorr

Pre-Press Coordinator
Steve Peake

Associate Pre-Press Coordinator
Tony Augsburger

Media/Archive Coordinator
Paul Belcastro

Project Editor
Stephanie Britt

Editor
Jeff Waggoner
Luci N. Miller

Technical Reviewer
H. Tate Holt

Associate Project Coordinator
J. Tyler Connor

Production Staff
Gina Scott
Carla Radzikinas
Patricia R. Reynolds
Melissa D. Buddendeck
Dwight Ramsey
Robert Springer
Theresa Sánchez-Baker
Linda Boyer
Jae Cho
Maridee V. Ennis
Angela F. Hunckler
Elizabeth Cárdenas-Nelson
Laura Puranen

Proofreader
Phil Worthington

Indexer
Anne Leach

Cover Design
Kavish + Kavish

Acknowledgments

I must acknowledge my wonderful wife, Debbie, who has brought so much joy into my life. I'm grateful for your patience and understanding when my life's work takes me away. I'm also grateful for your valuable input into my teaching, and particularly in this book.

I would like to thank Kathy Welton of IDG Books for contacting me about writing *Selling For Dummies.* I then would like to thank Judy Slack of Tom Hopkins International for researching IDG and the ...*For Dummies* books and persuading me that it was a good thing to do. Thanks, too, Judy for cheerfully accepting my reward (ahem!) of putting you in charge of the book and getting it completed in record time. Carpal tunnel syndrome is covered on our insurance, isn't it?

I thank John Kilcullen, IDG Books Worldwide's President, for his enthusiasm for the book and for putting together a team of wonderful, excited people who are dedicated to making *Selling For Dummies* a winner for all of its readers.

Special thanks go to my long-time friend, and business partner, Tom Murphy. I don't know what I'd do without his business savvy and negotiating skills in growing our business which allows me the time to do what I love most — teach.

In a serious world, I have two special friends, Dan and Jana Lepke. Dan, I've known since we were quite mischievous 15-year-olds. When he brought his wonderful wife, Jana, into our lives she gave Debbie and me a new, lighthearted perspective on nearly everything. Jana, thanks so much for helping to add humor to this book.

Thanks also go to Debi Siegel, the writer who kept the book moving forward at times when the rest of us had pressing matters that demanded our attention. Thanks so much for your hard work and professionalism. It's great to have someone like you we can count on.

Last, but certainly not least, I thank Stephanie Britt and Tate Holt, for their countless hours spent reviewing the book contents to ensure that it provided the best information in the most acceptable manner for the reader.

(The Publisher would like to give special thanks to Patrick J. McGovern and Bill Murphy, without whom this book would not have been possible.)

Contents at a Glance

Cartoons at a Glance

By Rich Tennant

"Don't you agree that a little style goes a long way in making a memorable sales presentation?"

page 229

PROVING THAT BIGGER ISN'T ALWAYS BEST, A CONTRACT TO BUILD A COMPUTERIZED SONAR TRACKING SYSTEM FOR THE U.S. NAVY IS AWARDED TO TROOP 708 OF THE BAYONNE, NEW JERSEY EAGLE SCOUTS.

page 311

"YOU'LL HAVE TO COME UP WITH A BETTER LINE THAN THIS, MR. LANGLEY, BEFORE I CAN LET YOU IN TO SEE MR. CODMAN."

page 141

page 65

"GET READY, I THINK THEY'RE STARTING TO DRIFT."

page 126

"I SENSE YOU'RE IN A HURRY, SO I'LL BE BRIEF."

page 259

"OH, I THINK WE'VE FOUND OUR MAN."

page 7

page 160

"FIRST HARRY SOLD BOWLING BALLS, SO HE TOOK ME BOWLING. THEN HE SOLD GOLF CLUBS, SO WE TOOK UP GOLF. NOW HE'S SELLING SURGICAL INSTRUMENTS, AND FRANKLY I HAVEN'T HAD A FULL NIGHTS SLEEP SINCE."

page 63

"Well, that takes care of the 'point' part of it, but I hate to even think of what you'll come up with for 'click'!"

page 140

Table of Contents

Introduction

Welcome to *Selling For Dummies.* In this book, I'm not just talking about selling products and services to businesses and consumers. This book is really all about people skills. Knowing how to get along well with others is a vital skill that we all need to learn as early as possible in life.

To be successful in sales, you must have cooperation, good listening skills, and a willingness to put others' needs before your own. That's why having selling skills in your arsenal will help you have more happiness and contentment in all areas of your life.

Selling For Dummies can help you get more happiness and contentment out of your life right now by helping you gain

- More respect
- More money
- More recognition for the job you do
- More agreement from your friends and family
- More control in negotiations and, of course
- More sales!

This book was written by the original dummy in sales, a guy who started his selling career in real estate at age 19. Real estate may have been a great choice for a career, but at the time I owned neither a suit nor a car. All I had was a band uniform and a motorcycle. Selling real estate on a motorcycle was not easy; I had to tell the prospective buyers to follow me to the properties and hope they didn't get lost along the way. When they finally came to their senses and realized that this kid couldn't possibly be for real, they'd keep going straight when I'd make a turn. To make things even worse, wearing a woolen band uniform in southern California's summer heat didn't allow me to present the coolest image, either. But I stuck it out.

I knew there was big money to be made in the selling business if I could just find out what the successful people were doing that I wasn't doing. I learned it all the hard way, by trial and error. Early in my career, a professional, experienced salesperson told me I had to learn how to close, meaning *to close the sale.* I responded, "I don't have many clothes." See why I only averaged $42 a month in my first six months selling real estate?

Needless to say, I've come a long way since then, and it would thrill me to no end for you to learn from the mistakes I made, as well as from the subsequent success I had.

Yes, I had successes. I achieved my goal of becoming a millionaire by the age of 30, beating my own deadline by nearly three years! At age 27, I was one of the most successful real estate agents in the whole country. Imagine that, for a guy who started without a decent suit or a vehicle with four wheels! That just goes to show you that it doesn't matter how much of a dummy you are on this subject when you start. Selling, persuasion, and people skills can all be learned.

Who Needs to Read This Book?

I wrote *Selling For Dummies* not only for the traditional salesperson who wants to learn more about his or her career, but for anyone who can use selling skills to change or improve his or her life.

- It's for you—whether you're beginning a selling career or just looking to brush up your skills.
- It's for you—whether you're unemployed and want a job or you're employed and want a promotion.
- It's for you—whether you're a teen wanting to impress adults or an adult wanting to succeed at negotiation.
- It's for you—whether you're a teacher searching for better ways to get through to your students or a parent wanting to communicate more effectively with your children.
- It's for you—whether you have an idea that could help others or you want to improve your personal relationships.
- It's for real people.

Students who have attended my seminars tell me about how they used a strategy or technique to get agreement from a family member on an important decision. They've told me about using a questioning technique to get their spouse or children to agree to do something they previously tried to put off. And some have used the skills to sell themselves into better jobs. The increased confidence gained by learning the material has caused other students to ask for, and to receive, better service.

As an added bonus, when my students applied the skills and strategies to personal relationships, many have found that those relationships became more rewarding.

How to Use This Book

I've laid out the basics of any "selling" presentation in a series of steps. You can go through the steps in sequence or you can skim the Table of Contents and locate a title or heading that strikes you as interesting. Read it first. Then go on to another area that you think will benefit you the most.

- If you are a new, serious salesperson who has gone into sales as a career choice, you may want to read the book from cover to cover.
- If you want to use these skills in an area of your life, find the appropriate topic to develop that particular skill and use the tips and the phrases I've included.
- If you want to use these skills for a special project or a particular persuasion situation, you can go through the book with a highlighter in hand and highlight what you find to be helpful.

As you get into the material, you'll read about real-life examples of people in various situations where they needed people skills in order to succeed. I tell you the good stories and the bad ones; that way, you will learn and remember them when you get into similar situations.

You may be surprised at some of the little things that made a big difference in negotiations for people around the world. When you think of the saying *It's the little things that count,* you probably don't even consider that the way you hand out your business card can make or break a sale. The way you walk influences people you try to persuade as well.

The methods, words, and phrases contained in this book are not put on paper in *Selling For Dummies* just because they sound good to the editors at IDG Books. They have been proven successful by me and my 2 million students around the world.

If you're truly going to benefit by persuading, cajoling, convincing, or selling someone else on what you have to offer, why not pull out all the stops and learn the strategies and tactics that have been proven to work for others?

How This Book Is Organized

Selling For Dummies is organized into six parts. The chapters within each part cover specific topic areas in detail.

Part I: The Art of Selling

In this part, you learn a little about what selling is and a lot about what it isn't. Because misconceptions are the root of understanding, in the chapters in The Art of Selling, I'll explore the realities of how selling affects your daily life. Millions of people in the world are involved in selling situations all the time, including you with your friends and family members. Part I makes you more aware of the various selling situations you find yourself in and how to learn from them.

Part II: Winners Do Homework

Okay. So now you admit that you participate in selling situations all the time and that maybe you want to be more in control. Preparation is the key to winning in negotiations, persuading others, and selling products and services. In this part, I'll cover the steps to preparation that will set you apart from average persuaders and help you get more *Yes* into your life.

Part III: Inventory Your Skills

Welcome to the nitty-gritty. You already have a certain degree of selling skills because they are part of normal, everyday communications. But you can develop these skills to a much higher level that will put you in a stronger position when you persuade, negotiate, or sell.

Part IV: Building a Business

If your goal is to build a long-term business or to take your career to great heights, this part is for you. It's where you begin to separate yourself from the average to become great. Average people make their presentations, they win a few, they lose a few, they move on. The great ones view every presentation as an opportunity to build. There are no great losses. Just because someone doesn't take you up on your offering now, that doesn't mean they don't know someone else who might in the future. Great ones build, not just businesses, but *relationships,* because relationships take you farther and bring you a lot more satisfaction.

Part V: You Won't Always Win

Rejection is a part of life. Learn to expect it, accept it, and get over it. Just because your idea or product is rejected, that doesn't mean that someone has rejected you as a person. This part helps you learn to be a duck letting things run off your back like water. It also helps you understand how best to use your time and keep focused on the big picture so the little negativities of life won't bring you down.

Part VI: Part of 10s

These short chapters are packed with quick ideas about selling and persuading that you can read any time you have a few minutes. They're a great way to get yourself psyched for a presentation or for making calls. They're good for pumping up your attitude and getting you excited. And remember: No one will ever want what you have if you're not excited about it.

Icons in This Book

This icon highlights the crucial pieces of information and skills needed for selling anything. I once had a college professor who told us, the students in his class, that he didn't care if we slept in his class as long as we learned the things he highlighted with red flags. Those were the areas we'd be tested on!

This icon highlights persuasive tactics and strategies that you can use to move a person off the dime to say *Yes.*

This icon highlights advanced strategies and tips to go beyond the basics and become a Champion at selling.

This icon highlights edifying stories from my years of experience in selling and from my students' experiences.

This icon highlights words of wisdom to use for all kinds of selling situations.

This icon is a friendly reminder of information discussed elsewhere in the book or stuff you definitely want to remember.

This icon marks things to avoid and common mistakes people make.

Where to Go from Here

Look through the book and find which part, chapter, or section flips your switch. That's the best place to begin.

Most people won't choose to start in the area in which they need the most help, primarily because they don't *know* that they don't know the material. Instead, they'll probably choose their favorite area, the one they're already pretty good at. That's okay. If you do that, you'll see some increase in your successes once you start to apply this book's strategies in such areas. But to benefit the most from this material, you need to do a little self-analysis to see where you're the weakest. I know it's tough to admit your faults, even to yourself, but doing so and learning the material in your weaker areas will bring you the greatest amount of success.

Studies by Tom Hopkins International have shown that most traditional salespeople lack qualification skills. They waste a lot of time presenting to people who can't truly make decisions on what the salesperson is selling. If you're in traditional sales and you aren't sure if qualification is your weakness, start studying Chapter 10 and see how that material helps you.

The most important point to consider right now is that you're already headed toward the winner's circle. I've long taught that the most successful people in life are those who continue to learn. The fact that you're reading these words now puts you into that realm because it isn't how much you know that counts, but how much you can learn *after* you "know it all."

Congratulations for believing in yourself, in your ability to change for the better, in your ability to improve your lifestyle, *and* in your ability to improve the lives of the people you help with this book's many tips on the art of selling. I wish you greatness!

Part I
The Art of Selling

"OH, I THINK WE'VE FOUND OUR MAN."

In this part...

What selling is and a lot about what it isn't. I'll explore the realities of how selling affects your daily life and how many times you're selling without even knowing it. Chapter 2 covers essential skills for anyone selling or persuading. Chapter 3 covers incorporating selling skills into your life.

Chapter 1

You Don't Need a Plaid Sport Coat

In This Chapter

- Selling in your everyday life
- Advertising as selling in print
- Who's in selling
- Everyone's doing it

I couldn't write a book on the subject of selling without devoting an entire chapter to its definition. Selling is so prevalent in practically every human activity that it's essential you have a very clear picture of it. Selling affects you every waking moment. Your new awareness will help you utilize the new skills you'll develop after reading the rest of the book to your best advantage.

What Is Selling — Not Always What You Think

In the strictest sense of the word, selling is the process of moving goods and services from the hands of those who produce them into the hands of those who will benefit most from their use. It involves persuasive selling skills on the part of the person doing the talking. It is supported by print, audio and video messages that sell either the particular item or the brand name as being something the receiver would want to have.

It's been said that nothing ever happens unless someone sells something to someone else. Products that have been manufactured would sit in warehouses for eternity. People working for the manufacturers would become unemployed. Transportation and freight services would not be needed. We would all be living isolated little lives, striving to eke out livings from whatever bit of land we owned. Or would we even own the land if there was no one to sell it to us? Think about it.

Look around wherever you are now reading this book. There are probably hundreds, if not thousands of things you can see that were sold in order to get where they are right now. Even if you're totally naked, sitting in the woods, you had to be involved in some sort of selling process to have this book with you. If you choose to ignore "things," then take stock of yourself internally. What do you believe? Why do you believe what you do? Did someone — like your parents — sell you a set of values as you were growing up? Did your teachers persuade you to believe — through demonstration — that 2 + 2 = 4? Or did you figure that one out on your own?

The paragraph you've just finished reading should have persuaded you to at least look at selling a bit differently than you have in the past. It was done, too, without pushing facts and figures on you. Good selling isn't pushing. It's gently pulling with questions, getting people to think a bit differently than they have before.

Advertising is selling

You know that radio and television commercials and shows sell you. But you might not realize how deeply their advertising campaigns register in your mind. For example, you may not drink Coca-Cola, but I'll bet if you hear the music from one of their current commercials you can probably hum right along. Better yet for the advertisers, you can probably picture in your mind the million-dollar graphics display they put together with that music when you saw the ad on prime-time TV last night.

Even if you don't buy Coca-Cola, if someone else asked you to stop by the store and pick up a six-pack of Coca-Cola for them, how long would it take you to find it on the shelf? Not very long. Why? Partly because Coca-Cola has premium shelf space in most supermarkets. Mainly, though, you'd find that six-pack easily because you know exactly what Coca-Cola's product packaging looks like.

We get so used to product messages that we often tend to blot them out. We adjust our psychological fine tuning to screen out unwanted information and only call our attention to ads that mention areas of particular interest for us. This applies to all types of advertising.

Why billboards are big

When you drive around a big city, billboard advertising bombards you from every angle. In any city, you can drive by — and see — signs of all sorts for various businesses. Do you really read those signs? Most people notice when the signs change but can't always remember what product was advertised previously in the same billboard space. If a new business starts up, the flags and special grand opening signs on the company's billboards are so obvious that you'd have to be blind to miss them. The point of advertising by billboard and other signage is to get your attention in a big way.

Suppose that you just cruised past an eye-catching, positively heart-stopping billboard for the fastest, the least-expensive, without question the best plumbing service in town, Joe's Plumbing. By making its ad larger than life on that billboard, Joe's Plumbing hopes you'll remember (drum roll, please) Joe's Plumbing the next time you need plumbing services. Have you been sold? Not yet. Do you have a certain familiar feeling about good old Joe even though you may never have had a need for a plumber? Probably.

So what happens when you do need a plumber? Chances are good that you may not immediately think of Joe. However, as soon as you turn off your water supply, mop up the mess and begin wondering how long it'll be before you can flush again, you'll go to the Yellow Pages and look under Plumbing. Then, if Joe's serious about his business, in the Yellow Pages you'll see yet another of his ads or at least a name listing for him. You'll get a comfortable feeling when you see it and probably call Joe before you make any other choices. Have you been sold? If the person on the other end of the telephone does a halfway decent job of handling your request, the answer is yes.

Even standard billboard advertising is improving in the 90s. Inventive new methods catch our attention all the time. Just the other day, as I was on my way to the airport, one billboard made me do a double-take. It looked like your family room vertical blinds and kept turning, showing the faces of some of our local newscasters and their channel number. The billboard achieved its goal of keeping my attention longer than the average billboard. What else will probably happen? The next time I'm home and turn on the local news, I'll probably look for that particular group of smiling faces to learn if the newscasters are as clever as their stations' advertising. If they are, I'm sold and the billboard did the trick.

You're a walking billboard

Do you realize that you yourself are an integral part of the advertising plans of many manufacturers? As a matter of fact, you have even become a salesperson for many of them. I can hear you now: *Okay Hopkins, now you've really flipped your lid. I'm reading this book to learn how to sell and now you're telling me I'm already selling — and for major manufacturers at that!*

Here's a test that will prove my point: Look in your clothes closet or dresser drawers and see how many of your clothing items have the brand name plastered across the chest, subtly sewn on the back pocket, or displayed on an outside strip of your pumped-up athletic shoe. Then think about how much you paid for the privilege of being a walking advertisement for them.

The term *display advertising* means much more than signs, banners, and billboards. Who doesn't think it's cool to get a free T-shirt, hat, or fanny pack from someplace where they do business? No matter who you are, free stuff is free stuff and it's fun to get.

But when you accept these lovely gifts, are you realizing that wearing them helps the business to get the word out about how great they are or to nudge your unsuspecting friends and acquaintances toward the opening of that business's six new locations? Probably not, unless you personally know the owner of the business. When you wear such branded items, do you think people really notice? Yes. Just think about it the next time you catch yourself reading someone else's T-shirt or hat.

Print ads

A glance through the daily paper will allow your psyche to be bombarded by news and print ads. Most magazines devote a good portion of their pages to advertising. That's what keeps a good magazine in business. It's certainly not those $12.75 per year subscription rates! Advertisers are willing to pay hefty space rates to get their message before you. And you are paying money to the publisher to be advertised to — besides reading their articles.

Direct mail

Every piece of mail you receive, whether it's a letter of solicitation, a coupon or catalog is devised for a single purpose — to sell you something. Companies play the odds that there'll be enough people who stop long enough to look at and actually order their products before the direct mail hits the trash.

It may surprise you to know that a 1 percent response rate for direct mail is considered average. That means only one out of 100 catalogs may actually have an order placed from it. Ninety-nine of those catalogs hit the round file without ever generating a penny to the company. In fact, they can each cost a good bit if they contain a lot of full color photos. If that's the case, why is there such a proliferation of direct mail? The reason is simple. Once you place an order, it's highly likely that you'll order something else from them in the future. You have become a customer and companies will work very hard to keep you coming back for more.

What Selling Skills Can Do for You

Selling skills can do for you what a way with words did for Cyrano de Bergerac and William Shakespeare. They can do for you what sex appeal did for Marilyn Monroe. They can do for you what powerful communication skills did for historical greats like Abraham Lincoln, Franklin D. Roosevelt, and Dr. Martin Luther King. Selling skills can make or break you in whatever endeavor you choose. They can mean the difference between getting the promotion/job/girl or guy of your dreams and having to settle for less.

Selling yourself to get a job

If you're stuck in a job that makes you pine for the greener pastures of a better job, then you need selling skills. What are you selling? Yourself. And to sell yourself, you need to know how to find and qualify the best prospects, how to present yourself to them, and how to close the sale. This should be the easiest sale you'll ever make. Who other than you has more in-depth knowledge about your talents, abilities, and desires than you do?

Outsmart your prospect's last objection

I found this approach to be a winner in landing my first serious job as an adult.

Construction work was my first job. It was tough, physically demanding, and ultimately unfulfilling work. In my part of the country, real estate was booming, so I studied and eventually got my license.

My next step was to get a job with a local company. There were two strikes against me at this point. First, my only means of transportation was a motorcycle, which made it tough to drive people out to view properties. Even worse, I didn't own a suit.

After being turned away by several real estate companies, I finally talked with a man who told me he probably could help me work around the motorcycle challenge, but having a suit was critical. It dawned on me then that this was his final objection. I asked, "If I have a suit, then will you hire me?" To my surprise, he said yes and told me to show up in "a suit" at the next company sales meeting.

He didn't specify what kind of suit I needed — so I took the liberty of cleaning up and wearing my band uniform. You see, when I was 16, I played in a band. We were greatly influenced by the Beatles — our band uniforms were silver lamé. Technically, it was "a suit." I walked into that sales meeting just as he was informing everyone that they had a new agent on board. You should have seen his face when he realized that my "suit" was my old band uniform. It got a lot of laughs and the guy agreed to let me stay on if I could produce. I was the only motorcycle-riding real estate agent in a band uniform in the country at that time, and my nonconformity turned out to be an advantage. People talked about "that crazy kid, Hopkins." It was free advertising.

Figuring out how to sell myself into that job—identifying and outsmarting my prospect's last objection to what I was selling — was a turning point in my life. It can be in yours, too.

As you sell yourself into a job, or even as you sell anything, you'll want to follow the seven steps in the selling cycle. These are the Seven Steps to selling anything.

1. Prospecting
2. Original contact
3. Qualification
4. Presentation
5. Addressing concerns
6. Closing the sale
7. Getting referrals

The first thing is to change your perspective about getting a job. Look at an employment situation as a selling situation. You'll play two roles in this interchange. In a job interview, you are both the salesperson and the product. Your goal is to match your particular features and benefits with the needs of a qualified employer. Where do you begin in the selling sequence? Believe it or not, a very good place would be Step #1.

Step #1: Prospecting

Prospecting means finding the right potential buyer for what you're selling. When you're selling yourself into a new job, it means finding the right potential employer.

You should already know what type of work you most enjoy. That word *enjoy* is key here: if you don't firmly believe that you would enjoy the type of job you're seeking, you'll have trouble being enthusiastic about your job hunting — a.k.a. your prospecting. It's a lot easier to be excited about a job that interests you than about one that happens to have the biggest ad in the Sunday paper or has the salary range you need in order to keep living in (or even improve upon) your current lifestyle.

To make an informed decision about which prospects to approach, it's important to find out some information about the people or companies you've chosen as possibilities. I strongly recommend that you do some research at the local library about any prospective employer. This is sort of a prequalification step in job hunting. More qualification is done once you get an interview, but why waste time on an interview with a company you wouldn't want to work for. Prequalifying will help you narrow down your best prospective employers just like market research helps companies determine their best target markets. You can learn a lot from newspaper articles, prospective employers' financial statements, and the advertising your prospects run. The person at your library's reference desk is an invaluable asset during this prospecting stage. Just ask the reference librarian for help.

Other valuable assets are your friends, relatives, and business acquaintances. Tell them what type of work you want and the names of your prospective employers. See what suggestions they come up with. Who knows, one of them just might know people at one of your prospect companies who would be happy to talk with you about job opportunities there. I discuss more of this subject in Chapter 13. If there's something good going on, people are always willing to share their stories with others.

Next, you search the paper for classified ads in your market. You may make phone calls or send out literature on your product. Product literature in this case is called a *résumé.* Have your resume professionally prepared. Chances are good that your résumé will be competing with quite a few others that have been professionally prepared. You don't want yours to look like a poor relation. Also, know that many employers do check references in depth so leave out the part about having a degree in nuclear science and quantum physics unless it's true.

A word of advice here that applies to all selling situations: *Never begin any selling cycle until you have taken a few moments to put yourself in the shoes of the other person.* I have long advised my students to take themselves out of the picture and look at the entire situation through the eyes of the buyer — in this case, the prospective employer.

If you find an ad that sounds great, go for it. Be enthusiastic about it. Commit to doing whatever it takes to get in front of the person who interviews for the position. Then, before you take action, mentally put yourself on the other side of that person's desk. The ad you responded to may have been so effective that hundreds of people got excited about it. Your poor interviewer may be getting swamped with résumés, phone calls, and appointments just to fill one or two positions. You need to do or say something that makes your cover letter and résumé memorable. Selling yourself is part of job hunting, but you can find more hints and specific tips on résumés and cover letters in *Job Hunting For Dummies.*

Here's a list of things that others have done. Use only what may be appropriate for your particular employment situation. Although the requested material — your résumé — may be much like everyone else's, by making your experience memorable you're more likely to get a second look.

- **Enclose a photograph of yourself, dressed appropriately for the position.** Having a face on the resume to put with the attributes of the candidate establishes a certain familiarity with the interviewer once you finally get the interview. Just make sure it's a recent photo, not your high school graduation photo from 1965!

- **Include a tasteful comic about job hunting or interviewing — but it should make light only of the process of job hunting.** Be careful not to include anything that shows any negativity about either party involved.
- **Add a clever quote or anecdote to the bottom of your cover letter.** Many books offer great quotes about leadership, quality, making wise decisions, and other topics appropriate to finding and hiring the right people. Taking a few moments to research this attention-getter could make your résumé stand out.
- **If your telephone number is 344-6279 and your name is Mary, you could use the alphabet on the telephone pad to ask them to call 344-MARY.** If your name is Agamemnon, this will not work for you.
- **Include a stick of gum, two aspirin in a sample pack, or a miniature bottle of eye drops with a short note about the trials and tribulations of hiring.** Any of these goodies shows that you understand what your interviewer must be going through.
- **Include a package of microwave popcorn attached to a photo of a La-Z-Boy recliner chair.** In a note, hint that the interviewer deserves to relax while poring over the information required for submission for this particular position.

Disclaimer: These ideas may be a bit gimmicky if you're applying for a teaching position or corporate management position, but have worked for some of our students applying for positions where they are required to be a bit creative and think on their feet.

To ensure that your name gets in front of the interviewer more than once, send a thank you note the day after you send your résumé. Thank you notes always get read and if they haven't had the time to review your résumé when they receive it, don't you think they'll go looking for your name among the stacks of others? You will have made a positive first impression that will very likely bring you closer to getting that precious interview, which leads us to the next step.

Step #2: Original contact

You've found the people. The next step, original contact, is when you actually meet them. Okay. You've passed the first hurdle and been invited to visit with a potential employer. You want to appear to be at ease so that they'll be comfortable with you. After all, the number one need of people is the need to be comfortable. If you're uncomfortable, chances are good that unless you're a really good actor, it'll show and your discomfort may make them uncomfortable, too. Any tension at this point will take a bit of doing on both sides to overcome. If you don't get past it, you could turn a potential win into a lose-lose situation. You won't get the job and the potential employer will miss out on having your talents and skills in their employ.

First and foremost, you need to consider what you look like to this prospective employer. We all know the old saying, "You never get a second chance to make a good first impression." When in doubt about what to wear to an interview, err on the side of conservatism. Skip the band uniform. You want to look your best, but also remember to be comfortable. If your new shoes are too tight or squeak, you'll be conscious of that fact and not put all of your concentration into the interview.

Don't dress in such a manner that the interviewer can tell that you need the job. In a prospective employer's mind, any shabbiness in your appearance translates into shabbiness in work habits. On the other hand, unless this is a high profile job you might want to leave your Armani suit in the closet so the interviewer doesn't get the impression that you don't need this job. Think twice before you wear your favorite cologne or perfume. Subtlety is the motto here. You never know if you'll meet someone who is allergic to your added scents. If the interviewer opens the window, goes into a sneezing frenzy or just plain keels over, you went a bit heavy on the fragrance.

A special concern for women is the jewelry they wear to an interview. If it's attractive, that's great. But if it could be considered distracting, like a diamond tiara, that's bad. You don't want to be remembered as "that woman we interviewed who had those humongous earrings." You want them to remember your competence and professionalism.

Because this is a business situation, be prepared to shake hands, make eye contact, and build rapport. Building rapport is the getting-to-know-you stage that comes with any interview. The person doing the hiring doesn't just want someone competent for the position: they need someone who has *people* skills, someone who plays well with others. Be prepared to talk about previous work and civic experiences that show your ability to communicate well and work as part of a team.

Step #3: Qualification

You need to know if you are qualified to work for them and if they are qualified to be your employer of choice. For you, *qualification* means finding out who they are, what they do, how they treat employees — and whether the answers to those questions are satisfactory for you.

You should prequalify a company before you agree to an interview. Doing so will save both you and them a lot of time.You should have done some prequalifying in the prospecting step to determine if this company is truly one you'd like to work for. If you haven't prequalified them, though, take a few moments during your interview to ask questions which would tell you whether you and the employer would make a good match. Interviewers respect proactive potential employees. I recommend that you go in with a list of at least five questions whose answers will help you decide whether a prospective employer would make an ideal work environment for you.

Here's a valuable hint: *Don't just ask about salary and benefits.* These two topics are most important to you, but when you're selling yourself, you need to show them how having you on staff benefits them. If you focus on what you can do for the company, what the company can do for you will follow.

So, avoid pointed questions, such as: How much is the salary? How often are bonuses given? Where's the company Christmas Party held? How soon can I take vacation time? How many holidays do we get? Does the insurance plan cover elective plastic surgery? Will my company car be a Porsche or a BMW? Too much self-interest can eliminate you rather quickly as a potential candidate.

- Ask questions specific to the position as well as about the company.
- Ask about the company's future plans for growth.
- Ask about the product line.
- Ask about the computers and equipment.
- Ask about the position.

If you've done your homework and looked up information about the company, you'll know what questions to ask. It doesn't matter if you're applying for a job in sales, accounting, or shipping. You'll eventually have to know a lot of information about the company, providing you get the job, so if you're truly convinced this is the right job for you, you might as well ask these questions now. The more specific your questions, the more impressed your interviewer will be with your expertise. Asking pertinent questions now shows that you're interested in more than just a paycheck.

They'll be qualifying you, too, during this interview. So be aware of what you are showing them of yourself. Most employers are looking for people who are dependable, loyal, trustworthy, intelligent, competent, and even a little fun. Does the person opposite you see that when they look at you? If it's a trait that's difficult to see, short of wearing your Scout uniform, figure out how you can bring those images to mind in the answers you give to their questions.

Sometimes, believe it or not, it may turn out that you are not comfortable taking a job. If it's offered and it's really not what you're looking for, be honest with them, thank them for their time, and decline the job.

Step #4: Presentation

Your presentation of your product — yourself — requires the most preparation. In your preparation, practice your answers to common interview questions with a family member or close friend. Make a list of the qualities you think are your strongest persuaders in getting the job. Then try to figure a way to work those points into responses to the common questions.

For example, suppose that you have a great memory and that you're applying for a job as an executive secretary. However, you have almost no experience in handling a high volume of telephone calls and this particular boss gets loads of calls daily. Instead of letting the phone challenge get you down or make you nervous, stress the strength of your memory and your ability to learn. The conversation might go something like this:

EMPLOYER (doubt oozing from voice)

We have very busy phones in this office, you know. It's important for me to receive my calls quickly and efficiently. So how are you on the phone with XYZ system?

YOU (confident after reading *Selling For Dummies*)

I've not used that particular system before, but I'm a very quick study. If you want to know about my phone skills in general, you can check with my previous employer. He appreciated the fact that my memory is so good that I could identify our clients just after hearing their voices only two or three times.

Notice what has happened here. You've bypassed the interviewer's concern about the XYZ system because you're confident you can learn it and you've given them a good reason to hire you. Who wouldn't want a secretary or assistant with a great memory?

To demonstrate dependability, tell the interviewer an anecdote from a previous job or even from an outside activity. If you were an Eagle Scout as a kid, that tells a lot about you, doesn't it? Even if you didn't make Eagle but were active in scouting for a number of years, that presents a positive image of stick-to-it-iveness. Find a way to bring it up. You may want to mention long term friendships that evolved from past employment experiences or how others call on you for assistance. Some industries are very small and the same group of people moves from company to company to company. By showing that you're not one of them, that you're seeking a long term opportunity, you'll make great strides in winning them over.

Amazing things can happen during the rapport-establishing phase of an interview. I know of someone who was in an interview and noticed a small golf figurine on the interviewer's desk. She asked if the interviewer liked to play golf — a fairly general and safe question. The guy gave her a brief answer that didn't carry the conversation too far in that direction.

Then she remembered a new type of golf club, just out, that her husband had talked about. She asked if he had ever heard of these new clubs and explained briefly why she was asking. Because her husband was so crazy about them, she wanted to get him a set for his upcoming birthday. It just so happened that the interviewer's son was a cofounder of the company that developed and marketed those particular clubs. Suddenly, this prospective employer was very interested in hearing the applicant's husband thought of the clubs, and a deeper level of rapport was established.

Step #5: Addressing concerns

How do you handle any negative traits or qualifications that might come up? If any objections arise, explain yourself in as simple, unemotional terms as possible. If you're the primary caregiver for your 95-year-old grandmother and you have to arrange nursing care in advance on weekends, let them know. If you're on a traveling softball team, you need to weigh the importance of continuing that activity against the requirement of this job.

If you sidestep obstacles in an interview, there's a good chance they'll come back to haunt you if you do get the job. I always advise my students to find a way to bring up and elaborate on any concerns about fulfilling the needs of the "buyer" as early in the presentation as is appropriate.

Step #6: Closing the sale

If you've researched the job properly, and given yourself enough valuable preparation time, and handled all the previous steps in a professional manner, it's likely you'll get the job. Closing should follow naturally and smoothly after addressing concerns. If you do want the job and it hasn't been offered, you may have to ask them for it. Don't panic. This isn't where you have to turn into Joe Typical Salesperson and apply pressure to get what you want. Getting the job can be as simple as saying, "How soon do I start?" At this point, if you're confident about being able to give them what they need, you should begin taking verbal ownership of the position with assumptive statements and questions.

Step #7: Getting referrals (if you have to)

It means getting names of others you can talk with about your product.

If for some reason you and the interviewer agree that this may not be the best job for you, yet you both know that you've presented yourself well, don't just say your goodbyes and leave. Take a moment, as a professional person would, to make the interviewer a part of your network of people who can help you find the right job (as I covered in Step #1 on prospecting).

There may be another job in that same company that you would be qualified for. This person may know of other companies hiring in your field. Don't ever just walk away from an opportunity to network. And, immediately upon leaving the premises, drop a thank you note in the mail to the interviewer. This will guarantee your interview will stay fresh in his or her mind for at least a few days and during that time, the right lead for you may come their way.

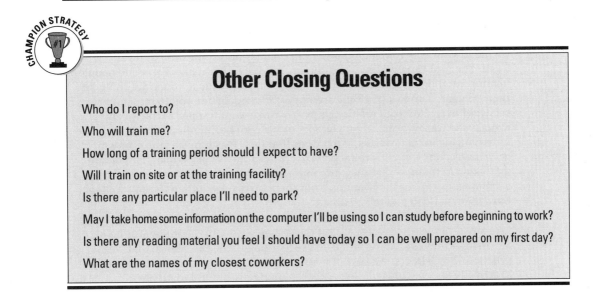

Other Closing Questions

Who do I report to?

Who will train me?

How long of a training period should I expect to have?

Will I train on site or at the training facility?

Is there any particular place I'll need to park?

May I take home some information on the computer I'll be using so I can study before beginning to work?

Is there any reading material you feel I should have today so I can be well prepared on my first day?

What are the names of my closest coworkers?

Selling yourself at your new job

If you're low on the totem pole because you're new, you'll have a lot going on besides learning your new job. Your boss and coworkers will have a natural curiosity about you as a person, not about you as, say, a computer programmer. They'll want to know about your family, your outside activities, what you like to eat, what fragrance you wear, where you shop — practically everything. Don't consider this an invasion of your privacy. What they're really trying to determine is how much like them you are. If you're like them, they'll like you and things will be a lot less complicated. If you're too much different from them, they'll need to adjust their thinking and your popularity as a new member of the team may take some time to blossom. This is not the time to bring up past UFO experiences or your fetish for sniffing used coffee mugs.

Size up the office

The best way to handle this situation is to use selling skills. To plan your "sale," you need to observe your situation carefully and make sound judgments about what you observe. Determining your plan of action requires some observation and judgment on your part. It's usually better to take it slow when you enter a new office or work environment. You don't know what has happened before you got there that may have charged the atmosphere negatively. You may be taking the place of someone who was the most popular person in the company who had to leave for personal reasons and will be sorely missed. It may take the rest of the crew awhile to deal with their feelings of loss before they can open up to you.

People skills will start the sale

Go out of your way to remember people's names and some little thing about them. The next time you see that person, use his or her name. For some people, hearing another person call them by name can be the most important thing for them to hear. It shows that they are important enough for you to remember; recognition is vital to all relationships. You may want to refer to the lovely brooch she was wearing when you met or his cool tie. Mention awards they have hanging in their offices. What does that do? Does it make you a brown-nose or kiss-up? Not if it's done properly. It tells the other people that you are interested in them — that they are important to you. People are proud of their accomplishments or they wouldn't put them on display if they weren't willing to have them noticed and talked about.

Like any other learned skills, at first these may seem put-on or unnatural. Surprise — they *are* put-on while you're learning them! But realize that, with practice, they'll become a part of your personality and your use of them will be practically unconscious for you and seem perfectly natural to others.

If you're stingy with compliments, praise, or thanks, people will perceive you as a cold fish or a hardnose. So don't be afraid to give kind words to the new people around you, even if it's uncomfortable at first. By following just a few simple rules of etiquette, you can overcome your initial discomfort.

- **Don't say things you don't believe.** Dishonesty shows through in your body language.
- **Praise or compliment at an appropriate time,** usually within 24 hours. After that, you'll both forget what they did to earn the compliment and your comments will seem affected.
- **Consider the person or people who are hearing your praise.** If you don't know how they accept recognition in a group, do it one on one.
- **Don't make a big deal about it.** Say it, let the person acknowledge it, and get back to work.

These actions require giant steps for some readers. If you're one of those people who doesn't already act this way, don't fret. Take baby steps. They will help you build to a level at which spontaneous praise is just like living and breathing. The easiest, least- involved method is to put the praise in writing. It takes only a moment to do the courtesy of thanking people when they have helped you or have done an exceptional job on a difficult assignment. Keep it simple, write something like this, *Thank you, Jill, for the great job you did on the Anderson project. Your efforts are greatly appreciated.* Don't tell Jill that she just made the company $10 million. Something like that could backfire later when she leaves for greener pastures feeling she wasn't compensated fairly for what the company earned from her efforts.

Don't ponder your kind words for days, though, because the appropriate moment can be fleeting. If you think you should acknowledge someone, do it within 24 hours. If you aren't inclined to the written word, take a moment to thank them personally. This can be done over the telephone if you're uncomfortable with a face-to-face situation. Or you could even leave a message in their voice mail or e-mail. This method delights most recipients because normally nothing but additional work shows up in voice and e-mail. The key point is this: *people will remember the time you took to say thanks or give them a positive stroke, and they will react accordingly.*

After you practice the note or e-mail thing awhile, your fellow workers will pass you in the hall, smile, and thank you for recognizing their accomplishments. They'll feel closer to you — which means that they'll be more open to discussing the important issues of your profession. At that point, you'll have won them over. The building blocks of commonsensical, ethical self-promotion will get you where you want to go.

Selling yourself in your current job

Okay. You've seen the importance of giving thanks and recognition when you're the new guy on the scene. But what if you weren't looking for a new job? What if you're happy where you are, but you want to be seen in a better light? Take advantage of what I just covered in order to help your boss and coworkers revise their opinions of you. It's easy to get into a rut with people you see every business day. You take it for granted that they do a good job. After all, they're still employed with you, aren't they? And they must know you like their work, right? Wrong! Very, very wrong!

Most of the employees at my little company have been with me for over 10 years. I've been fortunate to build a team of highly competent people who understand each other's strengths and weaknesses and thoroughly enjoy each other's company. We have a light-hearted attitude around our office even though everyone carries a heavy work load.

And do you know what I have the most fun with? Telling them that what each and every one of them does affects hundreds of thousands of students each year. Tom Hopkins International is not just me. Sure, I'm the person on the stage and my name is over the company doors, but I couldn't do what I do, at the level I work at, unless I had the confidence I have in my staff. And although I have a lot of winners on my team, I know they perform even better when I recognize them.

So don't ever assume that Mary knows she's doing a great job with purchasing — keeping costs down and quality up. Don't ever assume Jim understands how much you appreciate his ability to bring in new customers. It's wise to use the best of everyone's talents. However, it's even wiser to recognize the Marys and

Jims of the working world for what they do. When people know you appreciate their work, they will bend over backward to help and please you. They won't just climb the wall for you; they'll go through it if that's what it takes.

You don't have to be the boss or owner to give people recognition for a job well done. *Everyone* can and should do it. You make the other person feel important. You feel good for having made their day and, lo and behold, very likely you'll soon be on the receiving end of some recognition of your own. Wouldn't that be nice? There's an old saying that fits here: "What goes around comes around." I've seen it happen countless times in both my personal and business activities.

Why not be the instigator of good things in *your* place of business?

Who's Really in Selling — Everyone!

This isn't a trick question. The answer to the question "Who's *really* in selling?" is *everyone.* The person who isn't selling isn't living. At some point nearly every day, you are involved in a selling situation of some sort. You may call it by a different name or not even recognize it as an act of selling but, all the same, selling it is.

You may have persuaded your husband to put down the newspaper or remote control so you two can catch up on what's going on in each other's busy life — or your selling could be as complex as negotiating a multimillion-dollar land acquisition. You may have convinced your son to wear a piece of clothing that's clean and has no holes in it. You may have convinced your sister to join you for lunch at your favorite restaurant instead of hers. Getting her to pick up the tab is another thing.

In some cases, however, you may have been on the receiving end of these situations. If you're a spouse who'd rather read up on a vital piece of news than chat about an upcoming social event, a child who feels it's vital to wear what you choose, or someone who's tired of always eating at your sister's favorite restaurant instead of your own, you've still been involved in a selling situation.

In this second scenario, I want you to recognize that selling skills help you gain more control over your life when others have what they think are better things for you to do or different choices for you to make. You can present your side of the situation in a nonconfrontational and effective manner.

Show me the wrinkled-up little face of a 5-year-old, on the verge of tears, trying to get Mom or Dad to buy a toy. This little person is selling — big-time. If Mom or Dad says no, he uses a fundamental selling technique. He asks a question: "Why, Mommy?" "Why, Daddy?" He's trying to move them from saying "No" to saying "Yes."

Watch the teenager who wants to stay out late, go to the movies on a weeknight, or borrow the car. That's selling.

Show me a high school junior who's trying to get a date with a popular athlete and watch all the concepts of selling that come into play.

Obviously, we've all encountered career salespeople in business settings. That's a given. It's also easy to recognize when we are being romanced by the latest luxury car manufacturer on prime-time TV. But what about all those unexpected, overlooked selling situations we experience on a daily basis? We frequently come across excellent examples of selling, completely oblivious to the fact that selling has even occurred.

Actors and actresses

Have you ever thought about the selling abilities of actors and actresses? Actors and actresses are actually professional salespeople who only pretend to act. Look at the many ways they use their selling skills:

- They have to sell themselves. They need to convince themselves they have what it takes to fulfill a particular role.
- They have to persuade an agent that they are a valuable commodity to represent.
- They have to convince the casting director that they are right for the part.
- They have to give a believable performance so that you and I are sold on their portrayal of a character.

As with any selling situation, their incomes and level of personal happiness are directly proportional to their level of competence in those four areas. The sad part is that, once they're famous, the public often assumes that they came out of nowhere — that they got a lucky break. The stories of their early career struggles often don't surface until some interviewer digs them up. All the years of selling are what made them what they have become.

People who make fine dining fine

I'm switching to an entirely different profession now: restaurant servers. We've all heard the stories of how many actors and actresses supported themselves as restaurant servers while they waited for their big break. It's easy work to get. There's not much training required. The money can be pretty good. Not many restaurant owners expect you to make a career of it, so quitting when you get that break isn't too big a deal.

Where do you think the connection is? What do these people do during the course of their employment? Do they just take your order and carry food, or do they try to sell you on the enjoyment of your dining experience? Those two choices bring to mind very different pictures. The wise waiter or waitress gives you choices of drinks, appetizers, meals, and desserts. They don't just ask to take your order. Why? Because those who employ a bit of salesmanship are almost guaranteed to receive higher tips.

I know this from personal experience. No, I've never waited on tables. But, with all the traveling I do, I've certainly seen hundreds (if not thousands) of waiters and waitresses in action. I've trained some of the staff at an excellent restaurant chain in my hometown of Phoenix, Arizona. I've heard stories from students who have either applied the selling strategies to that type of employment or have helped others apply those strategies.

In one particular case a student's daughter, Kristen, had inadvertently learned some of our selling strategies on a car trip in which her dad listened to one of our audio tape series. She got a job part-time while she was in high school as a waitress in a restaurant/ice cream shoppe. Being the new girl on the shift, she had the fewest tables but, much to the surprise of the other waitresses, she was earning more tip money than they were. It wasn't just because she was a young, friendly blonde with a nice manner, either.

So what did make the difference? This: Kristen never asked her diners if they wanted dessert; she *assumed* that they did. She asked them which dessert or what kind of sundae they wanted. She smiled at them a lot, too. Not surprisingly, her diners placed more orders than the other waitresses' customers did. And, with higher dinner checks, her customers of course left her higher tips, too. So even though Kristen didn't have as many tables to cover, she was making great money and not running ragged for a lot of smaller tips as some of the other waitresses were. Selling skills helped her get the most out of her efforts.

Doctors sell you into saying "Ahh"

Doctors evaluate our health history, current health habits, and lifestyle. Then they make recommendations based on their experience and the latest proven medical advice. Dentists clean your teeth, make minor repairs, major repairs, and recommend certain types of treatment.

Tremendous benefits can accrue to both doctors and dentists when they learn — and use — selling skills. On the one hand, they will be better prepared to convince you and their other patients to follow their professional advice. On the other hand, they'll build their practices because you'll be so happy with their advice that you'll tell at least three people how great your doctor and dentist are, thus sending them referral business.

My dentist has invested some of his valuable time in learning selling skills, and now he has a much more rewarding practice. He's having an easier time convincing his patients to take advantage of preventive measures rather than letting them put off having the services performed and treating them later for more serious conditions. It's a win-win situation. His patients are happy to come in when it's for something of a preventative nature. As with most of us, when we have to go in for something more serious, we're not usually too happy about it. His use of selling skills has increased the level of confidence his patients have in him, which is building his business tremendously.

Lawyers set the stage for selling

Lawyers need selling skills in every aspect of their profession. They have to sell not only to get business, but to persuade a judge or jury that their client is in the right. They must cajole fearful witnesses to step forward with testimony that may significantly affect the outcome of a case. They instruct their clients on how to give effective testimony. They instruct jurors on the law, persuading them to remember to set aside their emotions and concentrate on the facts of the case and the relevant legal issues.

One of the strongest selling skills that lawyers use is *setting the stage* for selling. The highly successful lawyers know where to position themselves in the courtroom, when to pause for effect, when to raise or lower their voices to capture the attention of the jurors, how to use body language to influence the jurors' decisions, and how to appear calm and in control of the entire courtroom scenario. Unfortunately, like professional salespeople, lawyers struggle with a negative image that is often undeserved. If you ever get chosen for jury duty, watch the sales performances given by the attorneys representing each side. These people do practice their craft. If they can't sell, they won't win cases. And attorneys with poor track records don't last long.

Politicians sell, and sell, and sell

If it's not too agonizing for you to do, think about politicians for a second. When I say that politicians are professional salespeople, invariably the eyes of some of my students roll back into their heads. But think about politicians for another second: The single most important lesson they can teach us is the importance of following through on promises. Too many times, the public has felt manipulated or cheated by candidates who promised tax cuts, yet then introduced new budgets that increased spending as soon as the candidates got elected.

It doesn't take a scholar to recognize some politicians' contradictions, but I would never want to give the impression that all politicians are contradictory. That would be as unfair a stereotype as I have had to face all of my adult life about salespeople. However, I do want to illustrate the point that promises are best made when they can be fulfilled in a reasonable amount of time with mutually understood expectations.

How do we develop our expectations about political candidates? How do they get elected? They persuade the most people who actually go to the polls on election day that they can and will do the job those voters want done once they are elected. How do they do this? They find out what your hot buttons are — the things you're most concerned about, such as a balanced budget, crime, family values, or whatever. Then they build their platforms on those issues, giving you back your own answers to the problems. Because they agree with your opinions, you see them as being a lot like you and you probably vote for them.

Politicians' knowledge and use of selling skills enable them to persuade you to give them what they want.

Parents, our most important sellers

Mothers and fathers use selling skills almost every waking hour. Hopefully, they sell each other repeatedly on the value of their relationship with each other and with each of their children. Every day, parents move others by persuading, cajoling, teaching, and inspiring them. Those four skills should be at or near the top of the list as prerequisites to childrearing — as they should be for any other selling situation, too.

Whether by words or example, parents constantly sell their children values and beliefs. They convince or persuade the children on what to wear or eat, how to act, who to have as friends, how to be a friend, and thousands of other things children need to learn in order to grow into happy, healthy, well-adjusted adults. A good understanding of selling skills can make this tough job a lot less stressful.

Kids sell the darndest things

Children are some of the best, most persistent salespeople around. In fact, you probably were as a child, too.

Do you recall ever wanting something so badly that you would have done practically anything to get it? It might have been your first bicycle or that adorable, cuddly little puppy in the pet shop. You probably pleaded your case to every friend and relative you could think of, and maybe even to some people you didn't know well, too — anybody who could possibly have engineered a happy ending for you.

You probably found the bike shop with the best selection and the lowest prices or the pet shop's business hours and a smiling salesperson who answered all your questions about taking care of Puppy. Next you ventured the tried-and-true technique of reminding forgetful parents — gently, of course — or those who may have suffered from selective hearing syndrome or a slight case of memory loss. It was survival of the fittest, and your skill at selling very likely was fitter than your parents' skill at resisting. Most of the time, you probably got what you wanted.

If this scenario doesn't ring any bells for you and you have no children, watch someone else's child in a store sometime. Few children can go into a store and resist the things shopkeepers purposefully place on the lower shelves to tempt the young. Considerate of them, isn't it? Get ready, though. You are about to observe master sellers at work. Simply notice what they say and how they act when they try to persuade Mom, Dad, or Grandma to get them what they want. It's selling at its best.

We had a saying in our household when my children were young: "You've got to sell to survive." I began teaching my children selling skills when they were very young, and they are still benefiting from them today. Now we're working on the grandchildren.

When I took my children to the 7-Eleven™, for example, they would say, "Daddy, which should I have — a Popcicle® or a Fudgecicle®?" What was happening? If I chose either answer, they got ice cream. In Chapter 2, I elaborate on the questioning techniques that they so masterfully used.

Friendships, selling to and fro

How about your friends? Have they ever sold you anything? They probably have, but I'm not talking about a car or piece of stereo or computer equipment here. Do they ever recommend a movie to see? Certainly. They're your friends. If they see something they like, they think you'll like it, too, so they want to tell you about it. Sometimes they recommend a place to eat. Other times they persuade you to go to concerts or sporting events with them.

But what they're really doing is *building the relationship.* The more memories you share, the closer you'll continue to be. And so it is with the art of selling. The more rapport you establish with the prospective buyer or friend or lover, the better your chances for building a strong, mutually beneficial working relationship.

Spouses-to-be sell marriage & other bliss

If you are not married, but would like to be, you will put forth one of the most important sales presentations of your life in persuading your significant other of the value of spending the rest of his or her life with you.

Then, of course, the trick is to keep persuading that significant other to stay with you. This is one of the most important relationships in your life and you need to pay attention to it and build it. This will also help you get around "Do you want to?", "Do *you* want to?", "I asked you first . . ."

Getting happily involved at work

Do your business associates ever try to involve you in one of their projects — something that's outside your normal realm of responsibility?

What they're really trying to do is to sell you on doing what they need to have done. How do they go about this? They may invite you to sit in on a meeting, to give an opinion or feedback, or even to meet over lunch to discuss some ideas. Most of these scenarios allow you to give an opinion with no requirement of committing time and effort to the project. No one minds giving an opinion as long as there are no strings attached. But, what then happens in many business situations is that they get you interested or even excited about the project and, before you know it, your name appears on the project's list of people to keep informed. You are now a part of this project.

Chances are good that you have lunch with one or more of your coworkers every day. How do you decide where to go? Pay attention to the situation, and you'll see that one person probably has a taste for a particular type of food — and tries to convince the others to want it as well. Are they suggesting or are they trying to sell you on their choice? Have you ever been on the giving end of the suggestions? I'll guess that you have been at least once or twice. And guess what that brings us to? *You are in selling!*

The Moral: Sell Well, and You'll Go Far

The question now is *how good are you at selling?* If you're pretty good, you're probably making a satisfactory income and you have rewarding personal relationships. Those are some of the benefits of being a good salesperson. However, if you're not completely satisfied with your income level or with the quality of your personal relationships, make the development of selling skills a priority. Having those skills is like having an inside track on what the next batch of winning lottery numbers will be.

All you have to do is invest a bit of your time and effort to understand and apply these tried-and-true, proven-effective skills to your everyday life. Before you know it, they'll be such a natural part of you that no one, including yourself, will even recognize them as selling skills. People around you will see you as just a really nice, competent person instead of the stereotypical, cigar-chomping, back-slapping, plaid-coated, hand-masher, used-car salesman that most people associate with selling. And, believe me, you'll then be in the class of people who make the world go around.

Chapter 2

Questioning Your Way to Success

In This Chapter

- How questions draw your prospects in
- Why you need to ask what your prospects already know
- How four simple question methods can make all the difference
- Why ask why?

If you lack fundamental communication skills, you probably find it difficult not only to get your point across, but also to convince others of the value of your offering. The power of effective communication skills is extremely underrated in my estimation. All too often people assume that they are communicating only when they are talking. They fail to acknowledge the other half of communication, thus they never master even the lowest level of communication. Fundamental communication skills boil down to listening and talking. In the case of persuasion situations, talking should primarily include asking questions.

Asking questions is a vital sign of curiosity and we will never learn anything unless we are first curious enough to study it. In fact, noting the number of questions children ask is like taking the pulse of their intelligence level.

In today's society, children are encouraged to ask more questions than ever before. It's a method of discovery that has become part of the teaching process and I think it's wonderful. You may doubt that I, a salesperson, would praise a trend to encourage people to ask questions; everyone knows salespeople must talk, talk, talk in order to sell, right?

Wrong! My years of experience with millions of salespeople have proven to me that the top people have one very important characteristic in common: they are great listeners. They listen not only with their ears but with their eyes. They watch key body language signs that people give while they are speaking and they use the knowledge they gain from listening to their advantage.

There's a story Dale Carnegie tells in his wonderful book, *How to Win Friends and Influence People,* that I must share here. Mr. Carnegie once was invited to a party at which he knew few people. During the course of the evening, he spoke with several new acquaintances. The following day, the host of the party received several compliments on the new guest — specifically, that he was a wonderful conversationalist.

You probably picture Mr. Carnegie in the middle of a group of people, spouting hilarious stories and imparting interesting facts. Not so. *All* Mr. Carnegie did was invest a little time with several people one on one. When introduced to them, he asked them each a question about their backgrounds. The guests, of course, obliged with discourses in varying lengths about their lives. Whenever they paused, Mr. Carnegie asked another question or encouraged them simply by saying, "Go on." Mr. Carnegie actually spoke very little the entire evening, yet he was thought of highly by the others as a great "conversationalist."

People love to feel that what they are saying is important to someone else.

By questioning and encouraging others, you are in essence telling them that you're interested in them and their needs. You're again doing the opposite of what the stereotypical salesperson does. You're not being pushy by telling them things. Instead, what happens when you ask someone a question is that you are *pulling* answers out of them; there's no pushing about it. Top-producing salespeople and extremely successful people in life in general know this and benefit tremendously from the strategy. It's very low-key and works great in building personal relationships as well.

If you want visual evidence of the power of pulling versus pushing, try this simple experiment. Get a piece of string about six inches long and lay it on the table or desk in front of you. Using your index finger only, pull one end of the string and see how it goes wherever you lead. Now, try pushing that same end to get where you want it to go. This method works the same with people as it does with the string.

There's an interesting parallel here: those top people in selling are like Mr. Carnegie. They're not interesting *ex*troverts who control conversations by talking and pushing their knowledge and experiences upon others. Instead, they are interested *in*troverts who have learned to control by asking questions and listening to answers. The answers to their carefully crafted questions almost always prove to be to their advantage. This again applies to all areas of our lives. If others feel important when they are with us, they will make us important to them.

Why Ask?

There are many, many benefits to learning to ask questions rather than to drone on and on. If you're the person asking the questions, the first benefit is that you are in control. Watch Barbara Walters during one of her interviews. Or watch any law program on television and pay attention to the attorneys while they examine witnesses. By the very questions that they ask, they direct the entire content of what the judge and jury hear. That's selling.

When you try to sell or persuade, you want to ask questions that help reveal the other person's broad area of interest and then help isolate their hot buttons. This information is vital if you want to end up with a win-win situation. You won't be able to provide the best solution for someone's needs until you know everything you can about what those needs are. I'll talk more about determining just what those needs are in detail in Chapter 10, but here's an example.

If your children's current hot button is the fancy new athletic shoes they've seen on television and you're trying to convince them to become more active and perhaps try a new sport, that would be valuable information in your persuasion tactics, wouldn't it?

As a child, you instinctively knew this strategy worked. Once you became an adult, you assumed that you had control and stopped asking questions to ensure control. A kid who wants new shoes will approach you this way:

> *Gee, Dad, wouldn't it be great if I could run and jump like Michael Jordan?*

When Dad agrees, what's next?

> *Gosh, Dad, Michael has these great shoes that really help him. If I had those shoes, don't you think they'd help me, too?*

Of course, Dad can come up with a host of reasons not to buy the shoes, most of which require some explanation including the fact that the shoes cost almost as much as the monthly mortgage payment. However, in listening to that explanation, Junior grabs ever so tightly to any little inference that the shoes may soon find their way to his feet. He finds out what Dad's hot button is and uses it to his advantage. This may include

> *Gee Dad, if I had those shoes, and could learn to play basketball as well as MJ, I'd buy you a house.*

As illogical an argument as that could be from Dad's viewpoint, the sentiment may very well be the catalyst that makes the sale.

Little Questions, Big Agreements

You can use questions to acknowledge or confirm a statement your prospect made that is important to your final request — the decision you want your listener to make.

Say someone tells you that gasoline mileage is very important to them in buying a new car. When you're getting ready to ask them for a final decision, you would include in your summary of the reasons why they should go ahead a question like this:

> *Didn't you say that fuel economy was your primary concern?*

Such a question starts the *yes* momentum you need in order to encourage them to go ahead and agree with you. The *yes* momentum is what every persuader strives for. Once you get them agreeing to things, if you simply keep asking the right question — kind of like following a flow chart — they'll follow where you want to lead them and have enough information at the end to make a wise decision, which is hopefully that they can't live without your product or service.

Selling or persuading requires you to get a lot of little agreements that lead to a big final agreement. Face it: If your prospects don't agree with at least a few things during your initial contact and qualification, you wouldn't waste your time or theirs presenting your idea, product, or service to them, would you?

Questions help you get your listener thinking in the affirmative. Even a question like this gets the ball rolling:

> *A reputation for professionalism is important, isn't it?*

It may not look like much, but it gets you at least one minor agreement. I've never had anyone respond to that question with

> *Oh, no. We don't want to work with professionals. We prefer to deal only with con artists and liars.*

If you or your company is highly professional and competent, why not turn that statement into a question that gets your listener's agreement?

Questions Create Emotional Involvement

Questions also create emotional involvement. If you're marketing home security devices, you can ask

> *Wouldn't you feel more confident about entering your home knowing that if there was any danger, you would be warned beforehand?*

What does that question do? It raises a prickle of alarm on the back of your prospect's neck about the unknown possibilities of walking into an unprotected home. That's emotional involvement. It's a requirement in any selling situation. Think of at least two ways to build emotion into every presentation you make through the use of questions.

If you hear an objection somewhere in your presentation to what you are proposing, ask a question:

> *If I could show you how to turn that into a benefit, would you still be interested?*

Or

> *If I can overcome that challenge, is this service something you would be interested in?*

What do such questions accomplish for you? They help you avoid confronting your listener, for starters; causing them to raise their wall of defense against a charging salesperson. You need to do whatever is possible to keep the lines of communication open. You want them to see you as someone who is on the same side of the wall with them. You are interested in their best interests. When people give you an objection, it's often simply a stall or method of slowing down the pace of things. I cover this in great detail in Chapter 11 on addressing customer concerns. If the objection they've raised carries enough weight with them, it could tell you that this sale is not going to happen. If it's not that heavy a weight, they will have given you something of interest to them that you must address in your presentation stage. You should learn just how serious that objection really is so you can determine your next course of action.

Ask What They Know

Before you ask any question, remember this: *in order to sell or persuade, you need to make the other person feel important.* They need to feel smart, too. So never, never, ever ask a question that your listener cannot answer.

For example, if you ask someone what the available memory is on their computer and they don't know, you've just made them uncomfortable. Yuck! Avoid that result at all costs. If they haven't brought up the subject of available memory, you should ask whether they have the information available on their current computer. Chances are good that they do. If you tell them specifically the information you need, they can get it. But if you assume that they know it, and they don't know it, you've just embarrassed them. They may find someone else to buy from who may be a little more sensitive and able to make them feel important.

And where does that leave you? With no sale.

Selling on a Personal Level

An important area of your life is your personal relationships. Personal relationships are supposed to be mostly fun and rewarding. If you don't think that you have enough fun in your life, do something about it.

The major difference between average people who live average lives and those who have a lot of satisfaction and success is the ability to persuade others to accept their way of thinking. They love life and look for fun things to do that will create wonderful memories for them and their friends or relatives. They seek out adventure and convince others to join them on their journeys. They take charge of their lives, assuming full responsibility for their happiness and enthusiastically seek the means of achieving their dreams. They ask a lot of questions. Asking questions can make you happy, if they're the right questions.

Proven Questioning Techniques

I have my favorite techniques for asking questions that help you help someone else find what they're really looking for. These are my favorites: the tie-down, the alternate of choice, the porcupine, and the involvement.

Tying down the details

I teach many questioning techniques to my students at my live seminars, on my videos, and on my audio tape programs. One of the most popular techniques is called the *tie-down.* A tie-down does not involve tying clients into their chairs

Asking the right questions kept me in high school

I was in high school when I first realized the value of asking the proper questions. In those days, I was recognized as something of a leader, not academically, by any means, but in sports and some of the various clubs — definitely the more social aspects of school. I didn't always lead my classmates down the straight and narrow path, though. In fact, our class had a reputation for being pranksters. I was a great instigator and pretty good at hiding these types of "leadership" activities from the teachers.

For three years, I led my classmates to do things they probably shouldn't have done. At that point our principal, Father Wagner, learned of my part in the pranks and called me into his office. This was the first quarter of my senior year. Father Wagner listed about six "unusual occurrences" that had been attributed to me, so I knew that he had a reliable source of information. Father Wagner said that we were the worst class they'd had at our school in many years and that he'd decided to make an example of me: I was to be expelled from school! My heart and mind raced. What would my parents say? What would I do? I had to graduate with my class.

Father Wagner went on to say that our class was the first class not to have a gift to leave to the school at the end of the year. I was trying to think fast before he dismissed me and I was out of school forever. Suddenly I asked, "Would things be different if our class did have something to leave the school and I was the one to lead them to giving it?" He said he'd never considered that option. He left the door open for further discussion, though, so I told him I thought there was enough time for us to raise money for a class gift.

Then I asked another question: "What did the school need most?" Father Wagner challenged me with the biggest single item that the school had a need for — an electric scoreboard for the football field. As captain of the football team, I thought that was a great idea. Then he told me how much it would cost — $2,500.

This was 1962, mind you, and $2,500 was a lot more money then than it is today. I couldn't let the amount stagger me, though, because I was trying to resuscitate my dying senior year. So I asked another question: "If I raise the money for the scoreboard, will you let me graduate with my class?" Father Wagner again expressed doubt that it could be done, but I stuck to my guns. "If I make a commitment to doing this, will you let me stay in school with my class and graduate with them?" After what seemed an eternity, Father Wagner asked if I'd give my word to make it happen. I jumped at the opportunity and we shook hands on it.

Our class began with a car wash. It raised $200. We went to a junk yard and got the body of a car that wasn't in too bad shape, hauled it to the school grounds, and sold chances to hit it with a sledgehammer for $0.25 each. That raised $50. We were getting nowhere fast.

Then I heard a local car dealership advertising that they were giving away a new Thunderbird to whoever could find the right key. I knew I had my answer: all we needed was a car! I went to the dealership and talked with the owner. He was pleasant and offered to make a cash donation to our effort. I told him I didn't want his cash; I wanted to work with him to get him a lot of publicity while working toward our goal. He was interested all the way up to the point where I told him all we wanted was a new Thunderbird. He leaned back and laughed for a long time. Then he told me that I had a lot of guts asking for a car and that there was no way he could do that.

(continued)

(continued)

So I started asking *him* questions. "You do want to help your community, don't you?" Of course he did; he was a well-respected businessman. "Would you like to see the largest group of teens ever assembled, teens who will be car buyers in the near future, applauding your dealership?" Now I had his attention. How would I accomplish this great goal? I explained how we would give presentations at all the other high schools in the San Fernando Valley to invite their students to the biggest dance ever held in the area. Tickets to the dance would be $1.00, and each ticket held the opportunity to win a Thunderbird. He was interested, but he still wouldn't give us a car. I looked around the room and saw a gold-plated ashtray on his desk in the shape of a Thunderbird. I asked if he could donate the ashtray. He was puzzled by my sudden change in tactics, but he agreed.

The end result was that 2,450 teenagers showed up at our dance. It was the largest dance in the history of the San Fernando Valley at the time. We raised the money we needed and Father Wagner smiled the whole time he counted it. Our class gave the school the electric scoreboard and I gave one of the most winning presentations of my life the night of the dance when I had to present the winner with a gold-plated Thunderbird ashtray. Fortunately for me, it was a fellow student who held the winning number. He was so excited by the recognition from over 2,400 other kids, as well as by our feat of getting the scoreboard, that he didn't even get upset about the prize. In fact, he laughed. Then everyone laughed and had a great time at the dance. It was truly a win-win situation.

At the end of the evening, I got another call to come to the principal's office. This time a smiling Father Wagner gave me a talk I will never forget. He told me that if I could take all the talent I had shown in making that evening a success, and apply it to business, I would be a very successful man, regardless of how terrible a student I had been. That's when I realized how vital it is to ask the right questions. And, to this day, I thank Father Wagner every time the answer to one of my questions adds to my success.

until they say yes. Tie-downs involve making a statement, then asking for agreement by adding a question to the end of it. Some of the most effective tie-downs are these:

Isn't it?	*Doesn't it?*	*Hasn't he?*	*Haven't they?*
Don't you?	*Didn't you?*	*Shouldn't we?*	*Couldn't we?*

Here are some examples of how they're used:

- It's a great day for golf, *isn't it?* When your partner agrees, set a tee time.
- Cleaning up the area where our children play is important, *don't you think?* When this person agrees, sign them up for one hour of clean-up duty at your neighborhood park.
- Jet skiing at the lake this weekend sounds like fun, *doesn't it?* If they agree, call the rental place or get the jet ski tuned up — pronto.

- You had a great time the last time we went hiking, *didn't you?* Schedule a time to go again while your friends are in a positive frame of mind about the last trip.

The goal of using tie-downs is to get the person thinking in the affirmative about the subject you've just tied down. While they're agreeing with you, you can confidently bring up whatever it is you're trying to get a commitment on.

Professional salespeople often use tie-down statements such as this:

> *A reputation for prompt, professional service is important, isn't it?*

Who can say *no* to that? The salesperson who asks such a question has begun a cycle of agreement from the prospect who, hopefully, will continue to agree all the way through Steps #6 and #7 of the selling sequence, the same sequence I cover in Chapter 1.

The dinner alternative

You've certainly seen or heard the *alternate of choice* questioning technique used before, but you probably didn't recognize it as a sales strategy. It involves giving you two acceptable suggestions. It's most often used for calendar events such as appointments, delivery dates, and so on. Here are some simple examples:

- *I can arrange my schedule so we can visit on Thursday at 3:00 PM or would Friday at 11:00 AM be better?* Either answer confirms that you have an appointment.
- *We'll have our delivery truck at your home on Monday at 9:00 AM sharp. Or would 2:00 PM be more convenient?*

You also use the alternate of choice technique when you want to focus or limit the conversation to certain points. For example, if you are on a committee to revamp the playground in the neighborhood park, you may want to find a way to gather information without getting into a debate about other aspects of the project. Perhaps some of the neighbors want the playground placed on the Northeast corner of the park, while others want it on the Southwest corner. Your total involvement may be just to work with the construction crew — not to make or alter placement decisions. In that case, you could ask, "Which do you think would be a better surface under the equipment, wood chips or sand?" It helps you get right to the point of the matter and gives only the two solutions you need addressed.

Alternate of choice questions are particularly effective in surveys. The market researchers are seeking particular information, not general answers, so they build the questions in such a way that the prospect is limited in their responses.

The technique is great fun to use in your personal life as well. It works this way: You pick something you would like to have happen. Then you broach the subject to the person you'd like to have join you, giving them two options — either one giving you the go-ahead — and ask the magical question. Sounds simple, doesn't it?

If you'd really like to go out to dinner tonight with your spouse, don't say, *I'd like to go out to eat.* Don't even ask if they want to go out. Instead, ask, *What type of food would you prefer for dinner tonight, Mexican or Chinese?* Unless you or your spouse has the time, talent, and ingredients to prepare ethnic cuisine, chances are pretty darned good that you'll be eating out tonight. And how did you get there? Simply by making up your mind and gently persuading your spouse to go along with you.

Or take a more everyday example: If your daughter isn't thrilled with wearing dresses, but you have to get her one for a special event, don't ask her what type of dress she wants. Ask if she'd prefer pink or purple. You're no longer arguing about whether she's getting the dress, but you are giving her some choice in the matter.

Porcupine

This is one of my favorite questioning strategies. Many times, it has saved me from blurting out something that would have destroyed the *yes* momentum of the sale. You've probably asked a few loaded questions in your life. You were consciously or unconsciously trying to get information that may have proven favorable to you and not so favorable to the other side. If you're ever on the receiving end of something that might be considered a loaded question, picture this:

If I were holding a prickly porcupine right now and tossed it at you, what would you do? Instinctively, most people would either jump out of its way or catch it and quickly toss it back — kind of like a game of Hot Potato.

Try to remember this technique when someone asks you what could be a loaded question. You either want to sidestep it or toss it back. *How do you toss a question back? Ask another question about that question.*

Here's how it might go. Suppose that a prospective buyer of your vehicle ventures this seemingly innocent question:

> *Does this car have a warranty?*

How could this question be loaded? Consider: If you answer *yes* and they don't believe in warranties, what does that get you? A negative response, right? On the other hand, if a warranty is important to them and you simply answer *yes,* what happens? They register that fact and you don't necessarily move forward in the process of selling the car.

Instead of bogging yourself down with either a bad or dead-end answer to such a question, throw the porcupine back. Answer with a question of your own to clarify why they're asking:

> *Is having a warranty something you're interested in?*

Now you've thrown that porcupine back, and you've lessened the sting of its bristles by asking for clarification or elaboration. If having the warranty is a major decision, you'll know to bring it up again if they hesitate in making a final decision. And if the warranty is a negative for them, then you'll know to steer clear of mentioning it.

Getting them involved

Another questioning technique is called *the involvement question.* This simply means using questions to help your listeners envision themselves *after* they've made a decision to agree with you.

If you're marketing office equipment, you could involve them with a question like this:

> *Who will be the key contact for us to train on the use of the machine?*

Now you've got them thinking about implementing training *after* they own the product, not about whether or not they'll own it.

Similarly, if you want to involve someone in business with you, use a question like this:

> *What will you and Janet do with the extra income that our business plan says we'll generate in the next year?*

Is your listener thinking about whether to get into business with you? Nope. She's just envisioning spending the money she'll earn *after* she goes into business with you. If what she plans to spend the money on is something she wants badly enough, there's a good chance that she'll find herself *having* to go into business with you to satisfy a need she's been feeling without knowing how to fulfill it. Aren't you the good little fairy bringing her just the right solution?

How Questioning Techniques Get You to Yes

Now that I have covered the what of questioning strategies, I'll cover how they can best be used. Depending on what you're working with — a product, service, or idea — the right question will give you the information you need to persuade or convince the other party that they just have to be involved with it.

Selling products

When you're selling a product, whether it's tangible or intangible, you need to develop emotional involvement between the prospect and the product. The idea is to create ownership in the person's mind. Help them picture the product or service or its benefits in their daily lives. You do this with the help of questions.

If you were selling a new, more powerful computer hard drive to an office manager, you might ask, *Who will use the computer most often?* This question gets them thinking about what to do after they own it, doesn't it? (Recognize the tie-down?) They'll picture James hunkered down over his new equipment and getting more done than ever before. They'll picture the work area where they need to install the computer. *In their own minds,* they'll own the computer before they ever make the decision to go ahead. That's selling.

Real estate agents love the strategy of involvement questions. They use it most often when they show a home. They'll see the wife mentally measuring the size of the living room and ask, *Where in this room would you put your sofa?* Once she visualizes her largest piece of furniture in the room, she sees herself in that picture, too, which means that she sees herself the way the agent wants her to see herself — as owning that home.

On a more intangible level, some people are superb at persuading their spouses in their personal lives with involvement questions. You'll hear things like *Honey, where do you think we should put the new exercise machine, in the bedroom or in the family room?* "Honey" may not have known that he was even interested in an exercise machine or that he had to have an opinion about its placement. Nevertheless, if he's asked at the right time and place, his answer will probably be to give the go-ahead his spouse was seeking.

Selling ideas

Suppose that you have a great idea you'd like to have others share and get excited about. Take, for example, the issue of community safety. You want to start a Block Watch program, so you need to ask questions of your neighbors to determine their level of interest in such a program before you ask them what their commitment would be.

An effective tie-down might be this:

> *We're all concerned with keeping our families safe with the rising crime rate, aren't we?*

After they agree with you, you may want to get their commitment by following a statement with a tie down like this:

> *Nearly every family on the block has committed to one hour a week of involvement in this project. You do want to be a part of this valuable program, don't you?*

Used in a positive manner, peer pressure can be a good thing, can't it?

Chapter 3

Make Selling Your Hobby— It's All in the Attitude

In This Chapter

- Never mix business with pleasure — unless you know why you should
- How your life improves when you forget what you think you know
- How to keep riding the growth curve you're already on
- What pangs you feel when learning tugs at your comfort zone

Many people like to keep their business and personal lives separate. And, in some cases, that's necessary. For example, if you're a psychiatrist, you wouldn't want to limit your friendships to the people you've treated, would you? We have to have balance in our lives in order to fulfill ourselves. However, work and enjoyment shouldn't be two separate categories. Work and play can be separate since play usually consists of physical activity, however, there are those whose work involves teaching others to play, such as golf pros and coaches. I find it unfortunate, though, that so many people have jobs that fit my definition of work. As I see it, *work is anything you do when you'd rather be doing something else.* If you're doing exactly what you want to be doing, it should be called *fun* and *my favorite hobby.*

In most cases, treating your business as your hobby greatly increases your satisfaction and the enjoyment you get from your business. That's because you'll constantly be tuned into learning new things that will make business more fun *and more profitable*. I have to believe, from my own personal experience and from watching my students over the years, that learning something new stimulates the area in our brains that causes us to experience pleasure. When this starts happening, your business eventually *will* become your hobby. Someday you won't have to convince yourself anymore that business can be fun; the marriage of the two will become second nature.

Passion meets profession for the Golden Bear

Want a prime example of making your profession your hobby? Take a look at the Golden Bear himself, Jack Nicklaus.

Nicklaus has been doing the same thing to earn an income for many years. When he started playing golf as a young boy, though, I'll bet he wasn't thinking of golf as a career. But when he fell in love with golf, he was able to turn it into his hobby first, treating it as a career only secondarily.

He had to have had plenty of days when he didn't want to practice. He probably had plenty of days when golf was the last thing on his mind. But his passion to excel at golf outweighed any temporary lapses in his desire to practice.

Mastering his profession became the only way for him to satisfy his passion, and vice versa. Nobody had to convince Jack Nicklaus of the value of "loving what you do."

This merging of passion and profession has occurred for me with selling. For me, selling began as a career opportunity that would fulfill a need — the need to make money. When I failed miserably at first, I knew I needed help and started a journey of study. I knew that some people made huge incomes in sales, so I assumed that they must have learned something I'd not yet discovered.

It was at that point that I chose to turn selling into my hobby. Once I started to educate myself — by watching everyday people for little nuances of selling that worked, by reading up on the subject — I also started making a lot of money. Believe me when I say that, at first, money was my motivation for keeping up my selling hobby.

But since then I've managed to turn my job-turned-hobby into something much more: It has become a way of life. Today I live and breathe selling. I've built my business in such a way that I *enjoy* what I do for a living. I don't "work" anymore, if *work* means *doing some particular thing when you'd rather be doing something else.* Selling now pervades every communication I have with others, and I thoroughly enjoy my life these days.

If you're in a job you don't like in order to earn a living, stop a moment and analyze what's going on. Why don't you like what you're doing? Chances are pretty good that it's because you're not growing, achieving, or having fun. The reasons behind those feelings usually have something to do with how competent you are in your field. If you're not really any good at what you do, it's no wonder your life's no fun.

If that's the realization you come to, you have two ways out:

1. Change what you do to something that is fun.
2. Get better at what you do to make it more fun.

That's the great thing about living in our day and age. We have choices. No one is going to hold a gun to your head and tell you that you have to have this career and none other. If you aren't happy with what you've got, there are thousands of other choices available to you.

How the Cream Does Rise

The main factor that separates the top 5 percent of us in sales from those who struggle to accomplish their goals is elementary (you thought I was going to say *my dear Watson,* didn't you?). Highly successful salespeople actually *enjoy* the crazy business of sales. To Champion salespeople, selling isn't a "a job." Instead, Champion salespeople have learned how to turn their selling into a hobby.

When they prospect, go to appointments, have a chance to visit, and ask for sales, Champion salespeople are doing what they love to do. It just so happens that Champions get paid very well for their hobbies. If you're struggling with your ability to sell *and* with finding the desire to make it to the top, then be glad that you and I are having this bookside chat because I've just given you the key to excelling in sales: *Turn your job into a hobby.* Before you know it, your new hobby will be a way of life. You will live and breathe selling — all to your advantage.

It's interesting: the more involved you get with selling, the more selling you observe going on around you in all walks of your life. When you truly *study* selling, you see that selling pervades every communication you have with others; and, on a more purely business level, you notice and compare the selling efforts of others to your own. The fun part is that people never know what you're up to. You get to make all the mental notes you want and they get to be your teachers. The best learning often (if not usually) occurs in an informal, nonselling atmosphere.

In other words, get used to a new sensation. In times and situations that you may not see as sales situations per se, suddenly a realization creeps right up on you and whispers *Hey, there's selling going on here. You should be taking notes.*

Business? Pleasure? What's the difference?

You've heard the advice to *Never mix business with pleasure.* Whoever wrote that maxim must not have had work that was much fun to do — and the person certainly wasn't a Champion salesperson. Learning to make selling your hobby blurs the distinction between what you do to live and what you live to do. Once you get the hang of making your work your hobby, you *always* mix business with pleasure.

When you don't enjoy what you do to earn money, you make a draining trade-off — interminably long hours for incalculably short vacations. My question to you is this: *As short as life is, are those two fun-filled weeks every summer worth the fifty weeks of drudgery just so that you can get two weeks of freedom?* I certainly hope they are. We are on this earth for such a short time why not do something you enjoy?

Or, especially if you're in sales, you can learn to enjoy what you're already doing. Learning and practicing the communication skills that are a part of selling is guaranteed to make your life more interesting. When you're doing something you're interested in, there has to be at least a little fun involved or it won't hold your interest.

And another question: *Do you ever feel guilty about taking time away from your job when you have fun on vacation?* If you answer *yes* to that question, you need to take a long, hard look at what you do for a living. You might even want to seek professional advice. Don't do a job just because it provides for you and your family. Consider what kind of life you're providing if every day you leave the house unhappy to go slogging again through the trenches.

Wouldn't it be much more fun to take each day and enjoy it to its fullest — looking forward to getting up every morning, bright-eyed and bushy-tailed, vibrant with anticipation for what the day will bring? What would your life be like if you could enjoy your job as much as you enjoy your hobby? What kind of life would you be providing for those around you if the central element of your life was no longer drudgery but the joy that comes from self-fulfillment? It would be like going to Disneyland every day without your kids.

Some selling today Can even cement the family way

I hope I've already convinced you that selling is a vital part of everything you do; maybe you were already trying on selling as a hobby before you bought this book. Either way, any time now you'll start to notice how salespeople treat you in retail situations. And maybe you'll pay more attention to your family communications, too.

In fact, an increased awareness of family communications is one of the strongest benefits of learning selling skills.Your kids are probably the best salespeople around. Ever notice how attentive they can be when they want to borrow the car or need money for the latest style of jeans or athletic shoes? Ever hear this one?

> *Dad, will you be using the car Friday or Saturday night?*

How does the conversation go from there? About to get blindsided, you absentmindedly say,

> *Yes, on Saturday.*

Then your kid says,

> *Great, Dad! I'll take it on Friday.*

If you're a parent, you hear such examples of master salesmanship all the time as a matter of course. You may not have realized it, but in examples such as this the child has used the classic *alternate of choice* technique from Chapter 2. And you didn't feel a thing.

Hobbies versus Jobs

Take a look at the difference between how we treat our hobbies and how we treat our jobs. Maybe then it will become clear why it's often so much easier to be the best, the top of the heap, in your hobbies than it is to excel on the job.

I contend that if more people looked at selling as a hobby — with energy, enthusiasm, excitement, fervor, anticipation, devotion, and sheer fun — they would be leaders in all walks of their lives. In fact, we'd be watching them on *Lifestyles of the Happy and Fulfilled.*

What makes you successful in your hobby? Have you ever noticed the difference in expression and animation in people when they talk about their hobbies compared to when they talk about their jobs? If you haven't noticed this up to now, test this theory yourself. Ask a few people this question and pay attention to their answers: *How do you like to spend your days?* Rarely will you hear about people's jobs. Instead, the conversation usually turns to how they spend their recreation time.

People gladly talk about their children's lives. They talk about their last ski trip, their favorite authors, travel to fun places, friends they enjoy. They may show you their craftwork or even proudly invite you to the cabin they built in the woods. People always express attitudes toward hobbies positively, with much relish of talk of the latest doodad they hope to invest in (soon!) to keep up to date with their passion.

Get used to it, folks; we're becoming computer-literate. As with any other talent or skill, computers can easily turn into a hobby once you start to get the hang of them. You find yourself picking up literature on the latest hardware innovations. You peruse catalogs for fun *and* for effective software programs. You try to get other members of your family involved. Even toddlers today are learning how to point and click.

Computer manufacturers, suppliers, and support people have reached us at our base level by making the operation fun and pretty easy to learn. Because of that, sales of computers and all their related paraphernalia are skyrocketing. The industry as a whole has changed attitudes toward computers by bringing them to the level of the common person and letting us fall in love with them.

Attitude makes the difference

Studies have proven that *attitude* is one of the traits that separate so-so salespeople from their highly successful colleagues. I have to believe that it's true in life in general, not just in sales. Think about the happiest, most successful people you know. How do you usually find them? Are they depressed, negative, or even apathetic? I doubt it. They're probably upbeat, smiling, and positive about life.

Why not take the same positive, interested attitude you have toward your hobbies and transfer your passion to your ability to sell yourself, your ideas, or the end results of your hobby (if you're involved in craft- or handiwork)?

Instead of turning your selling job into a hobby, why not take the hobby you love so much and figure out how to market it or yourself? I'm not saying this change will make you a millionaire, but money isn't the only measure of success. If you could support yourself comfortably on the earnings from your hobby, I would deem you as having a successful life.

Success can fit many definitions — including yours

I always enjoy asking my seminar audiences for definitions of the term success. I've probably asked well over 500 people to define success for me over the years. I haven't kept strict records on their answers, however, I'd have to guess that I have rarely gotten repeat answers. That's because success is something like fingerprints; it's individual. Of course many of the answers I've received have reflected a desire for monetary riches, love and security, but few people have been able to put into words the specifics in such a manner as it would be understood by all who hear it. I've thought a lot about a definition of success and developed this one that I teach my students. It seems to cover most of the answers I've heard.

Success is the continuous journey toward the achievement of predetermined, worthwhile goals.

I like the phrase "continuous journey" because I don't think anyone really wants to arrive at success and be done. In fact, I don't think it's possible to reach a place called success and be happy there forever. Look at Olympic athletes. At very young ages, they achieve greatness, worldwide acclaim, and medals which many say show that they are successful. If that achievement was success, then what do they do with the rest of their lives?

The other phrase that I like is, "predetermined, worthwhile goals." Predetermined shows that there was a choice made, a course set. It was something that required thorough consideration and perhaps inspiration to commit to. Worthwhile is key because I truly believe in the good of all mankind and that the majority of people in the world want to do something of worth with their lives. Consider using this definition for yourself and lay a course for an exciting journey toward success!

Think about it! You already have the built-in enthusiasm, excitement, and knowledge of your hobby. Now all you need to do is show others why they need to feel the same way. If you do a little research, you'll find that many very successful businesspeople started out by selling their hobbies. Determine what you love to do, and then figure out a way to get paid for it. What could be better?

Emotional involvement supplies the meaning

Another important aspect of hobby enthusiasts that workers often lack is *emotional involvement.* Too many people who are disillusioned with their jobs develop a detached attitude about what goes on in their work environment. They become disinterested observers. They don't join in the company's extracurricular activities. They don't interact much with others, either.

To those who bring enthusiasm to their jobs, life is much more interesting and more fun. Even if you're not thrilled with what you do for a living, you must at least be pleased with living. Learn to bring that pleasure into your work and your work may just become more fun, too.

You must be able to find at least a smidgen of something you like about your job — even if it's just the cool telephone you get to use or having business cards. Maybe it's having someone besides a relative who calls you by name. Whatever. There must be *some*thing you like about what you do for a living.

If you're having trouble finding even one little thing to like about your job, then I suggest that you seriously consider making a change: either change yourself or change your job. There's no reason why anyone should have to suffer through a job they hate. Such people aren't doing themselves or their employers any good by continuing on with it.

Sport hobbies usually carry a lot of emotional involvement. If your hobby is an outdoor sport, such as mountain biking, nothing is more exciting than cresting mountain peaks at sunrise or soaring downhill so fast that you have a permanent grin on your face. It's not just a physical experience, either: it's charged with emotional involvement. When you schedule a biking event, it becomes a highlight that gives you a great feeling whenever you think about it. You involve yourself in planning every detail to make the outing the best one yet. You live and breathe for the next opportunity to get out there with your mountain-biking cohorts.

When you think about your biking events, you feel an emotional jolt. Mountain biking also involves a great deal of physical preparation and can be quite challenging. But if the emotional involvement is strong enough, you can hurdle those barriers with no sweat (so to speak). When you get right down to it, avid mountain bikers have become sold on their pastime because they want to experience the emotional involvement that others have shared with them.

Selling: It Goes with Everything

If your hobby is creating physical goods such as woodwork, quilts, knitting, and food, eventually you'll run out of room for all that you will produce. So how do you get the products of your hobby out of your house and into someone else's? You get them to want it and take it cheerfully and, in some cases, even to give you money for it. Hmm. Sounds like selling, doesn't it?

If your hobby is travel, do you go alone — or do you persuade someone else to come along with you? It's not too exciting to take a cruise without someone to share the fun with. So how do you get someone to come along on that cruise with you? You sell them on it.

Whatever your hobby is, it's bound to be more enjoyable when you share it with someone. And building relationships, as you just saw, always involves selling skills.

Trading Knowledge for a Sense of Wonder

Starting the hobby of selling is pretty simple. It doesn't require any special tools or equipment. There's no large investment. You don't have to travel far to participate, either.

What do you need to do to start? Pay attention to the way your children or parents communicate with you about family matters. Watch how retail clerks treat you and notice how you feel about the store because of them. Get into the habit of really *reading* billboards and newspaper ads. Which ones are talking directly to you and why? Listen carefully to radio spots; those that hold your attention the longest deserve some analysis.

In general, become a student of the selling that is presented to you daily by our country's top sales and marketing experts.

Time to learn, time to burn

Although we allow children the privilege of ample time to learn, we often don't allow ourselves as adults the same privilege. We assume we're too busy to take educational courses. Or that we learn faster on our own. Or that we don't really need to know much more than we already know. Tune into *Jeopardy*® sometime to find out exactly how much you don't know.

Did you realize that the large majority of people discontinue their conscious learning experiences in life when they complete their formal education? There are hundreds of thousands of mature adults in our country who have not learned in the past 20 years half as much as they learned in their four years of high school or college courses.

Studies have shown that developing the habit of listening to educational cassette tapes in your car during commuting time can provide you just as much information as studying for a master's degree. How hard can it be to carry some tapes around with you all the time? You probably already do it with music. But when was the last time your favorite music group taught you anything that made you more successful in life?

Learning means having productive mistakes

Giving yourself permission to be a lifelong student can change your life dramatically. Students don't always do things right the first time around. So giving yourself permission to be a student also gives you the right to make mistakes. It takes some of the pressure off: you don't have to be right all the time just because you're an educated adult.

Having the attitude of a student should keep you from beating yourself up over failures. Instead, look at your mistakes as learning experiences. As a student, you must admit that you are fallible. Until you make that admission, you won't move far off the mark you're currently standing on.

After you do admit that you can make mistakes, though, you will seek out others who can teach you, others who can help you grow into the person you want to become. When you open yourself up to the possibility that you don't know everything and don't have all the answers, you start a quest to discover what you don't know. It's an important step in the learning process.

One of my favorite reminders about learning is this: You can recognize true professionals by how much they learn after they "know it all." If you ever assume you know all there is to know about something, or even if you accept that you know enough, you have just doomed yourself to mediocrity.

The Learning Curve — Passing from Beginner to Butterfly

No one masters something new at first exposure. Of course there are those with some natural talents or skills from other learning experiences that apply to the new experience, but mastery cannot occur on initial impact. None of us learned to walk on our first try. Learning anything takes exposure and practice. It also takes a good psychological mindset that understands that there is a learning curve associated with most new things.

If you comprehend and agree with the preceding paragraph, then you are ready to read and hopefully accept the four levels of competency. Once you accept this as fact, you'll find it easier to identify and work from each level to the next.

Unconscious incompetence

There are four levels of competency in any area of life. The first level is known as *unconscious incompetence.* In this most elementary phase, you find people who do not even know that they do not know what they are doing. They are the hardest people to help because they haven't yet recognized or won't admit they need help.

These are the people who drift into your lane on the freeway and never realize you were there. They unknowingly leave grocery carts perilously close to new cars. They tend to live rather mediocre lives because they either haven't woken up enough to know there's more to be learned — more to be aware of — or they have simply resigned themselves to be whatever they are at the present moment.

There's a second type of individual that falls in this category. It's you and me. *What?* you say, *I never do things like that.* You may not now, but chances are pretty good that you did before you became aware. We are all at the Unconscious Incompetent level of learning whenever we first try something new. Unsure? Try juggling. Sure, it looks easy enough and any intelligent person with a smattering of motor skills ought to be able to handle it.

Watch a baby learning to walk. He doesn't know he doesn't know how to walk. He just tries it because everyone else is doing it. When he learns, by falling, that it's not as easy as it looks, he'll reach for helping hands. The instant he reaches for help, he moves to the next level of competency — the conscious incompetent.

Conscious incompetence

The second level is *conscious incompetence.* People abandon unconscious incompetence when they suddenly realize that they don't know what they're doing. You are very likely at this level of competency right now in the wonderful world of sales. You've admitted that you don't have all the answers and that you want to learn more. And how do I know such an intimate thing about you? Because I have the pleasure of your company now even as we speak. You wouldn't be reading this book if you hadn't admitted that you still have something to learn about selling.

But heed one word of caution here: Now that you realize that you need to learn more, take action now! Too many potentially great careers have been stalled at this level because people don't know where to turn for help or won't expend the effort to find the right help. Your lack of competency can be overwhelming if you don't take charge. Don't be like the deer you sight in your headlights at night, frozen to a spot on the road. You must *move* in order to rise to the third level.

Conscious competence

When you reach the third level, *conscious competence,* you find new challenges and new victories. By this point, your desire to improve has become strong enough to overcome the discomfort of learning something new. You're testing the waters now. Just don't place too high a level of expectation on yourself and you'll do better faster. Tensing up when you try new things takes your enjoyment from the experience.

The tension also clouds your judgment when you must analyze how well you did and how you can improve the next time. Remember how uncomfortable you felt in your first algebra class, or in any other class, on the first day? Why were you so uncomfortable? Because you were *acutely* consciously incompetent. But there you sat anyway, having committed to being there (or, at any rate, with your parents having committed you to being there) so that you could learn enough to reach the level of conscious competence.

Unconscious competence

All of which brings me to the fourth and final level of competence, *unconscious competence.* At this stage in learning, you apply all of your previous knowledge without making a conscious effort to do so.

You are smack in the middle of an example of unconscious competence right now — you're reading this book. You probably aren't reading it as would someone who is just learning to read. Instead, you're cruising along, seeking content, not uttering each syllable individually as you point-and-sound it out, hoping for eventual comprehension.

A tremendous advantage of being a lifelong student is that you no longer allow yourself the luxury of seeing yourself as a victim of circumstance. You take responsibility for your successes *and* your failures, and you're more likely to be honest with yourself when it comes to evaluating those successes and failures.

Once upon a time, a future Champion salesperson froze solid in his second-grade production of *Sleeping Beauty*

For an example of acutely conscious incompetence in action, remember the first time you had to give a presentation in front of a group? Probably not much fun, was it? If it was anything like my first time, you came out of it with strong misgivings about making public speaking your hobby.

My first public performance was in the second grade, when it was my honor to be chosen to be Prince Charming in our class presentation of Sleeping Beauty. This was pretty cool. I got to wear a neat costume and carry a sword. I was even going to get to kiss the Princess. At that point, I was definitely at the unconscious incompetent level of understanding about performing.

When it was time for me to go on, I walked out on stage and saw the smiling faces of everyone's parents — and froze. After I stood there for a couple of consciously incompetent minutes, my merciful teacher came out and led me off the stage. Needless to say, I eliminated public speaking from my list of potential careers. The irony is that my success in sales demanded that I give at least acknowledgment speeches at awards presentations so I later had to face my dragon in order to continue on my journey toward success.

Years later, a mentor gave me the advice of a lifetime

The first time I was contacted to give a formal talk, I responded with a reflexive but polite *No, thank you.* No trophy was involved, so I had little desire to get anywhere near a podium. But my dear friend, my mentor in sales, urged me to use the opportunity to overcome my fear of public speaking because the ability to speak in public is extremely valuable if you are to be a leader in any field. His words etched themselves upon my mind and I've been able to apply them to many situations in which I once was uncomfortable.

Do what you fear the most, he said, and you will conquer your fear.

You see, I was afraid of an unknown. The fear became so big in my mind that I couldn't see around it, over it, or past it to any sort of positive ending. I couldn't predict the outcome of giving that talk, so I convinced myself that there were too many ways it could go wrong for the talk to be worth the risk. All I could think of was that frightened second-grade boy standing frozen with fear onstage; I had determined that I'd never put myself in that position again.

My mentor encouraged me, though, and I reluctantly consented to give the talk. I prepared for hours. I made meticulous notes on 3×5 cards and rehearsed my speech many times over. When the day of the presentation arrived, I was so nervous that I was afraid the sweat from my hands would smear my notes. My heart raced as I walked up to the podium.

This time I survived the Prince Charming syndrome

I covered my well-prepared 45 minutes of presentation in 15 minutes. I still had half an hour to go and didn't know what to do! So I went through it all again — and my time still wasn't up! There still was nearly half an hour to go! Thinking fast, I said, *I can tell by the intelligence of this audience that you have some great questions, so let's hear them.* Luckily, they did have great questions and I was able to answer them.

(continued)

(continued)

Overall, my presentation wasn't great or even good. It was awful. But I did it, and my world didn't end. That huge fear that stood between me and the platform had just gotten a little bit smaller.

I realized then — just as I did when I figured out that selling was a learned skill — that effective public speaking is a skill that I could learn. I evaluated my performance and identified what about my speaking performance I could change for the better. In a way, that was the beginning of where I am today as a trainer.

I began to understand that public speaking isn't just public speaking. It is salesmanship in the format of a speech. And if there was one thing I did know how to do well, even then, it was selling. My greatest fear and weakness has become my hobby and the greatest love of my life.

The Value of Keeping Your Eyes and Ears Open

Most adults fail to continue the learning process, not because of a lack of desire, but because of a perceived lack of time. We expect youngsters to spend most of their time on education, with a strong dose of fun thrown in for good measure. Somewhere along our paths, though, that focus shifts to Responsibilities for Financial and Family Matters. Your desire for achievement overwhelms you. Taking time out for education just doesn't happen.

Look for educational events

From now on, challenge yourself to think of training seminars and educational events as professional necessities. Take these learning tools out of the realm of things to do "when you have the time" and put them into the category of things that you *must* do to reach the levels of success you set for yourself.

Shift your perspective only that much, and you will *make* the time to continue your education — you will become a lifelong learner.

Avoid brain cramps

When you begin to learn anything, you can absorb only so much before you experience what I call a brain cramp. It's best to learn, practice, learn some more, and then practice some more. You can internalize only so much information at once. Besides, you need to get past the conscious incompetent level gradually. If you take on a whole new subject such as selling all at once, it will overwhelm you and you'll be so uncomfortable at the conscious incompetent level that you may decide to give it up. Set a goal to get yourself to the unconscious competent level one piece at a time.

Many novices who choose to consciously develop sales skills want instant success. I think it has something to do with being an adult and the expectation that adults must be quick studies. It's an assumption many people make:

> *I'm an intelligent adult. I must be able to figure out something as simple as this rather quickly.*

Well, figuring it out isn't too difficult, but the application can be tricky. Don't look at others who are more successful than you and try to duplicate their sales techniques overnight. They are successful because they have practiced, drilled, and rehearsed the material over a long period of time. They've already experimented with the nuances of body language, voice intonation, and inflection that you're just introducing yourself to. It all goes along with the saying about not assuming anything about another person until you've walked in their shoes.

No Discomfort, No Learning

Remember earlier when I mentioned being consciously competent? To get to that point, you need to get past unconscious incompetent and his evil twin brother, consciously incompetent. Both encounters can be somewhat painful. However, in order to be successful you will have to step outside of your comfort zone. Your *comfort zone* is where you are today and unless you change who and what you are today, you will never change what you are getting out of life.

You cannot let the desire to be comfortable rule your life until you recognize it and learn how to use it to your advantage. You see, once you open your mind to learning something new, you're not the same old comfortable person you were even a minute before. With that realization, you make yourself *un*comfortable with the extent of your own ignorance.

But everyone wants to be comfortable more than anything else. So, even after you start your quest for growth, you set goals, do some research, and invest your time learning until you again reach a level of comfort with the knowledge you have and use in your everyday life. The trick is to learn to make yourself *keep* growing — to make yourself just uncomfortable enough about today that you'll better yourself for tomorrow.

This striving for knowledge can become wonderfully habit-forming. It's such a kick to learn and benefit from new concepts and ideas that the highest achievers in life have become addicted to it. They wouldn't think of facing a single day without the anticipation of learning something new.

In talking about stepping out of your comfort zone, remember to develop a picture of the new you who will take the place of that old comfortable you. I teach my students that at times it's extremely valuable to develop the "fake it 'til you make it" approach. I don't mean this in a negative way at all. I mean for you to think about the person who already has all the traits you desire; see yourself as the person who uses selling skills effectively to get the raise or promotion they want or as the person who gets great fun as a result of persuading others.

When you act like that person, you'll try to do and say what they would do and say. Eventually, you begin having small successes with the material and, before you know it, you are that person. You'll wear the suit of success. And the more you wear it, the more comfortable it will seem.

Professional athletes use this method all the time. Basketball players develop a clear picture in their mind's eye of just how the basketball will leave their hands for a three-point shot. They picture their fingers releasing the ball and see nothing of the crowd, only the net. When they first begin picturing this, their bodies may not be up to speed with the picture, but if they play the picture often enough, chances are good that their bodies get the hint and soon perform accordingly.

Make selling your hobby. Read about it. Watch those involved in it. Try it on for size. Talk with others about it. I think you'll enjoy how easy a hobby it is to pick up, how it heightens your awareness of what's going on around you, and how you can benefit from it as well.

"FIRST HARRY SOLD BOWLING BALLS, SO HE TOOK ME BOWLING. THEN HE SOLD GOLF CLUBS, SO WE TOOK UP GOLF. NOW HE'S SELLING SURGICAL INSTRUMENTS, AND FRANKLY I HAVEN'T HAD A FULL NIGHTS SLEEP SINCE."

Part II
Winners Do Homework

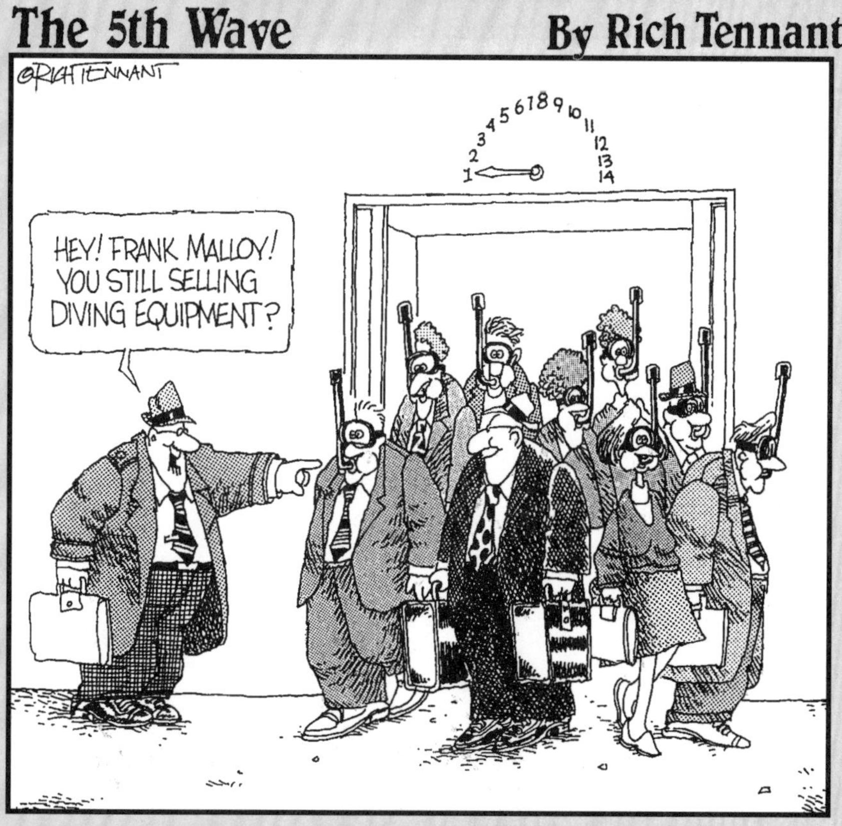

In this part...

Preparation is the key to winning in negotiations, persuading others, and selling products and services. In this part, I'll cover the steps to preparation that will set you apart from the average persuaders and help you get more *yes* in your life.

Chapter 4

Finding the People Who Need What You Have

In This Chapter

- Ten ways to find the *right* people
- Where to find them
- Tested ways to approach your prospects
- Phone, mail, and in-person prospecting methods

Prospecting is Step #1 in the selling cycle. It's a lot like the type of mineral prospecting that you use a burro, pick, and shovel for, except that the prospecting you'll be doing is finding the people to sell and selling the people you find.

If you already know whom you'll be selling to or persuading, you probably don't need this chapter right now. This chapter helps you when you have a great opportunity, service, product, or idea, but you don't know where to find other people who would be interested in getting involved with it.

Over the years, former students of mine have contacted me with news of what they thought were the greatest new products, services, or ideas. They were going to make millions, they said, with their new businesses. Their enthusiasm practically lifted them off the ground.

Some of their proposed businesses actually sounded pretty good. But, in the absence of proper planning — in the absence of the know-how for finding financial resources and the right end users — most of those projects turned to dust and my former students' enthusiasm dissipated like so many wisps of smoke. If you don't know who is the best person to contact to help you get from Point A to Point B, you doom your product, service, or idea right from the start. You'll soon lose your enthusiasm or invest too much of your own time and money without immediate payoff. You'll run out of gas before you even get on that road to success.

That's why this chapter is vital. You can master everything else in this book, but if you never get the opportunity to get in front of the right people, all the selling techniques you've learned add up to naught. You won't even make enough to feed your burro.

So . . . Whom to Prospect?

RED FLAG

The best place to start is with people who already have paid money for products and services similar to yours.

If you're selling exercise equipment, begin with people who jog, belong to health clubs, or join local sports teams. Why? Because you *know* they're already health-conscious. The convenience of being able to exercise at home may be just what they're looking for.

If you're selling graphic design, start with the people responsible for advertising in local companies. If you've already worked for people in a certain type of business, such as gift shops, you may want to concentrate on other gift shops in the area. The items in your portfolio will then be very appropriate displays of your work.

When you're finally prepared enough with knowledge about your product, service or concept and have a good level of selling skills, you then need to begin finding those people. Because you won't have a lot of qualifying, presenting, closing, or follow-up to do when you're new, your primary focus should be on prospecting. In fact, in the beginning, your daily plan should be to invest about 75 percent of your time prospecting. The other 25 percent of your time should go toward developing your product knowledge and presentation skills.

So . . . how do you find these elusive but absolutely essential prospects? Read on, and ye shall see.

Ten Strategies for Finding the Right People

In this section, we'll cover ten of the most effective ways we've used to find those people who are the best candidates for what you have to offer. Once you apply yourself to finding them, and continue to do so on a regularly scheduled basis, you'll be off and running on a successful selling career.

Strategy #1: Mine the people you already know

You don't conduct your normal daily activities in isolation (do you?). That means that you already know a horde of people who could be potential prospects for your product, service, or idea.

Think beyond your closest circle of friends and relatives. (Besides, you probably tapped them out during your first two weeks of selling, anyway.) If you bear any resemblance to an average person, you shop every week. You have neighbors. You might go to church or school functions. You may have a spouse who works or who is involved in other activities through hobbies.

Chances are good that several people in this wider circle of acquaintances may be able to benefit from your product or service in some way, or they may know others who do. In prospecting with them, your job is simply to communicate. Letting others know what you do opens many doors of opportunity for you. All you need to do is start a conversation.

Prospecting . . . an imaginative way

One student of mine always wore his company logo on a lapel pin — upside down. He made a specific point of having it upside down when he left the house. Hardly a day went by that some well-meaning do-gooder didn't tell him it was upside down, thus opening the door to a pleasant conversation about his business. As soon as he left that person's presence, he would turn the pin upside down again and move on to the next do-gooder.

How many people do you *really* know?

You already know lots of people who can help you if you only ask. Think about it!

- Your parents
- Your grandparents
- Siblings
- Aunts
- Uncles
- Cousins
- Coworkers
- Members of your sports team
- Fellow churchgoers
- Parents of your children's friends
- Neighbors
- Your hair stylist
- Friends
- Other members of business or civic groups
- The person who repairs your car
- The grocery cashier
- Your dry cleaner
- The pest control person
- Your pet's veterinarian
- Your doctor
- Your lawyer
- Your accountant
- Your dentist
- Your kids' teachers
- Your teachers
- Coaches
- Ex-boy- or girlfriends
- The teller at the bank
- Fraternity or sorority friends
- Your babysitter
- Your spouse's friends

If you put your pencil on paper and start listing all the people you know, you'll have more people to contact than you thought.

Strategy #2: Tap your business contacts

Whether or not you're new to selling, you've probably been involved in some sort of business. Even young people entering sales have held part-time jobs throughout their school careers. Business contacts can be easier to talk with than some of your more social contacts because they prospect all the time, too. You probably can cut to the chase more quickly with them than with your personal contacts.

Consider not only people you know in business, but also get involved in clubs or organizations for business professionals and prospect there. Excellent opportunities have been found in Sales and Marketing clubs and at Chamber of Commerce functions.

I can't recommend Toastmasters — a public-speaking organization — highly enough for anyone in sales. With them, you win through what you give to the group *and* you gain a lot of skill that can help you win as well. Check your local phone book for Toastmasters.

Many industries also have their own associations through which you can learn valuable new strategies for approaching people in your specific industry. Staking your claim in these groups can be highly beneficial.

Strategy #3: Talk to salespeople you currently buy from

This is one of the most overlooked strategies of prospecting. Other companies send you highly knowledgeable professional salespeople who already know loads of other people. They wouldn't be coming to you if you were in a similar business, right? So, since you're in a noncompeting business, why not talk with them about sharing leads or keeping you in mind the next time they call on their customers? Any extra sets of eyes that are out there for you are of tremendous value, especially when your only investment will most likely be returning the favor sometime down the road.

Strategy #4: Parlay your adventures as a consumer

Pretend you're at a restaurant and your server does an especially excellent job. And let's also say you're in network marketing. You're looking for someone to join with you in business, not work for you. If this person already has great people skills and is competent at performing his duties, he may be a good candidate for being in business for himself.

Be careful not to approach these people while they are working, though. Professional etiquette dictates that you don't interfere with other professionals while they are conducting business. You may, however, want to leave your card with the server, suggesting that they contact you if they ever consider making a career change. That's harmless enough, yet you've got their attention.

What do you say to such people? Here are some words that have proven to work in this particular situation:

> *I can't help but notice that you have a nice way with people. I'm curious,are you achieving all of your goals working here? The reason I ask is that the firm I represent is in an expansion mode and we're looking for quality people to take advantage of the opportunity. Do you have an interest in knowing more?*

If they ask, *What's this about?*, say

> *Ethically, because you're working now, I'm not at liberty to discuss it. However, if you'd like to jot down a number and time I can reach you when you're not working, we can visit and see if it's a win-win possibility.*

You would then either arrange a time to call or, at the very least, leave them with your card and a time to contact you.

Another way to prospect through other businesses is to send them a letter or thank you note for providing you excellent service. Many businesspeople publish or display these letters in their places of business or on their marketing literature. If they have your permission to use your name in promoting their business, they're also pretty likely to list your profession or business name. When other people read your words, they'll see how professional you are and, hopefully, remember your name when they need services such as those you offer.

Strategy #5: Benefit from the itch cycle

Face it: nearly every tangible product brought to market has a limited lifespan. At one end of the spectrum, we have computer software and hardware that can have a lifespan as short as six months. At the other end of the spectrum are things like refrigerators and freezers that have almost 20-year lifespans. No matter how long a product's lifespan is, every product's got one.

But here's the key to this strategy: the precise lifespan of your product doesn't matter. What matters is that you know what its lifespan is. Once you know, there's a goldmine of opportunity already there in your business waiting for your pickax to strike. If you're new to the product, keep a file or ask people already in the business.

When you review your past customer files (which I'll show you how to do anytime now, in Strategy #6), you'll soon see that Mr. and Mrs. Jones's microwave oven will need to be replaced in the near future. It's bound to happen if it's getting up in years — say, 10, 12, or 15 years old.

Don't wait for the Joneses' microwave to break down and then quietly hope they'll come see you again. Get in touch with them *before* their microwave breaks down and let them know you have some great new products with greater energy efficiency, space-saving designs, and other all-around better features. Your call may just help them move a little *quicker* in replacing that old microwave!

Chances are good that the Joneses know that their microwave is on its last legs and that they've just been putting off making the decision to shop. Maybe they've been waiting for a good buy or sale to appear in the paper. That doesn't matter. What matters is that they haven't acted yet. And these facts matter, too: the Joneses already know you and/or your product personally — and they know that you're the expert they turn to when the time for decision making arrives.

Real estate agents know that most Americans move every five to seven years. Therefore, real estate agents follow a plan to keep in touch with every customer in order to be the person there to handle the sale of the first home and possibly the purchase of the next.

Most professional people — such as doctors, lawyers, real estate agents, and traveling salespeople — replace their vehicles about every 30 months. They always want to be seen driving the latest model of their favorite car.

That's why wise automobile salespeople keep in touch with their past customers. And, when they know that a customer itch is about to happen, they get prepared to scratch it. About 60 days before these people start itching, automobile salespeople make their move. They select the make and model that the person is most likely to want next. Then they drive to the person's office or home with the new vehicle. Chances are good that prospects will need some sort of service work performed on their vehicles if their vehicles are at least 28 months old. The salespeople and the prospects trade vehicles for a day or two so that the prospects can try out the new vehicles for themselves.

I call this strategy *puppydogging*. How do you sell a little puppy? You let someone take it home for a few days to see how things go. Almost every time, the people — that is, the *prospects* — become so attached to the new puppy that they can't bear to part with it.

Before a few days are up, the prospect loves the new car and wants to keep it; if nothing else, they've started itching for a new car and need to get back in touch with that salesperson to return the loaner. What has this salesperson done? They've guaranteed themselves an itchy customer to serve. Such personalized service is guaranteed to keep customers coming back for more. There are even salespeople who will drop off a high-quality videotape of the latest model of the car you drive so that you can fantasize about owning it *from right in your own home*. Now that's nice!

If you don't already know the replacement cycle for your line of products, do some research to find out what it is. When do people begin getting that itch for something new? To determine this only takes a few phone calls to people who currently use your products or services. You can treat this like a survey or market study and simply ask for their help. If they know it won't take long, people love to help you. You begin by verifying that they are still using the product your records show them owning. Then you ask what they used prior to the model they bought from you (or the service that they are buying from you, as the case may be). The only time such research will fail is if the product or service that you sold to your customer is your customer's first foray into your market. If it's the second, third, or later piece of similar product or service that they've acquired, you ask how many years, overall, they've used such products or services.

A realistic example will illustrate this point. If you sell copiers and your customer has used your copiers for 17 years, trading in only four times during your association, you know they'll need a new copier after they've owned their present model for about four years. When that fourth year rolls around, you may want to ask a few questions about their current needs and get permission to drop them information about the latest and greatest models. If they won't need another machine for two more years, thank them for their help and make a commitment to stay in touch.

With replacement products, it's often the salesperson who gets to the customer at the right time who wins. Plan to be that person and you'll be doing a lot of the winning. Remember, it's the early bird who makes the sale.

Strategy #6: Use your customer list

Any business that's been in business for at least three years should have a pretty good customer list. The question you must ask the business owner or manager is how many salespeople have come and gone during that time? It could be that those salespeople haven't necessarily gone away, but are now in other positions in the company. If there were several, what happened to the people they sold to? If those customers weren't reassigned to another salesperson to keep in touch with them, you might ask to be given the authority to contact them yourself.

With the many changes that occur in business these days, managers don't always take the time to complete this task. If everyone is really busy and the company is growing rapidly, some customers may get left in the dust. Why not be the one to pick them up and take care of them? They've already bought your brand or service before.

If your company has lived up to its promises, your customers should want to continue to work with such a fine organization. If they haven't made any purchases lately, it could be simply because no one has asked. Don't leave the door open for a competitor to come in and snatch up valuable customers. Prospect your list of past customers and you could not only solidify *their* future business, but business that they will *refer to* you as well.

Strategy #7: Ride the wave of technical advancement

I talked earlier about people having "itch cycles" with various products. Why do you suppose they itch? In some cases, it's simply because the product wears out. In others, though, it's because of something more personal. It's a perception people have of themselves that is to great advantage to salespeople. Simply put, it's a status thing. They want to have the latest, greatest, shiniest, top-of-the-line products with all the bells and whistles you can provide. Having those products makes people appear to be doing well.

Few people really want to have the old model of anything unless they're collectors and the old model is a true antique or classic model. Because most businesses today sell high-tech equipment, peripherals, and support products and services, knowing and using this method of prospecting is tantamount to success.

Whenever you have a new model, an updated version, or even a price change, you have a solid reason to recontact people you've already sold to. Being the kind of people they are, it's only natural that they'll want to be kept apprised of the latest changes. The key to success with this strategy is in how you contact them.

Bill has recently invested in a top-of-the-line stereo system for his home, and now some improvement has been made in the product that wasn't available then. Don't just call up old Bill and say, *Hey, I've got something even better for you.* That would be both pushy and presumptuous and would very likely have the opposite affect of what you wanted — you could turn Bill off to even hearing what you have to say since you've just in effect run down his system.

Instead, call up Bill and ask him how he's enjoying listening to his favorite music on the system. It's critical for you to be sure that he's still happy with what he's got before you bring up anything else. If there's a complaint you didn't know about and you start talking about new products, you could lose Bill as a customer forever.

Once you know that he's happy, say, *Bill, I know how diligent you were in your research before investing in the T-tronics system. Because I value your opinion, would you mind evaluating something else our company is coming out with?* See the difference? How's Bill going to react to this? You've complimented him, acknowledged his intelligence, *and* asked for his opinion. You've made him feel important. *Of course* he'll be happy to look at your new toy now. And, if it's truly better than the one he has, it's a pretty good bet that Bill will want to upgrade his system.

If you take the time to know what's going on with your current customers, you'll know exactly when and how to contact them with new products or innovations and increase the volume and number of sales you make to each one. Now that's what I call working smarter.

Strategy #8: Read the newspaper

One of the greatest prospecting tools around can be delivered to your doorstep for under a dollar a day in most areas. It's got an intimidating, ultra-technical name; it's called a *newspaper.* I used to read mine with a felt marker so I could circle all of the opportunities I found. Unless you do business internationally, you'll probably want to stick to the local news, business, and announcements sections. Stay away from the latest crime statistics and headline-making stories unless that's your field of interest. For most people, the most beneficial portion of the paper is written about John and Jane Q. Public.

John and Jane are the people who get promoted in business. They have babies. They buy or sell homes. They start up new businesses. Do you get my drift here?

If John Q. Public has been promoted, what else usually comes along with that promotion? A raise in pay. And what do most people do with their raises? Invest in stocks and mutual funds? Some do. Most, however, buy new cars, bigger houses, nicer clothing, and season tickets.

Learning how to read your newspaper for leads only takes a few days of practice. Once you get started, you'll be amazed at the number of leads you used to glance over. Keep a highlighter pen handy.

People having babies need more insurance, bigger homes, minivans, delivery services and diapers, just to name a few.

Families who are moving into new homes need lots of new things, such as garage door openers, security systems, ceiling fans, homeowners' insurance, and landscaping.

New or expanding businesses need equipment, personnel, and supplies to fulfill their growth needs.

I know of one real estate agent who benefited tremendously from a single news item in his daily paper. The local football team had acquired a new player. This man sent a note to that new local sports figure before his arrival, congratulating him on making the move and welcoming him to the area. He included a copy of the news article and offered his services if needed.

Being new to the area and to the team, this football player didn't know anyone in town, but he did need a place to live — so he contacted that real estate agent. The agent not only helped him find a new home but put him in touch with an insurance agent, local doctors for his family, a dentist, hair stylist, and so on. Do you see how the newspaper can pay you much, much more than the few cents a day it costs?

Try this experiment. Take today's local newspaper and read every headline. Circle those with stories that may hold some business prospects for you. Then do what any top salesperson who's striving for excellence would do and *contact* those people. You do this by cutting out the article. Make a copy for yourself. Then send a brief note, saying, "I saw you in the news. I'm in business in the community and hope to meet you someday in person. I thought you might enjoy having an extra copy of the article to share with friends or relatives." Always include your business card.

People love seeing that they were in the news. And they love having extra copies of the articles to send to friends and relatives who are not in the local area. By providing this little service in a nonthreatening way, you can gain a lot of big business.

Strategy #9: Know your service or support people

We talked about the benefits of selling yourself on your job in Chapter 1. Another benefit not discussed there is that people inside your company will think of you when they hear valuable information.

For example, say someone in accounting knows that one of your clients has been late several times in making their monthly investment in your product or service. That's a valuable piece of information for anyone in sales. By reconnecting with that client, you may be able to make other arrangements for them. Perhaps their growth rate isn't as high they anticipated and your equipment or service just costs too much for them.

Rather than let information like that get away, help them cut back on their equipment or make other financial arrangements. They'll never forget you and will become loyal, long-term customers. If you let such information go unaddressed, you could lose them as a customer just because they're overloaded with unnecessary equipment and are too embarrassed to approach the company about it.

Get in the habit of periodically checking the company service and repair records. Ask customer service how many times your people call with questions. If there's a lot of activity there, you need to get back in touch with them. Maybe they're in a growth phase and you could help them acquire new services. Or maybe they're having some challenges with particular equipment. If they got stuck with a lemon, then you need to be the one to turn it into lemon*ade* — before they demand a replacement, refund, or your head and you get squeezed out!

Always strive to provide service above and beyond what the average salesperson would give. It will help you build long-term relationships, trust, and referral business.

Strategy #10: Practice the 3-foot rule

Many business people subscribe to the three-foot rule when it comes to prospecting. *Anyone who comes within three feet of them is worth talking to about their product, service, or business.* Once you get comfortable with what you're selling and in talking with people about it, I highly recommend applying this strategy. All you need to do is say, "Hello" and that it's nice to meet them. Pay attention to them. Notice something about them you can compliment.

Woman-to-woman: *That's a great purse. Where did you find it?* After she answers, go on with another question about her response or something else you have in common, such as why you're standing in line at the grocery store at 11:00 PM. Once you establish a little bit of rapport, it's only polite then to exchange names.

That's when you can bring up the subject of your idea, product, or service. Tell her by asking a question such as *Have you ever found a product to get gum off kids' sneakers?* if that's what you sell. Or use a question such as *Have you been to the new gift shop on 5th and Grovers?* if the new shop is your shop. If you market security products, here's another: *I see you carry Mace on your key ring. It makes you feel a bit more secure, doesn't it?* When she answers in the affirmative, talk about the great security product that you found (and sell). Personal testimony moves more products than any other method.

I know of one man who has gotten some of his best leads from fellow elevator passengers whom he knew for only six floors! There are a lot of business contacts that have been made while standing in checkout lines at the grocery store or order lines at the fast-food restaurant.

Car handlers at valet parking can be a valuable source of information. They learn a lot about people by their cars and how they treat the valets. They overhear a lot of conversations about business. I'm not advising you to encourage people to eavesdrop on your behalf, but you never turn away a valuable source of leads, either. If you've been trying to get an appointment with Mr. Warbucks and the valet knows he's in the restaurant and will be leaving promptly at 9:00 PM, do you think it would be convenient for you to be next in line at that time? Could be.

How do you handle these brief encounters with people and get leads to build your business? First of all, I have to admit that this method won't bring you great leads every time. Even so, why walk by a potentially beneficial opportunity without knocking ?

So here's what you do: Take all of your business cards — okay, maybe just a few at a time. (Salespeople are notorious for ordering thousands of business cards at a time. In fact, you can often tell the people who are newest to sales by the huge bulge of cards in their pockets.) Anyway, take the cards that you do have with you and very neatly write *Thank You* across the front of each one. Hopefully, you haven't printed every one of your vital statistics on the cards; if you did, you have no room to print your *Thank You.*

When you meet a new person — someone who has entered your three-foot space — be warm and friendly. Introduce yourself and ask them what their business is or why they're at that place. Making such banter sort of obligates them to do the same. When they ask what your business is, you simply hand them one of your cards.

Most people take whatever is handed them as long as their hands aren't already full. (Thousands of servers of legal documents requesting your presence in court can't be wrong!) When the prospect gives you the courtesy of looking at the card, she'll probably ask about that *Thank You.* Curiosity gets the better of most people and they blurt out their questions almost as a matter of reflex.

That's the moment you've been waiting for. At that point, you simply smile and say these words: *I guess I'm thanking you in advance for what hopefully will be the opportunity someday to serve your [whatever your business is] needs.*

Be certain to use those words exactly. *I guess* makes it sound spontaneous. *Thanking you in advance* shows that you're a nice person. *Hopefully* shows humility. *Someday* places your offer way out into the limbo of the future. It's a very passive, nonthreatening word. *Serve your needs* elevates your prospect to a place of importance in your life — and *everyone* needs to feel important. When they feel like they're important to you, they're more likely to make a move that could help you.

They'll most often do one of three things, any one of which is a move in the right direction for you:

- They'll agree to call you to discuss it further.
- They'll give you a time to call them to discuss it further.
- They won't be interested, but they'll refer you to someone who could be interested in what you have to offer.

What have you got now? A lot more than you had a moment ago, standing here in line waiting to order your burger. You've got a prospect with a side order of referrals.

Prospecting Your Way to Riches

When you're just getting started, don't be overly concerned about committing so much time to prospecting. After all, if you're new, you won't have anyone to go over the other steps of selling with until you find those prospects. The key to success in a people business like selling lies in how many people you can see in the time allotted or committed to. In the beginning, you'll probably find yourself working very hard. With every experience, though, you'll learn a little more, refine your strategies and techniques, and eventually find yourself working smarter. But there's no getting around that, in the beginning, you'll have to invest a lot of time in prospecting.

You're probably asking yourself, *With all this prospecting, am I a miner or a salesperson?* The two share many similarities. In each, you stake a claim; you bring with you the necessary tools to help dig out your own little niche of success; you have high expectations of success; you persistently and consistently work toward your goals; you have a firm belief in your ability to achieve those goals; and, finally, you refuse to let others' negative reactions to your work inhibit your behavior and beliefs.

Where to Round Up the Likeliest Suspects — or Prospects

So here you are ready to dig in. You have your schedule made out. You have encased yourself with a positive attitude and high expectations. Now you're ready to find those people who will benefit most from your product or service. The question you are probably asking yourself at this point is *Where — where do I find this mother lode of prospects?* The answer to that question depends on what it is that you represent.

If you sell products or services for a company, you should have learned during your product knowledge training where the likeliest places are to find your products or services in use. Those are, obviously, the best places to begin prospecting. Once you have some business under your belt, you'll have time to get more creative with staking out other claims.

If you're on your own, start with your local Chamber of Commerce or your local library, both of which have listings of all sorts available. All you need to do is ask the right questions to narrow down the list of potential prospects. If you have some money to invest in lists, you might want to contact a list broker. These are people who have all sorts of lists available and can review your particular demographic needs with you to provide you the best list of potential customers to contact.

The simplest place to start is with the people you already know. Talking with them first will help you find easy leads and give you an opportunity to practice your prospecting presentation with people who are less likely to give you a dose of rejection than complete strangers.

Among friends

When you're new, learning selling skills probably draws you out of your comfort zone. That's why I recommend that you begin prospecting among those people with whom you are most comfortable — your friends and relatives. I call this your "warm" or "natural" market. Be selective here, though. If you're selling exercise equipment, don't get discouraged if 90-year old Aunt Minnie doesn't buy two of everything.

With friends and relatives, you're less likely to be rejected or to fail, *the two biggest fears* of anyone who is trying anything new. They like you, they trust you, and they want to see you succeed. They're almost always willing to help. Besides, if you truly believe in the goodness of what you're doing and these people are candidates for your product or service, why would you want to deprive them of the chance to benefit from what you're selling? If you truly care about these people, they'll respond in kind and possibly become some of your best clients.

Contact them and tell them that you're in a new business or you've started a new career and that you want to share the news with them. Unless you've done this every six months in the past, they'll be happy for you and will want to know more. It's with them that you'll test your presentation skills.

If your friends and relatives are not good candidates for your offering, contact them anyway. *The first rule in prospecting is to never assume that someone cannot help you build your business.* They may not be a prospect themselves, but they may know others who are. Don't ever be afraid to ask for a referral. There's gold in them thar hills! A key phrase to use in getting their permission to share with them your new product, service, or idea is this: *Because I value your judgment, I was hoping you'd give me your opinion.* This statement is bound to make them feel important and be willing to help you.

After you've contacted all of your close friends, move on to acquaintances. Consider talking with your kid's baseball coach, other parents, your accountant, the clerk you always go to at the grocery store. If approached properly, most people are more than willing to give you advice. Ask the right question, and they can advise you right into a great connection with a big client.

In the wide, wide world

Unless you represent a unique product or service, the opportunities for making contact are practically unlimited. You simply need to test a variety of methods to narrow down those that bring you the best people.

If what you sell is good for businesses, begin with your local *Yellow Pages.* Those businesses invest their money in listings because they are serious about being in business. Their listing also should tell you that they're serious about *staying* in business. If your product or service can bring them more business or make them more efficient, you owe it to them to contact them. If you want broaden your field of prospects, check out an 800 number directory.

If you're computer-literate, you may be able to do some prospecting on the Internet. If you're not, ask someone to help you here. Post bulletins, get involved in providing valuable information as well as selling your product or service. Refer to *Internet For Dummies* to get a clearer idea of how you can use this phenomenal tool to your greatest advantage.

Through professional help

If you're starting a new business, get some advice from others who have already been there and are willing to share their knowledge. S.C.O.R.E., the Service Corps Of Retired Executives, has an excellent reputation for putting new people, or those who may be struggling, together with a retired or semi-retired professional from similar fields. It's a government program with contact offices in most major metropolitan areas. The experience these people can provide is exceptional, but you must be willing to learn. It's also important to remember that some of their experiences may not apply to your current marketplace. Still, the information available through this source can be like getting a life jacket thrown to you in the middle of the ocean.

If there's no S.C.O.R.E. office in your area, keep an eye out for a mentor who can offer similar assistance. A mentor is someone who has more experience than you, an interest in what you are doing, and a willingness to take you under his or her wing to guide your actions. Mentors want to help others overcome obstacles they faced — to help others learn from their experience. Mentors can be found through Sales and Marketing Executives, a professional support organization that has offices in most major cities. Of course, you can always contact your local Small Business Administration office for advice.

Most of the top companies will partner up a novice salesperson with one of their veterans for a brief training period. This type of company-sponsored mentoring program is working wonders around the world. It gives recognition to the vets for their knowledge and experience, while at the same time helping to train the new people in tried-and-true methods of conducting business.

You can also go so far as to hire an advertising agency and a public relations firm to handle much of your market awareness and prospecting for you, though that option of course depends on your financial situation. Agency assistance varies; an agency can take on everything for your business, or they can help you with occasional, one-shot promotional ideas.

Investments for agency assistance differ throughout the country, so do your homework. Ask prospective agencies to send you information on what they've done for other businesses. Always check out the people who give testimonials and references for a business. You never know when their best testimonial will turn out to be Grandpa Smith who may have a personal (and maybe even a financial) interest in the agency's success. If anyone hesitates to give you references, don't waste your time considering doing business with them.

From lists your company generates

When you work for someone else's company, you see that the company usually handles the details of advertising and marketing to generate leads. Many companies provide leads to their salespeople, and to be a great salesperson, you should always be prospecting on your own, too. That way, if the company lead program hits a lull, you'll be prepared. That wouldn't be the time to begin to learn prospecting skills. If you're prospecting all along, you'll barely break stride in your business activity level with a minor setback like that.

By phone, by mail, or face to face

These are the three major ways you can contact your prospects: by mail, by phone, or face to face. Through any of these three methods, you ask busy professionals to give up time that they may think could be used more productively — such as out on a golf course. So before you have a chance to convince them otherwise, they will try to shut you out.

And shutting you out is easy for them to do. They can just make a paper airplane from your letter, leave you on terminal hold, or put off your incoming phone call. Face-to-face prospecting can be very effective in those instances yet extremely time-consuming in other situations.

Most professional salespeople integrate the three methods into an effective prospecting strategy. For some, one method works better than others. Different situations call for different responses. You need some experience to determine the best methods for you at the appropriate times.

Between the rewards and pitfalls of telemarketing

It's easy to hate receiving telemarketers' calls — especially when you can hear the pages of their script turning as they read it at warp speed, hardly taking a moment to breathe. You may feel a telemarketing call is an intrusion or interruption in your daily life. The common reaction to a telemarketing call is to say *No, thanks* and hang up.

If that's your response to most telemarketers, you probably wonder why businesses keep using telemarketing. Why then do they use it? Because telemarketers can reach more potential users of their product or service in one hour than most salespeople going face to face can meet in a week. Another advantage: telemarketers' travel time is short — they don't have to travel from one location to another. They just dial the next few digits. It's an efficient method for prospecting for business.

But telemarketing comes with (more than?) its share of pitfalls. Salespeople who telemarket have to have skin as thick as the backside of a rhinoceros *and* they have to use a survey approach to the call rather than just trying to set appointments straight out. There's a certain amount of rapport-building that must take place with every new contact, whether it's on the phone or in person. People have to decide whether or not they like you before they'll consider doing business with you. The survey presents a simple, nonthreatening method for that.

If this is the method you choose to use, first of all, you need to create a brief but effective survey. Your survey needs to provide you information about whether to pursue a contact as a customer; it also needs to pique your prospect's curiosity about your product or service. Your goal is to get them talking — grunting doesn't count. The more they talk, the more information you'll gather that could point you toward or away from future contact with this person.

It's best to stick with five or fewer questions. Always tell the person on the other end of the phone that the firm you represent has asked you to conduct a quick survey and state that you need their help. If they say it's a bad time for them, acknowledge the bad timing, apologize, and try to get an appointment for a better time to call. If they say, "go ahead and ask," thank them and get right to your questions. Unless the person appears very interested in what you're saying, each call should take no more than two minutes. You have two possible goals for these calls:

1. To arrange a time for a face-to-face meeting.
2. To get permission to send information and make another brief follow up call.

If the prospect declines your invitation to arrange a face-to-face meeting, then at the very least you want her permission to send more information and talk to her again.

By relying on the U.S. Postal Service

If you choose to use mail as your primary method of prospecting, choose your mailing list carefully. Mailing is great, but mail sent to the wrong list of people is a tremendous waste of time, money, and effort. Nothing is easier to get rid of than a piece of paper that arrives amidst a stack of other papers. This is especially true if your *prospecting* piece of paper winds up in the mailbox of someone who wouldn't care about your product or service in a hundred years.

Instead of sending a piece of mail that talks about your product or service, mail a single-page introductory letter to the people you know who are most likely to want to get involved with what you're doing, indicating that you'll be calling on a certain date and time. Include your photograph on the letterhead or on a magnet or other novelty item you enclose. Magnets are great: every time your prospect goes to the fridge, he sees your smiling face. People buy faces. They aren't as likely, however, to buy from some anonymous voice on the phone. Again, it's a matter of establishing rapport.

By gettin' out and sellin' 'em eye to eye

Face-to-face prospecting is best, but it's also the most time-intensive. Walking from office to office or home to home trying to find someone to talk with is physically exhausting, which is bad enough. Worse, with most people having too much to do in our high-tech world, you won't get too many appointments.

What you will get, though, is a load of information from receptionists. They can be powerhouses who help you either to eliminate a company as a prospect or to advance your chances of obtaining an appointment for making your presentation with the right person. I've often thought one of the best places to prospect would be a secretarial convention rather than the one where all the executives meet.

When you think of face-to-face selling, think of how lucky you are that important people think enough of you to give you precious time from their busy schedules. They're offering something to you, too — an opportunity to show them how they can benefit from your product or service. In today's society, suspicion and distrust are rampant. When you professionally prospect with the methods covered in this chapter, your contacts will send you an *I trust you* message and welcome you into their homes and offices.

Although it doesn't guarantee you successful selling situations, professional prospecting helps you to enter each selling opportunity with a fresh face and winning attitude.

As a novice, you should try different types of prospecting to see which are most comfortable for you and are most successful for your offering. You'll quickly discover the ones that bring you success, and they will become your primary prospecting tools. It's also a good idea to keep your eyes and ears open for new prospecting methods from others in your field.

Hmm? Prospecting for prospecting ideas? What a novel thought. Soon you'll be able to trade in that old burro for something shiny and new from your local luxury car dealership.

Chapter 5

What You Don't Know Can Kill Your Chances of Success

In This Chapter

- Researching a business
- Nailing down an Evasive Ed
- Overcoming eight common fears
- Painting word pictures
- Listening twice as much as you talk

Sometimes the hardest thing in learning something new is breaking through old teachings or beliefs that we once felt were acceptable for successful living. I'm sure you remember the old adages of *Ignorance is bliss* or even *What you don't know can't hurt you.* Although they may have worked in people's personal lives in simpler times, such maxims were never sage advice for people who try to sell or persuade others. The loss of sales and personal career damage caused by ignorance can be so disastrous that some give up on selling altogether.

It's a shame that people with the potential to become great producers, people who have extremely satisfying careers, never get off the ground because they think they know everything or they excuse themselves for inadequate preparation. They justify their lack of knowledge by holding on to antiquated beliefs, old knowledge, and passé information.

When people look at the best of the best, the cream of the crop in marketing or business, people often don't see all the time put in behind the scenes. Of course, though, time behind the scenes is what it's all about. When a pro makes selling look *natural,* you can bet that there have been hours and hours of planning and preparation before those few minutes of face-to-face selling.

Obviously, it's impossible to know everything about everything, and when you do think you know it all, you're only setting yourself up for a gigantic fall. I've long taught that the sign of a true professional is how much they can learn *after* they supposedly know it all. The enemy of learning is knowing. Admitting that there are things you need to learn is the first step to achieving anything.

Starting at Ground Zero

Put aside old beliefs. To be successful at persuasion, you must be constantly on the prowl for information. What type of information? Everything and anything about your product, your company, your competition, and (most important) your prospect. Never forget: *Knowledge is power.*

The most important thing to remember is the benefit of being able to walk in someone else's shoes. It's not until you truly understand a prospect's situation that you can help him with what you're offering.

So where do you begin? Not at the shoe store. The business itself is a much better source. Leave no paperwork on a business unturned when you research a prospect. Your legwork will pay handsome dividends later.

- Gather as much literature and other information as possible on a company before approaching them with your offering.
- Get copies of their product brochures.
- Send for one of their catalogs. Talk with one of their customer service people about what they offer.
- Go to the library and look up past news articles on them.
- Check out their financial report if it's available. Get the names of the president and other key people — and learn how to pronounce and spell them.

Remember, knowledge *is* power *when* it's properly applied. And you should *always* apply that philosophy to research that will help you sell.

The very picture of diligent research

I know of one guy — I'll call him Sam — who went so deep into his study of the competition that he got to know the personal habits of the salesman who covered the same territory he did. Because the two directly competed for the same business, Sam had a chance to research his competitor just by talking to the prospects they shared. Sam learned his competitor's name, his method of operation, and his presentation style. What was the result? Because of Sam's detailed efforts, his company was number one in the territory. Seldom does someone take the process so far, but doing so paid off big for Sam and his company.

And just how far did Sam's knowledge of his competition go? He once showed me a photograph of that competing salesman from a piece of literature put out by that salesman's company. Sam carried that photo with him every day. And, he said, whenever he felt like quitting early or taking a shortcut, he would pull out that photo and remind himself that this guy would be the next one to talk with the customer if Sam didn't give his prospects 100% every time.

How Much Information Is Too Much?

It's tough to say how much information is too much; in the end, it's up to you. When you think you know enough to get the job done and make the sale, you've probably researched enough. But if something comes up during the presentation that you don't know, and what you don't know could hurt your chances of closing the sale, then you don't know enough. This is one of those things where experience dictates your actions.

Why do so much research? So that, at the moment of truth, you won't look bad. You do all your research simply to build for that final moment when your prospect gives you the okay to deliver your product and to start building a long-term relationship with him or his company.

As an example, say that you market air treatment systems to homes and businesses. If you know that a particular business must manufacture its products according to exacting standards, that's important to know. It means that they must have a high level of concern for cleanliness and precision. Your air cleaner can help them there.

If their company is growing, but they haven't expanded their work site, it's highly likely that their people are working in close proximity to one another. The closer the proximity, the greater the likelihood of a rapid spread of germs. No employer can afford to have its people taking a lot of sick time. The air treatment system can help there.

If their financial reports show solid growth and explosive future plans, you know that they're poised for change and probably are wide open to new ideas. Show them that your air treatment system is state-of-the-art, and you'll probably get their interest.

Bottom line: The more you know about a prospect, the more competent you will appear and the stronger you will be when you present your case.

The same principle applies to sales to individuals or families: the more you know about *their* background, the better. (Besides, what you learn could become great background material for that novel you're going to write after you retire.) You'll warm them up sooner when you talk about their hobbies, jobs, and kids than you will if you know nothing other than their address and phone number. If you're still selling air treatment systems, and you know that one of their children has allergies or asthma, then that's another bullet in your arsenal of benefits when you present your product.

Working with Buyers' Personality Types

When you work with companies, a key concern is who the true decision-maker really is. It may be the office manager, a purchasing agent, or a department head. You can usually find out simply by asking the receptionist *Who is responsible for . . .* the area of business to which your products or services apply.

Receptionists have to know all the ins and outs of the business. After they tell you, ask a confirming question, such as *So, Mr. Carter has the responsibility of authorizing purchase orders, is that right?* If Mr. Carter does handle the area, but he has to get approval on purchase orders from someone like the comptroller, you need to know that going in.

Once you have the name and position of this person, you need to know a little about their styles. My research has uncovered about nine different personality types of buyers. The earlier you recognize the personality-type, the sooner you can begin to work appropriately with each decision-maker.

Your delivery style must be flexible enough to relate to all the different personality types. Never settle for having one presentation style. Having only one style severely limits the number of people you can serve. I'm not advising you to become schizophrenic. Just remember that if you don't like the personality of the decision-maker, learn to like the opportunity they are offering you to do business with them.

Here are the nine types of decision-makers and my recommendations on how you can best work with each.

These personality types demonstrate characteristics of buyers. They have been exaggerated and are not limited to the gender of the example.

Buyer #1: Believing Bart

He's already sold on your company or brand. He knows just what to expect from them. He likes their reliability. He's easy to work with and loyal once you convince him of your personal competence. If he's not convinced that you're competent, he won't hesitate to call your company and request another representative.

How do you appeal to this type? Don't short-sell the product or service just because he's already sold on its quality. You need to exhibit great product knowledge to build trust and belief in your ability to meet his needs. Another important element in consummating this sale and gaining repeat business is to provide dependable service and follow-up.

Buyer #2: Freddie Freebie

Freddie is a real wheeler-dealer, the guy who won't settle until he thinks he has the upper hand and you've agreed to give him something extra. Today's market is full of these types. If you give him any extras in order to consummate the sale, he'll probably brag to and upset others who may not have received the same benefit.

How do you handle this type? Let him know that he's important and special—that he drives a hard bargain and that you admire his business savvy. If you think his business is worth giving something extra, consult with your manager or the business owner about the best way to handle it. You may not have to give away the company's back forty to entice this guy to buy. The enticement could be as simple as sending him thank you notes or making a few extra calls to let Freddie know how important he is.

Buyer #3: Purchasing Polly

Polly's a distant, matter-of-fact type who carries a high level of responsibility. As with many other purchasing agents, she may have little personal contact throughout the day besides the contact she gets from the salespeople who parade through her office. She can't risk liking you too much because she could have to replace you with the competition at any time.

This should be a no-fluff presentation. Don't try to become too familiar. Stick to the facts and figures. She'll be grading you every step of the way. By being low-key, you'll be different from the other all-too-typical salespeople she encounters. She'll remember you for that. Let her know that you understand how important and challenging her position can be. Send her thank you notes. Present all figures to her in the most professional manner possible. Do everything in writing; she needs the certainty of documentation.

Buyer #4: Evasive Ed

Ed is your most challenging buyer. He refuses to return your phone calls. He postpones appointments or reschedules at the last minute. He likes to shop around and keeps you waiting in the meantime. He tests your patience at every turn.

Enlist the aid of his secretary or support staff. They may be able to tell you how to get and keep his business.

Buyer #5: Griping Greg

Greg always has something to complain about or something negative to say; he wouldn't be your first choice for a companion if you ever got stranded on a deserted island.

You have to decide whether the income his business generates for you is worth all the energy he will steal from you. If his business is not one of your bread-and-butter accounts, you may want to consider finding other clients who don't take so much out of you. No client should ever be so important as to risk your mental and physical health for them.

The most important thing you can do is listen and be empathetic. Maybe he can't afford an analyst. To limit your exposure to his negativity, I recommend that you only call him a few minutes before his normal lunch hour or just before the end of the day, so he won't want too talk long. If he calls you at other times and begins to cost you valuable selling time, you just have to spend time learning polite ways to get off the line.

When you first get on the line, you might want to say something like this:

> *Greg! Glad you called, I'm just heading out for an appointment. What can I do for you in the next five minutes?*

Stay pleasant and helpful; after all, that's why Greg gives you his business. If Greg gets to be too much to handle, the easiest and least costly thing to do might be to refer him to someone else in your organization. The person receiving this new client may not be as strongly affected by Greg's personality and be able to get along just fine with him.

Buyer #6: Anna List

She knows exactly what she wants and she wants it written in blood or at least carved in stone. She will nit-pick everything and she is big on complete control.

Be *very* organized. She appreciates — nay, she craves — organization. Handle *every* detail in writing. Be punctual. Double-check everything. Once she knows she can depend on you, she will do just that. Confirm appointments, and always reconfirm details of your meetings with her in writing. Disorder in any form shatters her day. *Don't* be a source of disorder for Anna if you want to get and keep her business.

I recommend that you fax Anna a recap of every meeting you have with her. Also, fax ahead to let her know what information you plan to bring to your next appointment. In other words, treat her as she treats others. Everyone wants to be around people just like themselves.

Buyer #7: Domineering Donna

Donna is a strongwilled ball-of-fire who most likely has designs on a more powerful position in the company. She often hides her needs because she expects you to have done your homework; and if you have, she figures, then you already know her needs.

In talking to Donna, perhaps the most important thing you can do is to compliment her on her importance and remind her of the value of her abilities to her company. Remember: she likely bowls others over with her ambition for power — and most people try to avoid working with dominators. You don't have that option. Besides, she can become a positive force for you if you have challenges with billing or want to sell your product to another department or branch of her company. If Donna believes in you and your product, she'll be your best supporter throughout her company.

Buyer #8: Controlling Carl

It's Carl's way or the highway. He's a self-proclaimed expert. He's also poor at delegating authority. He wants everyone and everything to be reported to him. He may be rude and interrupt your presentation while he takes calls or gives directions to his secretary.

Be extremely polite. Be very prepared and concise. By all means, don't assume anything. Let him know that you value his time. If the interruptions become too distracting, pulling out your lunch isn't the best answer. Instead, offer to reschedule your meeting off the premises — for, say, a lunch appointment — so that you can have his undivided attention. Or you can enlist the aid of his secretary or assistant in keeping interruptions to a minimum during your appointment simply by asking. Unless Carl has a rule carved in granite that he takes all calls and sees all visitors, you're likely to get the assistance you want just by making a polite request.

Buyer #9: Cynical Cindy

Cindy's the first to say, "But we've *always* done it this way." She fights change. She's suspicious and questions your every move. She's very likely part of the old guard where she works, a long-term employee.

Welcome her objections; even brag that she was smart enough to bring them up. You have to impress Cindy with the names of people and companies she trusts; to relax her wall of doubt, she needs to know who else uses your product or service. For you, though, her hesitancy can become the best thing about Cindy. Why? Because if *you* have such a difficult time overcoming her objections, you'd better believe that your competition can get discouraged trying to win her over. It'll be hard for your competition to persuade her to change her loyalties once she sees the value of becoming your client.

Your Greatest Enemy: Their Fears

In all its forms, fear is the greatest enemy you will ever encounter in persuading others. The toughest part of your job is helping others admit to and overcome their fears so that you can earn the opportunity to do business with them. Fear builds those walls of resistance that we so often run into. You must learn how to climb over or break through those walls if you're to travel the road to sales success.

There are eight common fears that you'll have to help your prospects overcome. When you recognize these fears as barriers to your ability to serve your prospects with excellent service, then you're ready to learn how to dismantle those walls, one brick at a time, thus gaining your prospect's confidence and trust. Your goal is to get your prospect to like you and trust you. They do that when you serve them with warmth and empathy.

Enemy #1: Fear of salespeople

At first, every prospect is afraid of you. You're a salesperson. You want something from them. You're talking with them to get them to change something in their lives. Even if you are going to help someone you already know — friend, acquaintance, or even relative — when you meet them in the role of sales professional, certain fears arise. It's bound to happen in 99 percent of your presentations. I grant you a nonfear situation only with your parents or grandparents, simply because they probably believe in you and trust you no matter what role you play with them. To them you come across as you should to everyone — with a natural, nonsales personality.

Enemy #2: Fear of failure

The next fear you encounter is the fear of making a mistake. We all have that one, though, don't we? That's because we've all made mistakes. We all have regrets. Whether your mistake was in choosing the wrong hair color or style or to purchase a vehicle that wasn't right for you doesn't matter. Somewhere in our psyches we have a fear, not necessarily because of our bad decision but because we remember it as being associated with a salesperson. You must take the time to talk your prospects through every aspect of the decision very carefully. You are the expert. You know this business.

No one wants to handle a transaction in which the customer may be dissatisfied with the result. Believe me, there'll be times when the grief you get from a customer won't be worth the fee you'll earn on the sale. That doesn't happen often, but you must go into every presentation with a sharp interest in the who, what, when, where, and why of their needs. When you've satisfied yourself that buying your product or service is in their best interest, then it's your duty as the expert to convince them that this decision is truly good for them.

Enemy #3: Fear of owing money

Prospects are also tremendously afraid of owing too much money — to you, to your company, to a finance company. Your fee for service is almost always a point of contention with prospective customers.

Most people wouldn't attempt to negotiate with a company about fees, but you are not seen as an institution. You're not cold, forbidding concrete walls and walkways, but rather a warm, flesh-and-blood fellow human. *You* they will try to negotiate with. The challenge of haggling appears in many variations that depend on the negotiating skills of your buyers.

- They may put off making a decision and you'll have to draw them out. I cover this situation in more depth in Chapter 12.
- They may be point blank about it and you'll have to sell them on the value of the service you provide.
- They may go at it in a roundabout way such as saying, "Another company we talked with will charge a lot less."

When you hear that remark, here's what I recommend that you say:

> *You know, I've learned something over the years. People look for three things when they spend money. They look for the finest quality, the best service, and, of course, the lowest investment. I've also found that no company can offer all three. They can't offer the finest quality and the best service for the lowest investment. So, for your long-term happiness, which of the three would you be most willing to give up? Fine quality? Excellent service? Or the lowest fee?*

Most respond that quality and service are of utmost concern, which overcomes the concern about the fee. Your next move is to reiterate everything you will do for them. Again, sell the value of the service you and your company provide. If you run into a company that is truly concerned only with getting the lowest investment and you can't provide it, you may have to bow out of the picture. Do it gracefully and stay in touch. Chances are good that they'll get what they pay for and eventually see the wisdom in spending more for the quality product or service that you can provide them.

Enemy #4: Fear of being lied to

Another common fear in buyers is the fear of being lied to. As a rule, they doubt everything you are saying about how much they'll benefit from your product, service, or idea.

This is where strong past track records come into play. Having a long list of happy clients should help you calm this fear. If you're new and don't have an established track record, tell your prospect you made a point of choosing her company because it has a great track record. If you're doing something entirely new with a new company, new product or service, or new concept, you have to build on the personal integrity and credentials of those involved in the project.

Enemy #5: Fear of embarrassment

Many people fear losing face with anyone who could possibly know about the decision if it's bad. Have you ever made a poor decision that was big enough that most of your friends and family members knew about it (and then kept reminding you about it)? It demeaned and embarrassed you, didn't it? Bad decisions make you feel like a child again — insecure and powerless. For that reason, many potential customers put off making any decision.

Knowing that this fear could block your sale, your primary goal should be to help them feel secure with you. Let them know that they are not relinquishing total power to you. You are merely acting on their behalf, providing a product or service they need. If you're selling to more than one decision-maker, such as with a married couple, neither of them will want to risk losing face in front of the other. Chances are good that they've disagreed about something in the past and that they don't want to have that uncomfortable situation arise again.

Enemy #6: Fear of the unknown

Prospects are also afraid of the unknown. A lack of understanding of your product or service, or of its value to the prospect's company, is a reasonable cause for delaying any transaction. National name recognition will dispel some of this fear. If you work for a local company, however, I suggest that you join forces with your company's sales staff to earn a great local reputation as a competent business with great products. Over the years, a great reputation saves you a bundle of time in this business.

Former teachers often make the best salespeople — check that, former *good* teachers almost always achieve Champion status when they switch to careers in sales. The bottom line is that selling is educating people about the benefits of doing business with you. Once you educate them past their fear of the unknown, they feel confident about their decision to do business with you.

Enemy #7: Fear of past mistakes

Having a bad past experience generates fear in the hearts of some potential customers. If they've used a product or service like yours before, what kind of experience was it for them?

You need to know their answer to that question; to get it, you need to ask the proper questions. If they hesitate to tell you, you may assume that their past experience was bad and that you have to overcome a lot more fear than if they've never used a product or service like yours before. You may have to offer the product or service on a sample or trial basis. Get them to talk with satisfied customers who will give unbiased testimony as to the value of your offering.

Enemy #8: Fear generated by others

A prospect's fear also may come from third-party information. Someone they admire or respect may have told them something negative about your company, your type of product, or even another representative of your company. Either way, that third party will stand between you and them like a brick wall until you convince or persuade them that you can help them more than that person because *you* are the expert on your product or service. You'll have to work hard to earn their trust. You may even have to enlist the aid of some of your past happy clients as references.

Fear: Versatile, Stealthy, Persistent Enemy of Sales

In selling, your prospect's fear can assume more identities than Inspector Clouseau can imagine — and it's not nearly as lovable as Clouseau, either. Here they are once more for emphasis, the eight fears a prospect can have that can keep you from getting to *Yes. Know these eight fears.* They'll be on the test every day of your professional life.

Enemy #1: Fear of salespeople

Enemy #2: Fear of failure

Enemy #3: Fear of owing money

Enemy #4: Fear of dishonesty

Enemy #5: Fear of embarrassment

Enemy #6: Fear of the unknown

Enemy #7: Fear of past mistakes

Enemy #8: Fear generated by others

Do You Know What You're Saying?

Think about the effective power of language. Every word we utter creates a picture in the mind's eye of the listener. Do you use that power to your greatest advantage?

Every word paints a symbol or picture in your mind. When you hear a word, you picture a symbol of what that word represents. Each symbol often has emotions attached to it as well.

Words — spring, summer, autumn, winter — can generate positive or negative emotions in you. If you love gardening, the warm spring air brings to mind beautiful blossoms, the opportunity to get your fingers in the dirt, preparing your soil for a summer crop. If you are a hayfever sufferer, the picture painted by the word "spring" is totally different.

The same applies to the words you use in your contacts with customers. You don't know in advance which words about you, your product, and your company will generate positive feelings in your clients. That's why people in selling must become extrasensitive to the use of words if they want to have successful careers.

Words to sell by

Many words common to sales and selling situations can generate fearful or negative images in clients' minds. The experience of hundreds of thousands of salespeople confirms that it is imperative to replace such words with more positive, pacifying words and phrases.

For example, the first terms I recommend that you change are *sell* and *sold.* Many salespeople tell prospects how many units of their product they have *sold.* Or they brag about having *sold* the same product to another customer. What are the mental images here? No one likes the idea of being *sold* anything. The word reminds us of high-pressure sales tactics and usually turns people off. It makes the transaction sound one-sided, as if the customer really had little say in the matter. That's why you should replace *sell* or *sold* with *helped them acquire* or *got them involved.* Those phrases create softer images of a helpful salesperson and a receptive customer becoming involved together in the same process.

Another commonly used word in sales is *contract.* What images does that term bring to mind, especially when you picture yourself as a consumer? For most people, *contract* evokes negative images. It's something Mom and Dad have warned us about all our lives. It's fine print, legalities, and being locked into something. Where do we go to get out of contracts? To court — not a pleasant image for most people.

I recommend that you stop using the word *contract,* unless your particular line of business requires it. Instead, use *paperwork, agreement,* or *form.* Do those words bring to mind threatening images? Maybe, but those images are a lot less threatening than the ones you get with *contract.* Do yourself a favor and eliminate *contract* from your selling vocabulary. Use *paperwork, agreement,* or *form* instead.

What about *cost* and *price?* When I hear those words, I see my hard-earned cash leaving my pocket. That's why I teach people to substitute *investment* or *amount* for *cost* or *price.* When most people hear *investment,* they envision the positive image of getting a return on their money. For products for which *investment* would not be appropriate, use *amount.* That word, too, has been proven to be less threatening to most consumers than *cost* or *price.*

The same idea goes for *down payment* and *monthly payment.* Most people envision down payments as large deposits that lock them into many smaller monthly payments for, if not an eternity, at least a few years. They see themselves receiving bills and writing checks every month — not a pleasant image for most people. Replace those phrases with these: *initial investment, initial amount; monthly investment, monthly amount.* In the trade, we call these terms *money terms* and anyone who wants to persuade someone to part with money needs to use these terms well.

What about *buy?* There goes my money out of my pocket again. Use the term *own* instead. *Own* conjures images of where I'll put the product in my home, showing it with pride to friends or relatives, and many other positive thoughts.

Another term overused by salespeople is *deal.* This brings to mind something we've always wanted, but never found. Images of used-car salesmen (decked out in the plaid coat I mention in Chapter 1) are only too closely associated with *deal.* Top salespeople never offer their clients *deals.* They *offer opportunities* or *get them involved.*

Customers don't *raise objections* about our products or services. Instead, they *express areas of concern.*

I never have *problems with my sales.* Every now and then I may, however, *have some challenges with my transactions.*

I never *pitch* my product or service to my customer. Instead, I *present* or *demonstrate* my product or service — the way any self-respecting professional would.

And as an authority or expert on your product or services, you don't earn *commissions,* either. You do, however, *receive fees for service.* If Mr. Johnson ever asks you about your *commission* on a sale, elevate your conversation to a more appropriate level with language such as this:

> *Mr. Johnson, I'm fortunate that my company has included a fee for service in every transaction. In that way, they compensate me for the high level of service I give to each and every client, and that's what you really want, isn't it?*

The last but definitely not the least important term I recommend that you change is *sign.* If you change nothing else after you read *Selling For Dummies,* never again ask a customer to "sign" your agreement, form, or paperwork. What happens emotionally when people are asked to *sign* something? In most cases, a warning goes off in people's heads. They become hesitant and cautious. They want to review whatever it is they're signing, scanning the page for the infamous fine print. Anytime now, they may even head for the door. It's been drilled into almost everyone from early childhood to never *sign* anything without careful consideration.

So why would you want to create that emotion in anyone you were trying to *get happily involved* with your product or service? Instead of asking them to *sign,* ask them to *approve, authorize, endorse,* or *okay* your *paperwork, agreement,* or *form.* Any of those word pictures carries the positive associations that you want to inspire in your clients.

Don't ask 'em to *sign* when you can ask for an *autograph*

I know of one man who helps people acquire recreational vehicles. An RV isn't a minor investment for anyone. So when the moment of truth comes, he simply turns his paperwork around and says these words, "Bill & Sue, let me make you famous for a moment and ask for your autograph."

While he's saying these words, he's handing them a pen and smiling. Nice picture, isn't it?

It may sound foolish to you now to concentrate on what appear to be such minor details, but some of those details pack a hefty punch. You may consider such details minor and all my fussing over them misplaced. If you think about it, though, I think you'll see what I've been hinting at all along: language is a salesperson's *only* tool — period. The salesperson who uses language well, for the genuine benefit of other people, is a salesperson who sells, and sells, and sells. The words you use are not minor details at all. They are the very center of your profession.

So . . . when you write down and practice your own product presentation, go through it and make sure that your words stress ownership from your *prospects'* perspective. After all, satisfying your *prospects'* needs is what this business of selling is all about — and the words you send out to them are the only way that you, and not your competition, can earn the opportunity to satisfy those needs.

Jargon, by another name

Today more than ever, your selling vocabulary matters because of the phenomenon of trade talk, a.k.a. jargon. *Jargon* is words and phrases particular to a given field of work. If you sell medical supplies to doctors, you'd better know the trade talk and use it liberally. But if you sell stereo or computer equipment to the general public, limit your use of technical terms to the bare minimum until you can determine their level of knowledge about the product. There's nothing worse than alienating customers by using acronyms they're not familiar with. Remember, your goal is to make your customers feel important. It's tough to feel important when you don't feel very smart.

Words That Trip You Up, Words That Help You Out

Don't Say	*Say*
Contract	Paperwork, agreement, form
Cost or Price	Investment, amount
Down Payment	Initial investment, initial amount
Monthly Payment	Monthly investment, monthly amount
Buy	Own
Sell or Sold	Get them involved, help them acquire
Deal	Opportunity, transaction
Objection	Area of concern
Problem	Challenge
Pitch	Presentation, demonstration
Commission	Fee for service
Sign	Approve, endorse, okay, or authorize

The human mind can assimilate information rapidly only if it understands what is being said. If you're talking to Joe Consumer about bits and bytes and he doesn't understand those terms, his mind stops at those terms and tries in vain to find an image that fits them. Many people won't ask you for explanations for fear of showing their lack of knowledge; a negative feeling we all know as embarrassment. Others may get the gist of what you're talking about but struggle to keep up. While they're trying to keep up, they miss the next few valuable points you relay to them. In other words, you've lost them.

If your subject sounds more complicated than your customer can comprehend, you risk squelching his desire to ever own or use your product or service *and* you risk losing the sale. More often than not, you lose such customers to a salesperson who uses lay terms and simple definitions. Good things come to salespeople who take the time to learn how to speak their clients' language.

A whole vocabulary at your fingertips

Words are readily available to anyone who wants to control them. Webster didn't reserve certain words and their meanings for the rich. Everyone has access to the same dictionary. Everyone has the same opportunity to choose the words that make their speech outstanding and memorable. Every time you need to convey a concept to someone, you have a choice of any one of thousands of words to establish your meaning. We have no excuse *not* to choose our words carefully. Knowing that your words reflect the person you are, you should investigate the word choices you make and the reasons you make them.

Take the time to make a list of powerful but easy-to-understand words and phrases that are specific to your product or service. Then test them on a friend or relative — someone who is not a qualified prospect. If they don't have a clear understanding of the terms, prepare brief definitions of those terms in lay language. Then, the first time you use the terms with new or prospective clients, be prepared to give them the definition in lay terms if it's something vital to the transaction or will reoccur frequently in your discussion with these customers. I've stressed the importance of speaking their language; however, if you're offering something totally new to them, you have an obligation to educate them about the terms they'll need to know once they've gotten involved.

Anyone who wants to persuade others should recognize and choose appropriate language. Take a look at the two following examples. Be aware of the differences in language. Even though you cannot see these two salespeople, you will create a mental picture of each of them and their selling styles.

The manager of Continual Care Hair products has been courting an account with a major chain of salons (owned by one Mr. Dunn) for two months. These salons now carry a competitor's product but have agreed to hear a presentation by one of Continual Care Hair's representatives. It is now up to the manager to choose the salesperson who can consummate all the manager's hard work. The manager calls a meeting with each salesperson she is considering. The one who succeeds in representing the company could receive a sizable increase in earnings. Which one would you choose?

MANAGER: Now that you understand what will be expected of you, how would you give this presentation?

DAWN: I would just love the chance to tell Mr. Dunn how much better our products are than what he's using. I would go to Mr. Dunn's salon tomorrow morning. I know I could convince him to dump what he uses now and replace his stock with ours.

MANAGER: What's your next step?

DAWN: Well, after I got all the information, I would tell Mr. Dunn what we could do for him and I would try to get him on my side before the presentation to his staff so he could help me sell his stylists on the products.

MANAGER: I'm interested to hear how you would do this, Dawn.

DAWN: Well, I guess I'd tell him how much money he would save, and how much more he'll make by selling our products.

Same situation — hopeful salesperson talking to CCH's manager — except now the salesperson is Sue.

MANAGER: Now that you understand what will be expected of you, how will you handle this presentation?

SUE: I believe the first step would be to contact Mr. Dunn and request a meeting at his convenience. Then, with your approval, I would examine your files on the salon, so I'm prepared for the presentation.

MANAGER: What's your next step?

SUE: I will ask Mr. Dunn to show me his salons. I will familiarize myself with Mr. Dunn's needs, his stylist's needs, and those of the salons' clientele. Then I will offer Mr. Dunn the opportunity to use Continual Care Hair products and ask his permission to present the products to his stylists.

MANAGER: I'm interested to hear how you would do this, Sue.

SUE: Although it's important to consider his financial benefits, too, I will encourage Mr. Dunn to examine the improved condition of hair that has been treated with Continual Care Hair products. Making hair more beautiful will give Mr. Dunn happier customers as well as increased profits. Would it be possible to take a few company models with me on the presentation?

The two conversations have created two pictures in the mind of the manager. Who will represent her company with the most success? I believe it would be Sue. Sue radiated calm enthusiasm and a thoughtful manner. But the turning point in Sue's interview is her choice of the phrase *I will* instead of indefinite terms. Sue speaks as if she's already been chosen, while Dawn uses iffier, less-confident language. This is a subtle but very effective change in words. It isn't long before the manager agrees to send models out with Sue for her presentation.

Sue is an above average salesperson with a powerful command of language. She creates positive word pictures with every word she utters. Here are some words you might hear an average salesperson deliver. Think about the pictures they create in your mind.

SALESPERSON: All the kids in your neighborhood will love playing in your new pool.

PROSPECT: I'm probably going to have trouble getting my kids out of it.

SALESPERSON: When should we start digging? Would this Saturday or next Monday be better?

Was that a good question at the end? What was wrong with the dialogue between the salesperson and the prospect? What image comes to your mind from the salesperson's statement that "all the kids in your neighborhood will love playing in your new pool"? Loads of kids jumping, splashing, running, and yelling at the tops of their lungs comes to my mind. It's not too peaceful a scene.

Remember what I said earlier about the power of words. Be careful of the word pictures you paint. Just a few careless words can destroy hours of work. In this case, the salesperson would do better to say, *Most of our customers tell us they enjoy spending quality time with their families in their new pools.*

The salesperson's next words — "When should we start digging? Would this Saturday or next Monday be better?" — carry their own negative images. With *digging,* the prospect might envision a huge tractor roaring through his yard digging up plants and mound after mound of dirt, making a general mess of the prospect's home, and on a weekend to boot.

The salesperson would do better to say this:

> *Some people prefer to be present when we begin the first phase of their new swimming pool, others prefer to just tell us when and then have us tell them when the pool is ready to swim in. We can begin Phase 1 Saturday or next Monday. Which would you prefer?*

I can't emphasize enough how important your choice of words is to your selling career. Your words can make or break the sale without you even knowing it. In many cases, if you ask the customer why they didn't buy from you, they may not be able to put their finger on any one deciding moment. They "just didn't feel right" about going ahead. Words create images, which in turn evoke emotions, so start paying careful attention not only to your prospects, but to the effects your words have on them.

Know the regional manners

Another point to consider is your accent. People in nearly every region of the United States have an accent or a certain way of saying particular words. These accents can be charming or irritating to others, depending on their existing assumptions. If you do business in several areas of the country, you probably already know this.

For example, if you're from the South and must do business with folks in the Northeast, be prepared to talk a bit faster than normal in order to keep their attention. Also, you might want to train yourself to listen more effectively because people in that part of the country tend to talk faster than the people you are used to being around.

The opposite goes if you are a Northeasterner doing business with some Southerners or people residing outside major metropolitan areas. Some people from the South and in small towns handle business in a more relaxed manner than do folks in the Northeast.

Do You Know What You're Hearing?

The human body has two ears and one mouth. To be good at persuading or selling, you must learn to use those natural devices in proportion. Listen twice as much as you talk and you'll succeed in persuading others nearly every time. When you do most of the talking,

- You are not learning about either the customer or the customer's needs.
- You will not hear buying clues or concerns.
- You may be raising concerns the prospect might not have had.
- You shift your prospect's attention from your offering.
- You give them more opportunity to disagree with you, to distrust one of your statements, or both.

- You take center stage away from the customer.
- You can't think ahead.
- You can't guide the conversation.
- You cannot convince the other person of the best decision for them.

Most people don't think they talk too much, but if you'd listened to as many sales presentations as I have over 25 years of teaching, selling, and sales management, you would have developed a keen ear for how much talking is done compared to how much is needed.

To develop your ear, try these two simple exercises:

1. **Listen to salespeople selling others or trying to sell you.** Pay attention to what their words are doing. While you're listening, ask yourself these questions:
   - Do their words paint positive or negative mental pictures?
   - Do they say anything that could raise a new objection to their product or service?
   - Are all their words necessary?
   - Do they ask questions and then carefully listen to the prospect's answers?
   - Do they move forward with questions, or do they get off course by talking about features and benefits the customer has not expressed a need for?
2. **Record yourself with a customer.** You may be shocked at how much chatter you can cut out. To detect what you need to cut, ask yourself these questions:
   - What is the quality of the questions you ask?
   - Are they information-gathering questions to help you move forward with your sale, or are they just questions you are asking to fill a sound void? (Questions don't mean much unless the answers are helping you get the information to help you serve your customer better and keep the sale moving forward.)

Watch and listen to others and to yourself more carefully than you're used to listening. Acquaint yourself with what good listening really "sounds" like. It should sound like the voice of others, not yours. As you learn more and more about selling well, the phrase *putting your foot in your mouth* will gain new meaning for you. Remember: you can't put your foot in your mouth if it's closed. So close it, and listen more.

Chapter 6

Knowing Your Product

In This Chapter

- Knowing the importance of balance
- Getting the vital statistics
- Focusing on what's in it for them
- Making every negotiation a win-win

Product knowledge is one of the most important aspects of selling. In fact, when I teach people about mastering the fundamentals of selling, I use a triangle with equal sides.

On one whole side is *product knowledge.* On another whole side are the *selling tactics and strategies* we're covering throughout this book, while the base of the triangle is *attitude, enthusiasm, and goals.*

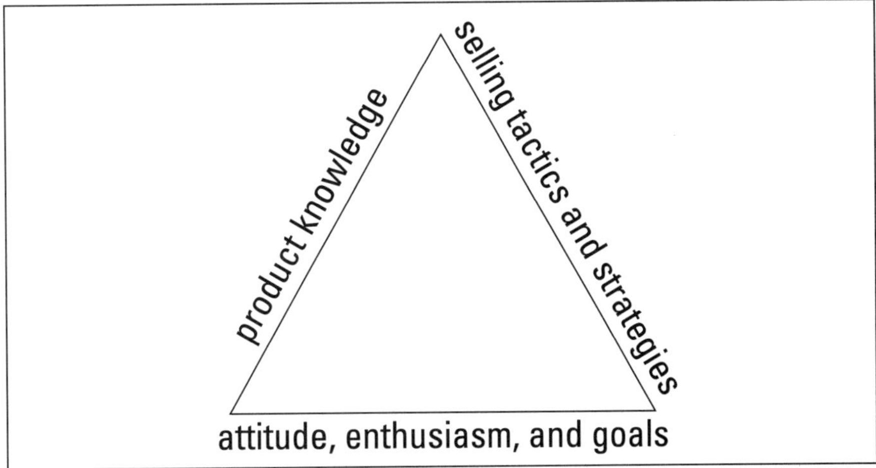

The three sides of the triangle are equally important. It's hard to predict the success of a person who is strong in two categories but weak in the third. A professional who has failed to develop any one side of the triangle is failing to reach his or her full potential with clients who expect to work with a competent person.

The Importance of Balance

You've all heard about the importance of having balance in your life. People who invest all of their waking hours only in business soon find themselves with disintegrating personal relationships. Those who use valuable business hours to keep up on the hour-by-hour events at home or with friends often find themselves unemployed or at the bottom of the list of income earners at their companies.

Since there are at least three aspects of a selling career, it's just as vital that you maintain balance within your selling career as shown in the triangle illustration on the previous page.

Too much product knowledge makes Jack . . .

If product knowledge were the most important factor in selling, then technical designers, manufacturers, or assemblers of products would make the best salespeople. However, being strong in one area without developing strengths in the other two parts of the triangle can doom your selling to career disaster.

Technical designers of products rarely make the best salespeople or marketers for their products to the end consumer. (Maybe it has something to do with a dress code that includes pocket protectors.) Of course, technical designers know the product quite literally from the inside out. But until they are trained in selling skills and understand how much a role attitude plays in sales, their sales approach is often 99 percent description of product, 1 percent relation of the product to the needs of the individual clients, and you can forget any attempt to close — it gets a big 0 percent.

Granted, sometimes technical people have to sell their designs to the Powers That Make Manufacturing Decisions (you know, the PTMMD). But in such cases they sell to people who already understand the lingo. Besides, they probably team up with marketing people who have conducted focus group sessions to get what the consumer response to such a product will be.

Most of the time, though, when technical people are put in traditional sales positions, the only thing accomplished is that the customer receives an excellent education on the product and its capabilities and knows exactly what to ask the competition when they come in for their demonstration.

Designers also tend to lack attitude and enthusiasm because they are used to being on the forefront of innovation in their industries. They know that bigger and better things are on the horizon; that knowledge can spell disaster if they need to move product today in order to earn a living. Involvement in the design phase requires them to move on to the next upgrade or model before the "present" model is even available to the end consumer. Focusing their attention so far ahead, on tomorrow's improvements and enhancements, inhibits their ability to get and to stay excited about the product that's available today.

Ice cubes to Eskimos?

Say you do have great selling skills. You are comfortable talking with practically anyone. You've invested a tremendous amount of time mastering the best words for creating positive pictures in the minds of your prospects. But, of what? If you don't have a clear picture in your own mind of what your product, service, or idea will do for others, how can you paint the right pictures in someone else's mind?

You would be selling for selling's sake — not for the good of the customer. In a very short period of time, that would get you nowhere — even if you had a great attitude and tremendous enthusiasm for what you do. It's still devoid of real purpose and will eventually bring you down. In fact, it could cause irreparable damage to your reputation and your career.

All pumped up but nowhere to go

What if you are what managers call an "Eddie Eager?" You're new to selling. You're excited. You've had a little product training and have heard about the big incomes the top people make. You've set your sights high and can't wait to get out there and make your first big sale. However, you have little knowledge or experience with selling tactics and strategies.

What happens to the "Eddies" of the world is that they get rejected a good bit because their enthusiasm will open the doors a crack, but they get their fingers slammed when they start pushing product. And *pushing* product isn't how you sell anything. Eventually, the many rejections will either bring Eddie back to his manager for help in acquiring selling skills or he may just quit and get a job with a lovely income ceiling, putting a cap on his dreams of earning a high income forever.

Caveat seller: An unbalanced triangle = an unbalanced life

Top people who move from one field to another, or even from one company to another, may have a tough time achieving their standard high level of success with a new product line. Since companies *always* want skilled salespeople to represent their product or service, headhunters seek champion salespeople every day. And they can be very persuasive. Although champion salespeople have been burning it up for their original companies, when they finally do change companies, their changes can devastate both themselves and the companies who recruited them to switch.

One of my students at an advanced seminar once came to me with the challenges he faced after making a change. He had been a young go-getter with a small and relatively unknown insurance company. From the moment he came to the company, their policy volume skyrocketed because of his talent and product knowledge. His proficiency, of course, earned him the respect of both the company leaders and his peers alike, not to mention the policyholders, who truly enjoyed working with him.

Naturally, it wasn't long before one of the larger, national insurance agencies heard of his track record and offered him a better opportunity with their company. Although he loved his current firm and their staff, he thought that he had exceeded his growth possibilities with them and made the change. That's when disaster struck!

He had chosen the largest, highest-paying bidder, the company he sincerely thought offered him the best opportunities for growth. What he failed to consider, though, was what his new offer really meant: because his new company had given him the best of everything, they also had the highest expectations for his success. They had come across with their promises, and now they expected him to come through on his and deliver bigger and better results than he had ever delivered. It was the pressure cooker school of hard knocks for him.

He had to suffer through a learning curve with the new company. He faced some serious challenges in working with the new, higher level of clientele this company served. The more involved products were a challenge to him as well. In fact, he never really recovered from making this change. His self-confidence and positive attitude began to falter. He shared with me his growing paranoia: he thought that other salespeople resented him and were out to make his life miserable. He continued for the next year to blame anyone or anything around him for his failure. The only place he failed to look for someone to blame was in the mirror.

As this student stood before me telling his story, the hurt and disappointment in his eyes were obvious as he went on to tell me about being dismissed from this highly prized position. Then he told me how happy he had been with that smaller company. As he spoke about it, his eyes sparkled and his old enthusiasm returned to his voice. I explained to him that what he had gone through was normal and that perhaps he just expected too much from himself.

He needed to rebalance the three sides of his triangle. By the time he came to me, he had weakened two major sides of the selling triangle. With the job change, his triangle lost its product knowledge side immediately. But, much more important, losing his product knowledge deflated his ego and soured his attitude. He needed to relearn one of the basic rules of selling: *Anyone who is proficient in both product knowledge and selling skills, but who is deficient in attitude and enthusiasm, will have trouble getting to — and staying at — the top of their chosen industry.*

Like other great salespeople, this man had a resilient spirit and was determined to succeed. Now that he understands what happened, his chances for success after surviving this experience are excellent.

Vital Statistics

The major portion of this book focuses on the selling skills side of the triangle. I cover attitude and enthusiasm specifically in Chapter 15, but for now the theme is product knowledge.

What must you absolutely, positively, truly *know* about your product in order to do well in selling it? Always begin with the obvious:

- What the product is called
- Whether it's the latest model
- How it improves a previous model or version
- How fast it is
- How to operate it during demonstrations
- What colors it comes in
- What your current inventory is for setting delivery dates
- How much it costs
- What terms and financing are available

Even companies with the most basic product training should cover those items with new salespeople before sending them out to talk with customers. It's sad, but true that some companies will provide only the bare minimum of information and salespeople have to develop the rest on their own. Much of this additional learning comes in the course of researching the answers to customers' questions and is built upon as needed.

Product information: yours for the finding

Hopefully, your company or the manufacturer of the products you represent hold regularly scheduled training sessions. If they do, then by all means *go to these training sessions.* They're your best opportunity for getting the scoop about your product from reliable sources. And *always* attend these sessions with a list of questions. If the speaker doesn't answer your questions during the presentation, find a way to ask your questions before this knowledgeable person gets away.

Your company probably will inundate you with brochures and technical information on your product or service. Schedule a specific time to sit and read such literature — but don't just read through them the way a customer would. Study them. Read them every day for at least three weeks. By the end of that time, you'll have them memorized and know exactly what your customers are referring to when they ask questions. There's nothing worse than having to look to a higher source when your customer asks a question that you should know the answer to, but don't.

If training sessions and product literature aren't available to you, and what you sell is a tangible product, get your hands on a sample at your earliest convenience. Be like a kid with a new toy. Play with it. Experiment. Read through suggested demonstrations and try them out as if you are the customer. Make notes on things you find hard to understand. Chances are good that at least one of your prospects will have the same questions or concerns. Resolve those concerns now, and you'll be well prepared for your demonstrations.

Customers & colleagues can put you in the know

If you work with intangibles, get as much feedback as you can from the people who already use and benefit from what you sell. If possible, survey some of those people to find out what they think of what you sell and what their experiences with it have been. For all you know, your competitors have already presented your customers with product options they didn't realize they had. Always remember: Your current customers are an extremely valuable resource — *if* you keep in contact with them.

Veteran and top salespeople have all kinds of information about products that they may never document. Talk with them as much as you can to learn from them. Be careful, though, to keep your meetings focused on product knowledge and information; otherwise, your time will not be well spent. When two or more salespeople get together, it's easy to slip into Miller time, get off the subject at hand, and descend into old war stories or other unrelated matters. If you want product knowledge, focus the conversation there. Now's no time for gossip.

Here is a learning strategy that has worked countless times: Ask to go on a demonstration call with the top person in your company or someone who is currently on the rise to success to see and hear how they present your product. Watch just how they handle everything: themselves, the client, the brochures, proposal, visual aids, the product itself. Listen to the word pictures they use in describing it. Notice the mood they set. The how of handling products and information is as important as the what and why.

One suggestion that has often been made is to handle all of your materials with courtesy and respect. If products or literature are tossed about or handled casually, that's the level of importance the receiver will put on them.

Create a respectful environment

When you are in a learning mode, it's important to set the stage for learning. That may mean gathering pen and paper, brochures, and a demo piece of equipment and locking yourself in the company conference room to study. It may mean setting appointments with a training director, company owner, or top salesperson and interviewing them. It may involve watching hours of product training video or attending classes on the products. It may involve interviewing current customers.

It doesn't matter what the type of education is, you must begin every session with a clear respect for what's to come. This means treating the sessions like gold — showing up on time, if not early. Have plenty of paper for note taking. Bring a couple of pens in different colors to highlight the most important information. Be courteous to those who are sharing their knowledge with you. What they are imparting will make you money. Treat them and their messages with the utmost respect. The better you treat them, the more they'll relax. You'll be making them like you and trust you, thus offering more information. Hmm, sounds a lot like selling, doesn't it?

Go directly to the source

Whatever type of product you sell, try to create an opportunity to tour the facility where your product is designed and built. Better yet, try to visit with the originator of the idea. Find out what he or she was thinking when it all came together. You cannot know too much about your product or service. Customers love to feel that you have the inside track on the latest and greatest products and services; they want to believe that you are the most competent person in your industry. Face it: No one wants to be represented by a dud!

The challenge is that changes in technology occur almost overnight. The rapidly changing face of our world gives you all the more reason to know everything you can now. What comes next will likely require you to build on previous knowledge in order to be prepared for the future. If you don't have today's knowledge when you need it, you'll just have more to learn to get back to scratch.

Competitors have products, too, you know

Most companies designate a person or department to gather information on the competition and to prepare analyses of that information for the sales staff. If your company has this situation under control, sing their praises and encourage them to keep up the good work because such research is a voraciously time-consuming feat.

But don't rely on just one source for information. If you're in business on your own, you may want to enlist a family member to find juicy tidbits of information on competitors' products for you. As another option, clipping services provide professional readers who research topics for you — for a fee. Because you're the one who's out there every day slogging in the trenches, facing off against the competition, you need to keep your eyes and ears open for any information available.

If you call on customers who've had past experiences with your competitors, ask them if they would mind sharing their thoughts on the product and service with you. When they tell their tales, take good notes and keep them handy for future reference. If a new customer has just switched from the competition to your product, find out exactly what the deciding factor was and work it into any presentations you make where circumstances are similar.

What's In It For Me?

There's an old sales training lesson that goes like this: What's everyone's favorite radio station? The answer is always WII-FM. The call letters in this case stand for *What's In It For Me?*

People have a WII-FM mentality, whether they admit it to themselves or not. Human beings are selfish creatures whose natural propensity is to make themselves as comfortable as possible.

Be painfully honest! When was the last time you did something for someone else with absolutely no expectations of getting anything in return? Now before you tell me what a self-sacrificing person you really are . . . think about that answer for a second. I'm asking you to remember a time when you did something for someone else without expecting *any*thing in return for what you did — no thank you, no undying loyalties, no promises that the object of your benefactions would someday return the favor . . . nothing, zip, zero, zilch, nada, nienti, goose egg.

If you're like the rest of us, you'll have a tough time remembering such a time. Most people are motivated to do for others only if they themselves expect to receive compensation that they value. The compensation may not always be monetary, but people *always* want something, anything, even a crust of bread in exchange for their efforts. Even if the sought rewards are intangible and emotional — hugs, kisses, pats on the head, a warm smile— a reward is a reward is a reward.

And that's the same philosophy your customer holds every time you contact her. She sees you as someone who can eliminate a discomfort from her life. To her, you're someone who can give more than he receives, which is why she expects you to provide customer *service*. You contact your customer for one reason: to serve her needs, whether you do it by providing information, a service, or a product.

Better Yet, What's in It for Them?

I've always taught that salespeople need to get themselves out of the picture when selling a product or service. Clients don't care if you like the product or service. They want information that'll help them decide whether or not they'll like it.

Whenever you enter a potential client's premises, try to imagine yourself as a fly on the wall — observing things from varying angles yet barely being observed yourself. I recommend this strategy because unless you're there to sell yourself into a job, that's about how much impact you personally will make on the overall business. Let's face it, unless you're selling funky Muzak you won't have the entire staff dancing in the halls.

Walk a mile in their shoes

Here's an excellent exercise to develop your face-to-face selling strategies.

Imagine that you are your customer. To do this, you must have done your research on your customer's company, its history, its products and services, and its decision-maker. To do this exercise well, ask yourself questions like these:

- What would this offering do for me?
- Could it make me more efficient or productive?

And here's a good question to ask yourself when you reverse roles before a presentation to a prospect whose position does not allow her to make final decisions in her company. If you're scheduled to meet an executive who has to answer to a Greater Force (that is, one of her higher-ups) to justify owning your product, prep yourself by imagining that you have to answer this question: What will the upper-management think of me personally if I invest in this product?

If you don't have enough information to answer these questions, it's back to the research role for you. You must be able to go in with confidence that your product or service will truly benefit the people you present to or at least their staff members.

Help them get ahead (and you'll get ahead)

Obviously, if you represent a more personal product, you can appeal to your customer's emotions, her self-esteem. How will your product make the other person feel better, look better, or appear more professional in the eyes of those they want to impress? If you know, you need to build that into your presentation.

On the other hand, if your product is a company product and the decision-maker is in a lower position, talk to their egos. Let them see how wise and businesslike they will look for recognizing all the benefits of your product for the company. Ask if they know their company's goals; if they do, find out what those goals are. Show them how your product or service will help the company meet its goals *and* help your contact rise a notch or two on the company ladder. Trust me on this: your customers can have fragile egos. Once you learn to bring your product to light as the answer to their concerns, you'll begin to increase your sales and number of clients.

Get the dollar signs out of your eyes

Getting yourself out of the picture and getting the dollar signs out of your eyes are the two toughest aspects of learning to sell successfully. If the other people recognize even a hint of selfishness or desperation in you, they will question your tactics. They will doubt you and you will begin a long, slow slide into obscurity in the selling profession.

It's a funny thing about money: the more money you have, the less important it becomes. I've talked to many very successful people in my time and, believe it or not, money has ceased to be their main motivation. At some time during their careers, money certainly was a motivator for them (as it is for everyone). But once they reached a certain level of success, other needs took over.

Some like the challenge of winning that negotiation or persuasion provides. Some like the contact with people who later become their friends as well as business associates. Some even like the tightrope excitement and constant activity that surround successful people.

But rarely is money the number one reason successful people just keep getting more successful. Not that it isn't an important factor. Few of us would maintain our hectic paces if money were not a positive benefit — but there's so much more to succeeding than just the promise of financial gain. When others can sense in you a sincere desire to help them, they will trust you and allow you to do just that.

Two Tested Ways to Meet Their Changing Needs

There are two things you want to have happen with every selling or persuasion situation:

1. You want to maintain control.
2. You want to display professionalism.

Negotiation is a give-and-take business and keeping control can only be done with knowledge. You have to know pretty well what cards your opponent holds or at least be able to make a reasonable guess at what they'll show you before you can make your best play. However, no matter how the game ends, it's vital you keep your professional demeanor.

Make every negotiation a win-win

There's an old adage in sales: *Always underpromise and overdeliver.* If you've done your homework, you'll know exactly what your product or service can do for each and every customer you meet. You'll also have a good idea of what they expect. This is where you decide how to play the hand you hold. If you know you can deliver exactly what they expect, it's always best to tell them.

But if you know you can deliver more than they expect, it's not always a good idea to tell them that in your first presentation. It may be a card worth holding in case the competition comes in with something better than you. In setting the stage so that you can *over*deliver, you retain control of the situation and maintain the option of pleasantly surprising your customers. Never underestimate the power of surprise in delighting and solidifying customers.

Follow up no matter what the outcome

The best time to plan for follow-up is before you even get the sale. Effective follow-up is too valuable a tool to misuse.

You know your product. You know what types of questions come up about your product during the first week, the second week, and after 90 days of owning it. Establish some sort of tickler system so that you follow up properly and effectively with each and every customer on each and every contact. Just don't tickle too often. Customers get leery of too much attention.

Every gladiator goes into battle expecting a win. So your system should anticipate that. But remember that you won't always make the sale. When you don't make a sale, though, don't toss an unsold prospect's file into the garbage and move on. Nonsales require follow up as well. No matter the outcome, be prepared to follow up. It can only enhance your professional image and keep the door open for future opportunities.

You know, or at least you should know, how much and how often your product changes. So consider this: The needs of customers or prospects who didn't become customers can change just as rapidly. They should have your name and image pictured in their minds when those new needs arise.

Chapter 7
Winning Presentations

In This Chapter

- Getting in the door
- And now we learn our ABCs of presenting
- Letting the product shine
- Helping prospects see their way to ownership
- Demonstrating — smoothly, persuasively

This is the show. This is where you get your potential client's senses involved. This is what major companies prepare for by investing hundreds of thousands of dollars and hours in graphics, models, and samples.

Presentations can be as simple as giving out a brochure with a quick explanation or as complex as what you might see at a trade show — including bells, whistles, food, clowns, and fireworks. How you present your show depends on what you represent and the potential investment.

A Foot in the Door

Once you've earned the right to give a prospect a demonstration or presentation of your idea, concept, product, or service, you're nowhere near done. What has happened is that the decision-maker has chosen you — probably from several other contestants for the honor, for the opportunity to prove that your offering is as dazzling as you've been saying.

But having an appointment to give a presentation doesn't automatically grant you favored status or guarantee you a warm welcome. It doesn't mean that you will become their favorite supplier, designer, or whatever. What many of them are saying is, "Okay, wonderboy. Impress me!" or "Okay, wondergirl. Now back up your claims." No pressure here, is there?

In any selling situation, it's vital that you understand the perspective of your contact person. (I cover this point at length in Chapter 4.) Every day, people much like you probably bombard them with overtures for their business. Your contact person may be a real decision-maker or a researcher who has temporary authority to study suppliers for a particular need. They may not be the final decision-maker, but rather someone designated to narrow the field to two or three potential suppliers for the real decision-maker to talk with. Many times a purchasing agent will bring in several competing companies for presentations to a committee. If you've done your homework well, you'll know exactly who'll be present and why each one of them is there.

Find the power players

When you begin the presentation, thank and acknowledge the person who invited you, make eye contact with each person in the room, and see if you can tell which member of your audience is the power player. There's one in every group. It may or may not be the person you've already been talking with. Just by watching how the other members of the group treat each other should clue you in. Workplace behavior isn't much different from what you see in a documentary about the social habits of wolves.

Just as in wolfpacks, in most workplaces the subordinates usually defer to the power players when important issues arise. And another hint for identifying the top dogs in a workplace: they also often take the best seat in the house for presentations. This is usually at the head of the table or at the 12:00 position at a round table with you being at 6:00. Or, they may sit closest to the door in anticipation of an interruption for a vital call or message. It's not a perfect call every time, but as you hone your skills at the people game, you'll start picking them out in minutes. Beware, though, that some power players don't play the game the way you'd expect and may sit unobtrusively in the back of the room. By watching everyone else's body language, though, you still should be able to recognize that person.

Be quick or be sorry

In today's world of the 10-second television commercial, it's become brutally obvious that few people bother anymore to develop their ability to concentrate. In fact, the average person in our society has a short, downright gnatlike attention span.

That means that you must compress the heart of your presentation down to a matter of only a few minutes. After those few minutes, spend the rest of your time involving your prospects directly in the presentation through questions, visual aids, or a hands-on demonstration.

I've long taught my students that they should practice, drill, and rehearse their presentations to get through the nitty-gritty in just under 17 minutes. Go past 17 minutes, and your prospect's mind wanders and his eyelids droop. Besides helping to keep your audience awake, brevity and conciseness demonstrate concern for their valuable time. They may not realize that they appreciate your concern for their time, but on some level they *will* appreciate it and the concern will make a difference.

This time constraint may challenge you if your product is, say, a complicated mechanical system. If that's the case, you may want to plan for a short break or a summary or question-answer period after the first 17 minutes are up. Letting them stretch their legs will increase the level of concentration they give you. When the blood stops circulating in your extremities, it's tough to pay attention.

The magic 17 minutes do not begin the moment you enter the room or while you're building rapport. The 17-minute period begins when you get down to the business at hand and cover the finer points of your product's features and how those features can benefit your client.

Break well, and prosper

If you do choose to schedule a break, or even if an unplanned break occurs, here's a vital piece of advice you must take to heart:

> Always do a brief recap before starting back into your presentation.

A brief recap is just a restatement of the major points that you've covered so far, a quick way to bring everyone back to where you were before the break. You see, any break in the action allows your listeners' minds to wander. People start looking at their watches, they think about lunch or their next appointment, or they wonder what the rest of the office is doing. They may even leave the room to make a call; if they do, their mind focuses on the other end of the call, not on your presentation. And you'd better believe that the emotional level they were at when the break came will not be the same when they come back. You must take a moment or two to bring them back to where they were before you can move on.

Studies have proven that, after any interruption, it will take you ten minutes to get back to the same level of concentration and emotional involvement you were at before the interruption. Just thinking about all of the interruptions each of us has in a normal day makes you wonder how we ever get anything done, doesn't it?

"GET READY, I THINK THEY'RE STARTING TO DRIFT."

The ABCs of Presenting

The rule of thumb for giving effective presentations is simple. It's the same one you learned in English class for writing a good story:

1. **Tell them what you're going to tell them.** Set the stage.
2. **Tell them.** Present the benefits of your product, service, or idea.
3. **Tell them what you've told them.** Summarize the benefits you just presented, and then move into any special financial considerations (if there are any) of transferring ownership to your prospects.

This method serves the same purpose in oral presentations as it does in written ones. It helps the person on the receiving end understand and remember the story. And, when you're selling, you do want your presentation to be a memorable occasion for the decision-maker. Master the four basics of presentations — talking on your customer's level, pacing your speech, using words that give your prospect ownership, and interpreting body language — and you're on your way to earning favored status in the mind of every prospect who hears your presentation.

Be multilingual (even if you're not)

Another vital point is this: *know enough about your prospect — going into the presentation — that you can talk with them on their level.*

What does this tip mean? Consider this example.

Suppose that you're in your 30s. You're trying to sell a refrigerator to a mature couple who want to replace a 20-year-old appliance. What do you say to them? Well, with these prospects you'd probably talk about dependability and the new features that your product displays. You'd also point out the benefits that would accrue to the couple if they owned those features. The benefits would be lower utility bills with increased efficiency of new appliances, longer food storage time — less waste, convenience of getting at things — if it has one of those outside drink doors, and so on.

Now cut to a different scene: You're trying to sell the same refrigerator to a newly married couple for their first home. Do you talk to them the same way you did to the mature couple who were replacing an old appliance? No, you'd accent the features and benefits that apply to *their* situation and satisfy *their* present needs. The features are the same, but the benefits are seen in a different light when viewed from their perspective. They may want something less expensive because that's all they can afford, but if you can show them the overall savings of getting a bigger or better 'fridge now, versus replacement costs down the road, you'll be farther ahead because they'll be happier once the decision is rationalized.

I call this versatility of message being *multilingual.* You speak senior citizen. You speak yuppie. You speak single parent. You speak high end. You speak economy. It pays big to be able to converse with someone at their level.

If you want to test this theory, try talking at your normal business level to a 5-year-old and see how long you keep her attention. Then talk with her on her level and watch the animation in her face as she realizes that you've just entered her world.

Recognize the posted speed limit

You need to be sensitive enough to recognize the proper demeanor to have with each client. It's kind of like what happens with stage actors and actresses. They play off of the attitude and enthusiasm of the audience. If you are too energetic for your audience and speak at too fast a rate, they'll be turned off. Then again, if you're too mild-mannered for them and speak too slowly, you may lose them as well.

The ideal is to pay attention to the rate and pitch of their speech and then closely match it. When this happens, on some subconscious level, they get the message that you're like them. They also will understand you better. Be careful if the other person has a Texas accent and you don't. If you adopt their accent, they'll think you're mocking them or that you're insincere. Also, if their pacing is slow, you can speak at a level slightly above theirs. Forcing yourself to get down to their level can have an adverse effect on your entire presentation. As with most of the strategies in this book, you'll develop a good sense for what's right with a little practice.

Let 'em function on assumption

Speak as if they already own what it is you're selling. Don't say, "*If* you join our neighborhood safety awareness group . . ." Instead, say, "*When* we meet, you'll enjoy the value of participating in our neighborhood safety awareness group."

Giving your prospect the ownership of your idea, product, or service helps to move them closer to making a decision. This is called *assumptive selling.*

Assumptive selling is not the same as "suggestive selling" — when you order nothing more than a chocolate shake but your friendly McDonald's server oh-so-sweetly asks if she can get you an apple turnover today anyway.

With suggestive selling you're being offered something you haven't yet asked for or about. Assumptive selling is operating as if you have made the decision to own a product or service you *have* expressed interest in.

Learn the human body's grammar, syntax, vocabulary

You don't necessarily need to learn to speak Spanish, French, or Russian to conduct business (though in our global marketplace, it wouldn't hurt you to do so). What I'm talking about here is *body language.*

The study of body language has been around for a long time. In fact, most of us are aware of body language, but we don't consciously read it and benefit from it. I recommend that all of my students pick up at least one book in the library on body language and peruse it. Once you learn a little bit about it and start studying others (as part of your full-time hobby of selling), you'll quickly see how to benefit from it. Studying body language gives you a perfectly valid alibi the next time you look a second or two too long at someone you find attractive.

Let me give you a few examples:

- **Leaning forward.**

  If the person sitting across from you leans forward, that's obviously a sign of interest or attention. When you recognize that positive sign, *you should keep moving forward, too.* In fact, you might be able to pick up the pace a bit.

- **Leaning back/Glancing away.**

  When they lean back or glance away from you, that means you're losing them. What do you do? Well, you should pause if you're in the middle of a long monologue, summarize the last couple of points, and ask them a question to bring them back. Or, if it's a group presentation and you see several of them displaying this body language, suggest a short break or a question-and-answer period.

- **Crossed arms.**

  Crossed arms indicate that the person doubts what you are saying. When you receive this sign, move to a point-proving demonstration, chart, graph, or diagram.

Just from those three examples, I think you can recognize the value of learning a new language — body language. Just as important as learning to read the language, though, is learning to "speak" it. Once you understand positive body language cues, you should practice them as a part of your presentation. They can be as critical as the words you say. You need to be able to give positive, warm, honesty-projecting gestures if you want to successfully persuade others. Such gestures include these:

- **Sitting beside the person you're trying to persuade instead of opposite them.**

  You're not on an opposing side. You're on their side.

- **Using a pen or pointer to draw attention, at the appropriate times, to your visual aids.**

  Some people hesitate when they use a pen or pointer, and that hesitation says that they are uncomfortable. (Avoid any suggestion of discomfort during demonstrations.) If you wonder about the effectiveness of this technique, watch a magician. They would never be able to keep their "magic" if they didn't master the ability to draw your attention to (or away from) what they want.

- **Using open hand gestures and eye contact.**

  Open hand gestures and lots of eye contact say that you have nothing to hide. Beware that you don't use the palm out — pushing — gesture unless it's when you're trying to eliminate a negative concern of theirs. Even then, push to the side, not toward them.

These are the basics of body language. There is a whole field of study on body language that can help you so much more. Once you begin paying attention, you'll find that many other body language cues will become obvious to you. I highly recommend that if it piques your interest that you research what's available at your local library.

Let the Product Be the Star

The first key in presenting or demonstrating anything — a new hobby, a multimillion-dollar piece of high-tech equipment for a Fortune 500 company, or anything in between — is really pretty simple. *Let the product shine. Let your product be the star.*

In Chapter 1, I tell you how to sell yourself in hiring situations. In those situations, *you* are the star because you are what your prospect is buying. When the item or service they end up with is not a part of your body, talents, or skills, though, you need to let that item be the star. You're just the host who introduces the key players to each other and then fades into the background to let them get acquainted.

In your case, one of the players may be an inanimate object, even an intangible one. But you need to think of that object in someone else's terms because the future primary relationship will be between the product and its new owner. And you need to let the possibilities for that relationship develop (with your encouragement, of course).

As a salesperson, you are not unlike the matchmakers of old. You may help me find a bride, but, once we've met, you step out of the picture. Of course, you may occasionally monitor the progress of our relationship, but you won't be coming to live with us.

Get out of the picture

In fact, that is some of the best advice I can give to real estate people: *Get yourself out of the picture.* I mean this specifically when people are viewing homes. Learn to turn yourself into a wallflower. Never precede a prospective homeowner into a property because you want them to see it as they would see it after they take possession. Chances are pretty good that you won't be in each room they enter once they own the home. You're not there as a tour guide, controlling their every move — herding them from room to room. You need to be a host, graciously inviting them to experience the home for themselves, yet available to answer whatever questions may arise.

Stay in control

One key point we must cover here with regard to presentations is this: *Be careful not to let your prospects see what you want them to see until you are ready for them to see it.* The product has to be the star, but you need to be the guide — or the bodyguard — letting them close only when it's appropriate.

If your demonstration involves the use of a piece of equipment, don't let the customer come in and begin punching buttons or demanding answers to a lot of questions — taking control of the presentation away from you. Just tell them that they have great questions and that most of them will be covered in your presentation. Then, ask that they hold their questions until after the demonstration. Once they recognize that you've planned something special for them, they'll usually settle down and let you do your thing.

Keeping control can also become a challenge when you have several things to display. I suggest that you bring something to cover your display items with, uncovering only those items you're prepared to discuss. If you're using a video or computer screen, be sure to have an attractive screen saver or blank that you can go to when you need your prospect's attention focused back on your planned presentation.

As I cover in Chapter 9, the primary need of all humans is the need to be comfortable. If your prospect isn't comfortable with what you're offering, they'll never part with their money for it, give their commitment to it, or follow through. So, your number one goal in any presentation is to get the prospect to an acceptable comfort level with your offering.

It's a Visual Thing — See?

The majority of people learn and understand best when they involve as many of their senses as possible, however, there is usually one dominant sense for each person. Some learn best by closing their eyes and listening. Others have a strong need to touch and feel things. Most people, however, gain the best understanding by seeing things.

I'm sure you've heard the phrase "seeing is believing." It comes from the desire of most people to be shown — proven — that what they are being told is reality or at least that it can come true. Take a moment to picture the difference between telling someone about a new product and letting them see it either in picture form or demonstrating the actual product. Obviously, letting them see it will involve more of their senses. Thus, the creation of visual aids.

The company gave them to me

If you represent a company's products or services, you've probably been exposed to their visual aids. These are usually slick, high-quality sheets with graphs, charts, diagrams, and photos. Such visual aids often contain quotes from various well-thought-of authorities about your product or service. For storing these visual aids, many companies provide you a great-looking binder that also stands up like a miniature easel.

But maybe you work for a company that's much more high-tech than this. If that's your situation, you may get computer-generated graphics that appear on a projection screen and include music and professional announcers.

Or it's possible that you work with videotapes for your presentations. Videos often include recorded testimonials from actual customers whom your prospect can relate to. When they see someone just like them who is benefiting from your product or service, the relationship between them and your product grows a little stronger.

Visual aids should show three things to new clients:

1. **Who we are.**

   Visual aids should identify your company and the industry to which it belongs. If you're worldwide suppliers of your particular type of product, put that information here. The story of your company builds credibility.

2. **What we've done.**

   If the Space Shuttle uses software developed by your company, brag about it in this portion of your visual aids. Be careful not to belabor the point, though. Being proud of your company is one thing; being a bore is something else.

3. **What we will do for you.**

   This is the part your customer is most interested in. This is where you tune in their favorite radio station, WII-FM, on which they will ask the pressing question, *What's In It For Me?*

Hopefully, your visual aids cover all three of these points. If they don't, try to incorporate these points into your presentation verbally.

Ways to master visual aids

Whatever your specific visual aids depict, the important thing to remember is this: Your company invested in the creation of your visual aids for a reason. And that reason was not to make your life more complicated by carrying all this stuff around and keeping it updated. No, they did it because many, many years' experience have proven that visual aids are very effective *when they are used properly.*

What's the proper way to use visual aids? Most likely, it's the way your company recommends. Few companies succeed in business by putting out garbage as visual aids. Normally, they rely on a task force of some sort that includes top salespeople, manufacturing people, marketing people, and all of their suggestions usually have to be approved by a director or manager of the marketing department — someone who will ultimately be held accountable if the brochures, videos or sample products do the job of moving product into the hands of consumers. Or, if they don't.

If for some reason you don't like or have trouble using the company's visual aids, talk with the people who trained you on how to use them. If their suggestions don't satisfy you, get with a top salesperson, someone who does use them effectively. You may even want to go on a customer call with them to watch how they handle things.

After you master their suggestions for using the visual aids as well as possible, if you still think there's room for improvement, ask to meet with the people who put them together; they'll probably be glad to offer you constructive suggestions. Please note that I didn't say *constructive criticism.* Read Chapter 1 and take it to heart, and you'll know how to sell yourself and your ideas on the job. If you don't know what I'm talking about here, you'll benefit from thumbing over to that very chapter now.

No Visuals? Develop Them Yourself

If you aren't involved in formal selling and have no visual aids, take time to put some thought into what you can develop. Involvement of the senses in attempting to persuade others is critical. In fact, I recommend that you involve as many of a prospect's senses as possible.

Say you want to sell the family on vacationing in the woods, when you know they'd rather go to the beach. You might want to rent a video on all the outdoor adventures available to them. Many vacation spots now offer them as promotional items in information packages. Or get a video on nature in general with flowing waterfalls, gentle breezes blowing in the trees, canoeing, horseback riding, whatever appeals to your audience. Such a video would involve two senses: *sight* and *hearing.* And what's that I smell out front — smoke? If it's feasible for you, you may even want to have a little campfire going in the yard while the family watches your video.

The Olfactory Trigger

The sense of *smell* is only recently being recognized as the powerhouse it is. If you're not sure about this, read up on the studies on worker productivity and how it's affected by different aromas in the officeplace. A fun experiment is to come up with an aroma from your past and notice how quickly old memories come to mind. Whenever I smell chalk dust, it reminds me of Sister Mary Joseph's classroom because cleaning the erasers was my primary duty the year I had her. But even better are memories of the names of my classmates that year and some of the funny things that happened to us. Without the olfactory trigger of chalk dust, I have a hard time calling up those memories.

Consider cooking some hot dogs over that campfire we mentioned in order to involve the sense of *taste.* Invest in hiking boots, lightweight canvas backpacks, or canteens filled with spring water for everyone in order to get the sense of *touch* involved.

All of these things are visual aids that are vital to your presentation if you are serious about persuading your family on this type of vacation. Once they accept ownership of all of these feelings, it'll be an easy sale (unless you have a family member with a very strong phobia toward bugs or wide open spaces).

The same goes for formal business sales presentations: *the more senses you can involve, the better.* If your visual aids limit you to sight and hearing, find ways to get additional sensual involvement (no, I don't mean that kind of sensual involvement, either). You can involve your prospects' sense of touch just by handing them things. Smell and taste are a little tougher, especially if you're selling an intangible. With intangibles, you may want to paint visual pictures that bring those senses into play.

As an example, say you're selling a cleaning service to a working mother. You may not necessarily want to have her smell the cleaning agents you use — but you *can* talk about how fresh the home will be after your professional crew has completed its duties. And, to get a homeowner prospect's senses completely involved, always refer to their residence as their *home* — not their *house.* A house is made up of lifeless bricks and boards; a home is made up of the people who live there and the events of those people's lives. Bringing a small box of candy or mints as a "new client" gift involves the sense of taste in your presentation, even though it doesn't directly apply to your service.

Demonstrating Products

When you demonstrate a tangible product, you have to be like a game show host. You want a lot of excited contestants, and the way people get excited is through involvement. Who cares if Pat Sajak knows all the answers to the puzzles on Wheel of Fortune? He's a nice guy and all, but the fun is in spinning that wheel and playing the game.

Selling is not a spectator sport; it's an involvement sport.

If you sell copiers and you don't have the people you are demonstrating to push the buttons, change the paper, and open and close the machine, you're not selling. You're showing. Let them perform the functions and they will feel involved.

It won't matter to the office manager that you, Jo(e) Salesperson, have won all the time trials at your office for making the most complicated copying challenges come out perfect. Instead, what matters is how simple it is for everyone on your prospect's staff to meet those challenges — and you should build the proof that they can do so *right into your demonstration.* Right in your demonstration, Susie Staffer should be able to make her normal copies simply and to learn something about a new feature that's going to make her job easier. The key contact person should see exactly what all the warning lights are on the machine and what to do about each one.

The same goes for all office equipment, whether it's for the home office or a place of business. The best computer salespeople stand or sit at your shoulder, giving you instructions on how you can do whatever it is you just asked about. They make sure your hands are on that keyboard and mouse. That way, you have a win and build your confidence in the capabilities of the machine. What's really happening is that you are learning something new and building your confidence in your own ability to use the machine. You may even be overcoming a fear of computers altogether.

You see, one of the greatest fears we all have in selling situations is that we will trust what the salesperson tells us, buy the product or service that's for sale, and then, once we own the product or service, it won't fulfill our expectations or meet our needs. The best demonstrations give us the opportunity to prove to ourselves that what the salesperson is telling us is true.

How Not to Crash and Burn

Let me tell you about Jim. Jim is a manufacturer's representative for a line of products sold to automotive service shops. He travels a great deal around the country servicing his clients.

Once or twice a year, Jim coordinates large-scale presentations of the latest innovations in equipment from his company. He invites two or three representatives from each of his best, noncompeting clients' companies. Into each presentation, Jim puts weeks of work that includes building models, coordinating slides, conducting interviews with end users — doing whatever's required for his presentation to succeed.

Jim is so detailed in these presentations that he's often invited to company headquarters to show other representatives his demonstration methods. Jim's customers always enjoy his presentations, and he often leaves with much larger orders for product than he would if he were to meet with them one-on-one. Besides placing orders for the latest and greatest products for their stores, his various clients can compare notes with each other on the latest industry trends. The Big Presentation is a win-win event for everyone involved.

At one of Jim's last presentations, however, he stayed at a new hotel. He heard it had a great reputation and thought his repeat attendees would enjoy the change. All was going well until the alarm clock in Jim's room failed to work. He overslept the morning of his presentation. Waking up with only 10 minutes to go before showtime, he quickly showered, dressed, and dashed to the meeting room. He was going to start on time, thank goodness. However, about 10 minutes into his well-planned presentation, the light bulb burnt out in his slide projector. Being the detail person he is, he had put a new one in the evening before, but didn't count on a new bulb being bad. It took him half of an embarrassing hour to find the correct staff people to find a replacement bulb so he could move on.

Luckily for Jim, his clients already knew his track record and they all ended up having a good laugh about it later in the day. However, if Jim had been giving this presentation to new clients, his credibility could have fallen to such a level that it would take many hours of follow-up in order to gain their business — if he ever got it at all.

The best thing of all in this incident is that Jim took the time to analyze what went wrong and how he could prevent it from happening again. He's a professional who sees every experience, good or bad, as a learning experience. Today Jim's checklist for presentations includes at least two extra light bulbs, learning the name of the audiovisual person who can help in case of an emergency, and carrying a *backup alarm* (or even two). And probably a keywind alarm clock, at that, to beat power failures.

It would take me several hours to tell you all of the horror stories I've heard about failed presentations that salespeople could have avoided. Hearing so many stories has helped me develop effective suggestions for avoiding your own demonstration *faux pas*. Here are just a few things you might not think of, but all of them should become a vital part of your preparatory checklist.

Find the plug-ins; know how to reach them

If your demonstration requires the use of electrical power, find out in advance exactly where the available electrical outlets are and how you can plug into them.

A woman I know of once invested hours in preparing her computer-generated demonstration with high-quality graphics, customized charts, graphs, and diagrams. Her only problem: the power cord she brought to her presentation was too short. She had to place all of her equipment right next to a wall, which was about 20 feet from her audience. She lost vital eye contact and other rapport-building closeness with her audience, and probably the sale, too — all because she brought the wrong extension cord.

Be sure your visual aids are clean and in order

Food stains and bent corners give the impression that you don't care about details. Almost as bad, a roving band of evil, invisible little gremlins often infiltrates your presentation materials, mischievously rearranging presentation items into a state of utter chaos. Never use your materials after someone else has been through them. The misplacement is rarely intentional, but it does happen.

Test everything

You may have a very dependable demo model of your computer software. It could be one you've used for several weeks or months without any challenges — yet, the day of your big presentation, Murphy's Law may strike. You remember Mr. Murphy. He's the poor bloke who deduced the most prevalent law in the known universe: *If anything can go wrong, it will.* Having a bad cable for your equipment or your computer can wreak havoc on the best laid plans. Always arrive early enough to test your equipment on-site.

Customize as much as you can

Don't you just love it when someone gives you a generic presentation that you just know they've given, word-for-word, to at least 40 other people? I didn't think so. No one does. By making the extra effort to customize your materials, you will appear competent and knowledgeable about your customer's specific needs. There's a good chance that that's just the kind of person they're looking for.

A word of caution: Don't customize by skipping over materials in your generic, full-blown presentation. People will feel slighted. Instead, remove pages or slides you won't need. Page past graphics on your computer screen that are unnecessary. If you can't skip them, go ahead and show them; just make sure you offer a brief explanation that you know those particular graphics don't apply to your present audience's needs and that you won't waste their valuable time going over them in detail.

Always bring a protective pad

If you're scheduled to make a presentation in someone else's office, don't take a chance that any of your equipment will mar their furniture.

I know of a guy who, when it was time to fill in his order form, placed it on the client's table and, because it was a three-part form, printed heavily on the paper. The only problem was that the table was made of a fine, soft wood. Because the guy didn't have a pad of paper under the form, his heavy printing etched itself into the tabletop. Needless to say, his lasting impression wasn't favorable. To prevent damages from a similar source, always check the bottoms of your equipment before placing anything on a potential customer's furniture. Rough edges can easily leave scratchmarks.

You can present well only what you know well. Invest the time to eat, breathe, and sleep your product until you can answer nearly every question your customers will raise. Talk with current users of the product to find out why they like it so much. Relating stories of others who have benefited from the product, idea, concept, or service is an excellent way to close a sale. I cover that in more detail in Chapter 12.

Know Before You Go (Or, The Foiling Mr. Murphy Checklist)

1. You know or have discovered where the power supply is. Usually the most inaccessible place in the room. Naturally.
2. All your presentation materials are ready for prime time and no one can tell where you've actually been keeping them.
3. Each and every single piece of equipment you bring with you — works!
4. Your generic speech has been beautifully customized and is down at the shop being detailed.
5. You have dedicated yourself to protecting other people's furniture and will always always, always use a pad of paper when writing things down.

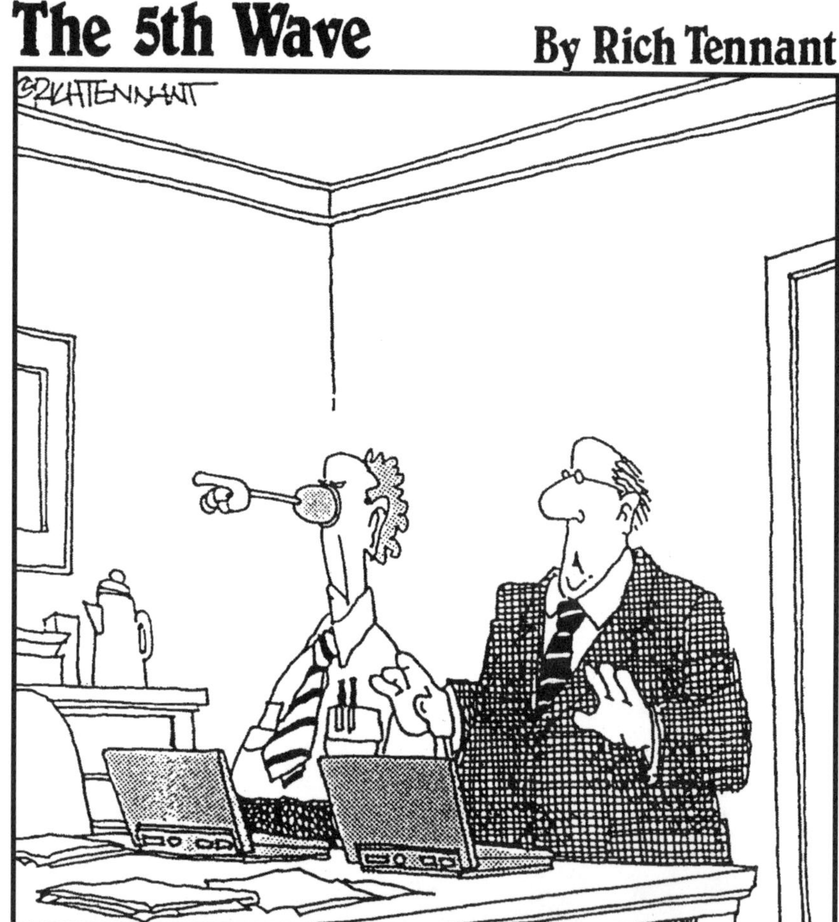

"Well, that takes care of the 'point' part of it, but I hate to even think of what you'll come up with for 'click'!"

Part III

Inventory Your Skills

"YOU'LL HAVE TO COME UP WITH A BETTER LINE THAN THIS, MR. LANGLEY, BEFORE I CAN LET YOU IN TO SEE MR. CODMAN."

In this part...

This is the nitty gritty. You already have a certain degree of selling skills because they are a part of normal, everyday communications. This is where you should take a close and honest look at what you do well and what you don't do well. These chapters develop those skills to a much higher level that will put you in a stronger position when persuading, negotiating, or selling.

Chapter 8

Getting an Appointment

In This Chapter

- Getting face time
- Making the telephone your best friend
- Seven steps to making contact
- What to say, what to say . . .
- Handling negative responses like a pro

I'm going to start with the bottom line. The first thing you have to do is get an appointment. Most people cringe at the word appointment. What you should always use is *visit* or *pop by* instead of the very formal appointment. The key points in all contacts for getting appointments or opportunities to pop by and visit are these:

1. Always be courteous.
2. Do anything to meet them.
3. Reconfirm all the details.

You may think these instructions are too simplified, but many a novice salesperson or persuader have gotten so excited about getting an appointment, they've let their etiquette slip and said, "#%*! yes I'll be there!" They've given up too easily when a customer was tough to meet with and they've failed to reconfirm details about when and where to meet that lost them what was potentially a big opportunity.

Face-to-Face Time Is Critical

With the exception of telephone sales, in every situation in which you can use selling skills, if you don't get face to face with the right person, all of your hard work developing your selling skills goes for naught.

So how do you get face to face with these people? Nearly every question I ask in this book has to do with selling, whether you call it persuading, people skills, or educating. So, *in order to get face to face with people, you first must sell them on scheduling the appointment.* And you must schedule an appointment before you can ever earn the right to persuade your prospect to own your product, start your service, or consider your idea.

To begin with, you have to find the right people to contact. (I discuss the many methods for finding the right people in Chapter 4.) And you have to be firmly convinced that what you have is right for those particular people. If you're not convinced of that, you won't deliver your presentation with enough conviction to persuade them to give you the time of day, let alone consider your product or service.

The Telephone: Best Friend or Worst Enemy?

Most appointments today are made by phone. That powerhouse of an electronic device can be your best friend or worst enemy. It's a friendly little lightweight device when potential customers call in for information and to set appointments. There's no threat of rejection involved.

But that same lightweight little device can transform into a nasty, 60-pound ball and chain when you make outgoing calls to people you've never met to set appointments. Making calls under such conditions is often called *cold calling,* partly because it can send shivers down your spine. It needn't be so scary, though. Just think of it as a slot machine. Eventually, it's going to pay off. If you use it right, it could bring you a jackpot!

It all depends on your perspective. Remember this: *The best way to sell or persuade anyone is in a face-to-face situation, and today the most effective way to get face to face is through the telephone.* If you focus on that simple point, you will overcome those clammy hands, the beads of perspiration dancing on your upper lip, the churning in the pit of your stomach, and all those cotton balls rolling around in your mouth when the time to make the call arrives. With practice, you can easily overcome those emotional reactions to your fear of saying the wrong thing or of being rejected.

If you doubt that, think back to when you first started talking with members of the opposite sex — probably somewhere in your preteen or teen years. Your physical reactions then probably resemble those you experience now if you're not used to cold calling, don't they? Your reactions were pretty much the same then because you wanted to impress someone and you were afraid you'd look like a fool.

Your fear arises partly because you know how you've treated people who have called you; now, you fear, it could be payback time. People who hate being called at home by salespeople tend to feel put-upon and interrupted. Now, as a cold-caller yourself, you're on the giving end of the situation. No one wants to deliberately bother anyone. And no one wants to be on the receiving end of a lot of rejection, except insofar as it comes with the territory when you cold-call.

And do keep that parka handy. You may need it.

How to Reach Mr. or Ms. Consumer by Telephone

Remember your belief in what you're offering, the happiness of people who are currently involved with you, and your desire to serve others. This advice remains the same whether you're selling yourself as an employee, your skills as a freelance writer, or a million-dollar computer system as a career sales representative of a Fortune 500 company.

So what if you have to contact 20 people to find one who wants just what you have to offer? Every one of those other 19 calls does nothing more than bring you one call closer to the right person. It's a matter of keeping focused on your ultimate goal and not letting a little bit of rejection send you scurrying to the nearest hidey-hole.

But now, here you are, on the telephone, waiting for the person at the other end to pick up. What do you do and say *now?*

You take a deep breath, and start hitting these seven points:

1. Greetings
2. Introduction
3. Gratitude
4. Purpose
5. Appointment
6. Thank you (by phone)
7. Thank you (by letter)

The rest, as they say, is selling.

Step #1: Greetings

Begin by using the most important thing for anyone to hear — their name. It's best if you use a formal approach such as *Good morning, Mr. James.* Such a greeting conveys respect. (But check your watch first. You don't want to look like a complete boob by saying "good morning" when it's 1:00 PM.) Or you might say, *Good afternoon. I'm calling for Mr. James.*

I recommend the use of *Good morning, afternoon, or evening* because it sounds more professional than just saying *Hello.* Again, this usage distinguishes you from all those other people who call the decision-maker — and this time the difference definitely favors you.

Too often, we're tempted to use a person's first name. The use of the familiar *Bob* or *Judy* doesn't bother some people (especially those whose name is Bob or Judy), but it does bother others. So don't risk being too familiar with Mr. Robert James, whose mother and friends always call him *Robert,* by souring the conversation at its beginning by calling him *Bob.* Wait for Mr. Robert James to say, *Call me Bob, why don't you?*

Common courtesy goes a long, long way in making initial contacts. If you aren't confident in your level of skill in this area, attend one of the many classes offered on business etiquette. If you can't find an etiquette class in your area, pick up a book on the subject at your local library. There aren't many situations in which you can be too polite, except maybe at cockfights and wrestling matches.

Step #2: Introduction

Next, introduce yourself and give your company name. If your company name doesn't explain what you do — as it would if your name were, say, Jensen Portrait Studios — then you must also mention briefly what type of business you're in. The key word here is *briefly.* I once asked a salesman what he sold, and I got 45 minutes on the features and benefits of owning my very own magnetic resonance imaging scanner. Gadzooks!

To keep them on the line and awake, you may not want to say that you're in carpet cleaning, for example. Instead, *describe your business in terms of benefits to them.* Remember to paint a tantalizing picture with the words you use. Just keep it simple. If you hear snoring on the other end of the line, you've gone on too long.

Carpet cleaners may say,

> *We're a local business that helps companies like yours enhance their image with customers and reduce employee sick time.*

Clean carpets give a good impression. Dirty carpets harbor germs. Is Mr. James ready to hang up? Probably not yet. Your description is creating all kinds of pictures in his mind because you weren't so specific as to mention carpet cleaning. Your business could be anything from sneeze guards to high-tech air-cleaning systems. Since he probably doesn't have that clear a picture yet, he is probably curious to know more. No one likes to end a conversation with all of the blanks not yet filled in.

This all happens in a matter of seconds. You're trying to get Mr. James to give you anything that you could extend the conversation with.

Step #3: Gratitude

Acknowledge that their time is valuable and thank them for taking your call. This lets them know you consider them to be important people.

Say something like this:

> *I appreciate your giving me a moment of your valuable time this morning. I promise to be brief.*

Or you might try

> *Thank you for talking with me. I'll only be a moment, and then let you get back to the important work you do.*

It won't matter if they were just walking into the room with nothing in particular planned for the moment. Acting as if you've just called them from a meeting with the President never hurts the impression you make. There's no need to gush at them with gratitude, though. Just be professional and businesslike in your manner.

Step #4: Purpose

Now get right to the heart of the matter. You need to let them know why you're calling. This should be done with a question.

Something like this may be appropriate:

> *If we can show you how to reduce employee sick time, while improving the image your company presents to its customers, would you be interested?*

If they say *yes,* then ask permission to ask them a few brief questions. Once you have that permission, go ahead with your questions.

Many students have benefited from a strategy that I call the *survey approach.* In it, they use the steps above, and then they say,

> *The company I represent has given me an assignment to conduct a quick two-question survey of just ten people. You're the sixth person I've contacted. We would greatly value your opinion. Could you help me by answering these two brief questions?*

When you ask for their help and show that you value their opinion, most people comply. After all, who among us doesn't have an opinion?

And, by informing them that your company is having you do this, you're likely to gain their empathy and cooperation.

The purpose of conducting this brief survey is to get the person on the other end of the line talking. Hopefully, what they tell you will give you the information you need to build their curiosity enough to commit to that vital face-to-face visit.

Be careful not to just go from one question to the next without really listening to their answers. They know by how you phrase the next question whether or not their last answer was heard. If they think you're just waiting to pounce on them with a canned list of questions, rather than sincerely trying to get valuable information, they'll quickly hang up and send you off into the void.

The best thing to do is to paraphrase their responses before moving on to the next question. When they hear that you cared enough to listen, they'll be more inclined to continue, and *you* escape your instant journey into the vortex.

Step #5: Appointment

If Mr. James seems inclined to set a time for a visit, be prepared to tell him just how long you'll need. I recommend that you keep your initial contact as short as possible. People will balk at giving you 90 minutes or even half an hour sometimes. Twenty minutes or less seems to be an acceptable time commitment for most people. When Mr. James agrees to give you the twenty minutes you need, you would then give him an option of when with an alternate advance question such as, *Would tomorrow at 10:20 AM be good for you, or is Wednesday at 2:40 PM better?* This lets him choose, yet keeps you in control. What's he doing if he chooses either one? Committing to the appointment, which is what you want.

Notice that I mentioned off-times. I didn't say 10:00 AM or 2:00 PM. Using off-times differentiates you from all the other salespeople who call. It also shows that you must know the importance of punctuality if you can keep a schedule using those times. If your visit will last only 20 minutes, it also lets them schedule other appointments around you in the more standard time slots. It all goes back to courtesy.

Step #6: Thank you (by phone)

Now you need to thank him again, reiterate the time that has been agreed to, and verify the location of his office. There's nothing worse than showing up late and presenting the excuse of getting lost. If the location is difficult to get to, *now* is the time to ask for explicit directions. If it's The Big Sale you've dreamed about for years and you finally have the appointment, drive over there the day before and get familiar with the area. Learn at least one alternate route. Don't risk having a traffic tie-up make you late. I recommend that if an appointment is important enough, that you at least schedule the earlier part of that day in their part of town. You never *ever* want to take a chance that you'll be late for a first appointment because you don't know where you're going or because of circumstances beyond your control.

Step #7: Thank you (by letter)

If your appointment is more than two days from when you call, immediately send Mr. James a thank you note or letter confirming the details of when you spoke and what was agreed to. A professional-looking piece of correspondence can solidify any doubts he may have about this commitment.

It won't hurt to have your picture on the letterhead or on your business card, which you would enclose with your thank you note. Get a professional portrait taken if you choose to use a photo. Sending something that looks like your driver's license is bad news. Knowing what you look like increases the prospect's comfort level when he meets you.

Keeping Forward Momentum

With any luck, if someone else designed your telephone presentation, they built in some flexibility for you. If you have that flexibility, try asking the second question based upon their answer to the first.

This technique is called *piggybacking.* It's a fun strategy to practice with friends or family members. It's also a great method for keeping a conversation going with people you've just met. You simply ask a question. When they give you an answer, acknowledge it with a nod or an *I see,* and then ask another question based on their response. As an example, if you meet someone at a party, the piggybacking might go like this:

You: How do you know the hostess?

Chris: Julie and I went to high school together.

You: What high school did you attend?

Or

You: How do you know the hostess?

Chris: I don't, actually, I came with a friend.

You: Who's your friend?

When you piggyback, don't make a hog out of yourself by asking too many questions unless you think that the other person is agreeable to answering more.

We rehearsed this technique at one of our company staff meetings. I had my people pair off and gave them the first question. It was amazing to walk around the room and hear the many different directions the conversations went — and all from the same initial question. Some of these conversations rambled all over the place. Other staff members directed their questions to get a specific response from the other person. It's a valuable strategy to master.

Telephone presentations — from scratch!

If you have to create your own telephone presentation, here are the steps you need to include:

1. Send a pre-call letter of introduction explaining that you'll be calling soon to ask them a couple of survey questions. Specify the date and time at which you'll call.
2. Make the call at the date and time specified in your letter.
3. Introduce yourself and give your company name.
4. Give your reason for calling.
5. Ask permission to ask them questions.
6. Ask your questions as soon as the other person gives you permission to do so.
7. Listen to the answers.
8. Paraphrase the answers they give you.
9. Get their approval to

   a. send more information and stay in touch

   b. arrange a time to visit

   c. and close the sale.

You may need to ask several questions to get enough information from the people you call to tell if they're good candidates for your product or service. Make a list of your questions and have it in front of you before you make the call. Nothing is worse than winging it when you're trying to conduct professional business.

How appointments cut into *Gilligan's Island*

If you call people at home, rather than at businesses, don't use the word *appointment*.

Appointment sounds like you want people to see the dentist. Stereotypical salespeople call all the time for *appointments,* and you don't want to have the person on the other end of the call create their image of that stereotypical salesperson in their minds (you know the image — "another plaid-suit"). *Appointment* just may keep you from seeing the person at all.

Instead, I suggest that you use the phrase *pop by and visit*. See the difference? For most people, *pop by* means that your visit will be quick and won't eat into their valuable time. *Visit* itself is a warm and friendly term.

But if you tell someone that you'll be over Thursday night for a half-hour *appointment,* you'll probably get a lot of hang-ups or cancellations. The word just sounds too much like a typical sales presentation that would keep the people you call from doing whatever else they think is important in that time slot.

Besides, isn't Thursday night when the reruns of *Gilligan's Island* are on?

What to Ask

You need to try to qualify this person a bit before determining if he or she is a good candidate for hearing your entire presentation. Ask our basic N.E.A.D.S. qualification questions from Chapter 10 to determine the following essential information about your telephone prospect:

- What they have now
- What they enjoy most about what they have now
- What they would alter about their current product or service
- Whether they are really the decision-maker on a matter like this
- When you can get together to present an effective solution to their needs

You have to customize your questions to your particular product, service, or idea, but that's the basic system you follow when you customize.

If you're trying to get an appointment to do an insurance evaluation, ask questions like these:

What do you like most about your current insurance provider?

That question gets them talking.

> *Does your current provider do a complete reevaluation with you every time your circumstances change?*

And that question gets them thinking about how good the service really is.

> *If we could show you a way to reduce your monthly investment while not reducing the amount of coverage you have, would you be interested?*

You won't find many people who wouldn't be interested in an opportunity like that.

If your product is family portraits, paint these word pictures to pique their interest — pun intended:

> *When was the last time you had a family portrait taken?*

If their last portrait was recent, then ask any of the following questions:

> *Were you satisfied with the quality of the portrait you received?*
>
> *Was your business handled professionally?*
>
> *Would you go back to that studio again or refer others to them?*

These are conversation-starting questions. Their answers are like little trail markers showing you the way to go with getting your information to them in a manner that's most acceptable to them.

Sometimes a "no" opens the door

If you hear *no* after any of those questions, that's the moment you've been waiting for. You now have *an obligation* to tell them about the great product or service you offer. They've told you they're not satisfied with what they have now and if you know you have something better, you should tell them about it. You, after all, are in the business of helping people make decisions that are good for them.

If you can capture them with information that will show them they can get better service or a better product, they'll be interested. What you're looking for is that chink in their armor that will open the way for you to meet them.

Earn the right to future business

If they say, *Yes, I just loved the studio and will go there forever* don't waste their time or yours. But try not to burst into tears, either. Remember: you're a pro. Simply ask for permission to send them information on your studio for consideration. I suggest that you send your information right away, while the call is still fresh in their minds.

And, as a true long-term business professional, you will set up a *tickler file* to send the information again in six months, which is about how often people think about having portraits done. You also should make a follow-up call in six months. Who knows? The other studio may have moved to a less-convenient location or gone out of business in the interim, leaving *you* to fill the customer's need.

Cancellation Rates for Appointments

When you set appointments for people to come to your place of business or to a meeting, give yourself a reality check and expect only 20 percent of those who committed to you to actually show up.

Their circumstances will change between the time you hang up and your appointment time of, say, Saturday at 11:20 AM. They may decide to sleep in. An important call may come in. They could just be running late. Or maybe the dog needed an emergency walk right then.

The only way to guarantee that a person will come to an appointment with you (short of offering them a bribe), is to go and fetch them to the appointment yourself. When your appointment is at their place of business or their home, your odds improve tremendously.

Getting to a Tough Decision-Maker

There'll be times when people like Mr. James won't be easily accessible. In fact, they may have so many people contacting them that they've established a hierarchy of people around them who screen calls quite heavily for them. This may cause you to wonder exactly where Mr. James is and what he's doing. Images of him jetting to exotic locations for meetings or floating in a sensory-deprivation tank may come to mind. It doesn't matter what he's doing, though, as long as you can eventually get to him.

This is where selling gets fun and you get to be a little creative. Yes, it's going to take more work, but remember: those people who are hardest to get to will be tough on your competition as well. Once you get in there and win their business, you'll be on the inside of that same protective wall and those support people will keep, not you, but your competition at bay.

Begin with the receptionist. If at all possible, get that person's name on your first contact. Then, whenever you make follow-up calls, use that person's name. Tell the receptionist that you need his or her help and ask *who would be in charge of the decision-making process if your company were to consider getting involved in a* whatever-your-product-or-service is. The receptionist is the person who has to know what each employee's area of responsibility is in order to direct calls properly.

Also in these initial contacts, always ask for the correct pronunciation and spelling of names. Never guess about names and write them down incorrectly; business practices like that tend to haunt you later. If the receptionist is especially helpful — as receptionists tend to be — take a moment to send a thank you note with your business card. Businesspeople often tout the value of a good receptionist when they need to hire one, but only smart businesspeople reward receptionists quite well. A little bit of recognition here can prove valuable later on.

If the decision-maker has an assistant, the receptionist probably will put you through to that person first. Expect it. Don't be put out by it. Treat this person with the same respect and courtesy you would use with the decision-maker. This person can make or break your chances of ever getting an appointment. The best thing to do is to ask for their help as well. You can do a great deal of research with this person. You may even be able to prequalify the decision-maker through them.

Tell the assistant something to the effect that you have a way of increasing efficiency while decreasing the costs of a service the company is already using. This provides that assistant with just enough information to want to know more or to want to help. If you can truly fulfill a statement like that, the assistant could be a hero by taking your proposal to the boss right away. Finally, tell them you need their help. Simply ask how to get an appointment with Mr. or Ms. Decision-Maker.

In most businesses, there is an established procedure for this. By asking what that procedure is, you show that you're not trying to beat the system, just to learn what it is so that you can work with it. By showing respect for what is in place, you rise a notch in their estimation.

Unless the procedure for meeting the honchos is too complicated or your offering has a stringent time deadline, try it their way first. If it doesn't work, then consider how much effort the prospect company's business is worth. If it's a once-in-a-lifetime proposition, then you need to get creative.

Whatever unusual method you choose, always consider how the other person will receive it. You need to find an inoffensive method for getting people's attention — yet your method has to be creative, too. You don't want to risk alienating anyone, yet if they are important enough to contact, you need to find out what their hot buttons are and build your contact method around that. Again, this is where receptionists, secretaries, and assistants can come to your rescue.

I know of another salesperson who sent a loaf of bread and bottle of wine in a basket to a hard-to-reach decision-maker. She included a note that said, "I hate to w(h)ine, but I know I can save you a lot of dough if you'll just meet me for ten minutes."

An offer to bring in coffee and rolls for a before-business-hours meeting works with many busy people. More and more business professionals are staying away from long lunches that eat into (ahem) valuable work time and break up the day so much.

If the decision-maker's schedule really is strict and you have a tough time getting face to face with the person, try instead to arrange for a telephone meeting. You have to adjust your presentation to give it impact over the telephone. But, if all else fails, a telephone meeting may be a method worth trying.

Chapter 9
Putting Others at Ease

In This Chapter

- Making a positive first impression
- Winning at the name game
- Establishing common ground
- Getting down to business

Being in a selling or persuading capacity immediately brings with it certain responsibilities. You start with three: to know your product, service, or idea really well; to display good etiquette; and to master all the selling skills covered in this dynamite new book, *Selling For Dummies* (ahem).

But beyond those responsibilities lies another: the need to put people at ease. No one wants to be in a situation in which they feel pressured into, or uncomfortable about making, a buying decision.

So leave the brass knuckles and thumbscrews at home. People make more and better decisions when they're relaxed. It's your job to set aside any nervousness you may have about doing your job and to concentrate instead on making your prospects feel comfortable with you.

Let's Get Comfy

Others feel comfortable around you when you learn how to establish *rapport,* a state "marked by harmony, conformity, accord, or affinity." How hard should you work, how far should you go, to achieve a little rapport? It's hard to say, but I can give this guideline: offering somebody a teddy bear and a blankie or (for the more sophisticated) champagne and caviar would probably be overkill most of the time.

What does Webster's definition of rapport mean for you? In selling situations, rapport means *establishing common ground.* People like to be around people who are like them. Bringing out the similarities you share with your prospects proves that at least one salesperson is not an alien being from another solar system. You're not even from the dark side of the moon. You're just like them. You have a family. You have a job. You have similar values. You need products and services, too. You are a consumer — working with salespeople — when you're seeking any product other than the one you represent. You just happen to be more of an expert on the particular product line or service you represent than they are and you're happy to help them.

In fact, I have a phrase just to get that point across. If you sense that the other party is concerned that you're on the same page as they are, say something like this:

> *Mr. James, when I'm not helping people get involved with my product, I'm a consumer, just like you, looking for quality products at the best price. What I hope for when I'm shopping is to find someone who can help me understand all the facts about the item I'm interested in so I can make a wise decision. Today, I'd like to earn your confidence in me as an expert on state-of-the-art stereo systems. So feel free to ask any questions you might have.*

Please don't wince at the thought of using this phraseology. It's been proven to work successfully in lowering barriers to salespeople in many countries. Until you are good enough to create your own successful phraseology, you will have to learn and master someone else's. Otherwise, your road to success will have many more detours than necessary.

No one likes hearing "canned" material, but it's only canned if you let it sound that way. Someday there will be books with built-in audio. I look forward to that day because the "how you say it" is as important as the "what to say" in sales. Always remember to speak with a sincere concern for your customer. If you're not truly concerned for them, you shouldn't be in this field.

The key point here is that you have to truly be interested in the other person. They must feel your sincerity in wanting to get to know them well enough so that you can help them have more, do more, and be more once you know them better. Even if you're selling to a loved one, they need to feel that high level of personal concern as well. If they believe you're being real — talking from your heart — they'll put their confidence in you much more quickly.

Just a Few Seconds

People make many decisions about you *in the first ten seconds after they meet you for the first time.* That's right. Within ten seconds, you're either chopped liver or Prince or Princess Charming.

Take a stopwatch or check the second hand on your watch right now and learn what ten seconds feels like. It seems like a long time. You now must come up with a way or ways to help people who meet you for the first time to think that they made a good choice in seeing you. They must immediately see some benefit from investing their time with you. You need to learn how to maximize those first ten seconds to give the impression you really want to give so that you can comfortably move forward in your selling sequence.

Dress for success

Before you arrive for your appointment or visit with a potential customer, it's important to consider the way you dress. To ensure that prospects like you and see that you're like them, how should you dress? *Like them* is a good answer.

But there's an even better answer: *dress like the people they turn to for advice.* Remember, some folks turn to their minister or priest for advice . . . you might want to rethink this one. A cleric's white collar under a suit may not be the best way to dress for success. And some folks turn to good old Mom. I'd caution you against a house dress and a pair of sensible shoes.

Use good judgment and common sense and you can't go wrong. If you sell farm equipment and show up at work dressed like a banker, you won't have many farmers getting comfortable around you. In the past decade, bankers have been foreclosing on farmers. Or, if you sell a product to a corporate purchasing agent and you show up in slacks and a casual shirt, you won't make the impression you want to make, either.

If you're new, notice what other salespeople at your company wear and dress like them. If your company has a dress code, it probably has a good reason. It's probably done some research and determined that it's what customers expect to see. Abide by it.

If you are in a situation where you're unsure or perhaps your company has no dress code, and you show up wearing something that's a good bit different from what the prospect is wearing, then you must work during the first few minutes of your meeting to find a way to get yourself on even footing with them. After that, it's too late.

What does your body language say?

I've talked about reading other people's body language. This may be the right place to cover what you say with your body language. Consider some of the other concerns besides clothes that profoundly affect first impressions. You may want to look at what your briefcase, jewelry, hairstyle, and pen say about you.

Your carriage, your facial expression, your placement of your hands (and the length of time you leave them in any one place — in your pockets? at your sides? clasped behind your back? all three options within any 20-second period?), the amount of bass in your voice, the frequency with which you have to pry your tongue from the roof of your mouth as you talk . . . All of these concerns also govern first impressions.

Like Me and Trust Me

When you meet people, your main goal is to have them relax with you. No one gets involved in a decision-making process when they're uptight. You want them to like you and trust you because, if they don't, they won't do business with you. Always remember that your goal is this: *to be a person people like, people trust, and people want to listen to.*

Five steps to stellar first impressions

You have five steps to cover in those first ten seconds. If you handle those steps properly, they'll earn you the opportunity to continue building rapport and lead into your qualification sequence, which is vital. If you can't get to where you can determine whether or not you can help this person or company, all of your previous efforts will be about as useful as a box of wet Cracker Jack's.

Most of the time, people will be the kind of people you expect them to be. That's because your demeanor — what you say and how you say it — sends them a distinct message of what you think of them. People are, for the most part, reactive and will respond according to what's given them. Therefore, expect them to be cordial, open, and friendly. When your body language and opening statements are pleasant, they'll very likely respond in kind.

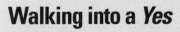

Walking into a *Yes*

There was a study conducted by U.C.L.A. of 10,000 people. Each was asked what their initial impressions were of someone they later said *Yes* to. The results were

> 7 % said the person had good knowledge of the topic, product, or service.
>
> 38% said the person had good voice quality — they sounded confident and intelligent.
>
> 55% said it was the way the person walked. They had an air of confidence and self-assurance rolling off of them even as they approached the customer.

If you doubt the power of projecting positive body language, think again.

Winning Over Hell's Angels

One of the most dramatic examples of this basic principle happened after about my third year in sales. I had worked hard and done pretty well in business. I was driving a brand-new Cadillac, which was *the* real estate car of the '60s. It was long, sleek, and beautiful. I'd even earned enough to invest in a few nice suits.

I received a call from a woman who asked me to come by and look at the home she and her husband were thinking of selling. Driving over in my new Caddy and nice suit, I was feeling pretty good about myself. When I pulled up to the house, there in the driveway leaned six Harley-Davidson motorcycles parked in a line the way serious bikers park their bikes.

Judging from the looks of these hawgs, my Cadillac and suit weren't going to help me establish much rapport. A huge, bearded man wearing a Hell's Angels jacket answered my knock. Glancing into the home, I could see five other guys just like him sitting in the living room. If there was ever time that a salesperson did not have instant rapport, that was it.

Nervous, I walked on into the home and decided to stick with what I normally did for starters. I said, "Before I can give you any figures on what your home is worth, I need you to show it to me." We started in the living room and went into the kitchen. Because the garage was just off the kitchen, it was the next stop. As we went into the garage, there on the floor was a motorcycle all in pieces that they were obviously customizing. I asked them how they distributed the weight when they extended the front wheel, explaining that I had a motorcycle, too, and that I had been riding for years. Of course, it wasn't a Harley, but I was a motorcycle enthusiast.

We talked bikes for about 10 minutes and all of a sudden the entire situation changed. I was no longer a guy in a fancy suit, but a fellow motorcyclist. I did end up listing the home and getting them happily moved and learned an interesting lesson about making others comfortable.

Step #1: Smile, deep and wide

Smile to the point of almost a grin.

Some people forget how to smile because they don't do it much. I've had to ask some of my salespeople to go home, stand in front of a mirror, and practice smiling for a solid 30 minutes. A little tip here: Make sure the door is closed when you practice, or someone may just throw a net over you!

Do you know why practicing your smile is so important? When you first meet a person, a smile radiates warmth. If you're not smiling, or if it looks like it hurts when you do, they'll want to avoid you and a wall of doubt and fear can go up in two seconds flat.

Always remember: *long-term relationships begin in the first ten seconds.* So . . . smile! And keep it pleasant. You don't want to look like a grinning hyena.

If you're contacting people over the telephone, smiling still counts. A smile can be heard in your voice. When I was a manager, I put little mirrors by the telephones of each salesperson. I wanted them to see themselves when they were talking with clients. If my people saw that they weren't smiling, chances were good that the person on the other end of the phone could sense it and it would certainly have a negative effect on the relationship. We had our people turn the mirrors over or slip them into drawers when clients were in the office, but, believe me, having those mirrors made a big difference in telephone contacts in our office.

Step #2: Let their eyes see your eyes

Look in their eyes.

This is a body language thing that builds trust. People tend not to trust people who can't look them in the eye. People usually glance away when they're lying to you. It takes a good bit of intentional practice to develop the ability to look someone in the eye and lie to them. That's what a con artist does.

So looking them in the eyes is very important — but don't go to the extreme and lock onto their eyes, either. Getting into a staring contest is dangerous in any selling situation. Give your prospect a couple seconds of solid eye contact while smiling and they'll most likely be the first to glance away.

Step #3: Say hi (or something like it)

Greet them.

The style of your greeting depends on lots of things. It depends on whether you're calling a longtime friend, a new acquaintance, a total stranger, or the Pope. The greeting will also be affected by the particular circumstance of how you're meeting this person. The appropriate opening should be the most formal if you have any doubt at all about what would be right.

Depending on the situation, any one of the following greetings may be appropriate:

- Hi.
- Hello.
- How do you do?
- How are you?

- Good morning. / Good afternoon. / Good evening.
- Thank you for coming in.
- Thank you for seeing me.

If you already know their names, use their names. If you don't know their names, don't rush to get them, either. Pressing strangers for their names so they're no longer strangers is fine in many parts of the country and in many situations. In others, though, it's viewed as being pushy. If you're in a situation where it's obvious you're a salesperson, be atypical and establish a bit of rapport before asking their names. Then you can ask with a "By the way, my name is Jane Parker." Then, you give them a pregnant pause that the other person will normally use to give you his or her name.

Step #4: Shake hands, not dead fish

Shake their hands — but only properly, and only if it's appropriate.

Salespeople are well known for having a tremendous desire to press the flesh. So most people expect to shake your hand when they meet you.

But, to avoid appearing awkward with those who don't feel comfortable shaking hands, I recommend that you keep your right arm slightly bent and held by your side. If you see the other person reach toward you, you're ready. If they don't reach toward you, then you haven't committed the grand *faux pas* of reaching out too eagerly.

Some people don't want to shake hands because they just don't like touching other people. Then there are those who go to great lengths to avoid physical contact for health reasons; maybe they're unusually susceptible to germs and don't want to touch anything they don't have to touch. Many people suffer with arthritis and shaking hands can be extremely painful for them. Rather than opening a first meeting with their list of woes, they'll simply avoid shaking your hand.

The handshake is appropriate in most instances, but only if you do it properly. You may wonder how much handling a handshake properly matters. If you're skeptical about the value of spending time learning and practicing a good handshake, take some time to notice when others shake your hand. If you ever have shaken a hand that feels like a dead fish, you'll understand what I mean. Or, if you have a bone-crushing handshake, you will also get my meaning.

To convey the highest level of trust, confidence, and competence, you need to grasp the whole hand of the other individual and give it a brief but solid squeeze — not too tight, but definitely not loosey-goosey, either. Keep it brief. There's nothing more uncomfortable than to have someone keep holding your hand when you're ready to have it back.

Be aware that it's appropriate to shake the hands of both the husband and wife if you're meeting a couple. If they have children with them, it's a nice gesture to shake their hands as well. If the product you're selling involves the children, you want to earn their trust, too. If you can tell the children would be uncomfortable with having their hand shaken, simply give them a moment of eye contact as well. And no cheek-tweaking or hair-tussling of the kids, either. Remember how you hated it when Aunt Minnie did it to you?

Step #5: Your name for their name

The handshake is the most natural time to exchange names. Depending on the situation you may want to use the formal *Good morning. My name is Robert Smith with Jones & Company.* If the setting is more casual, you may want to give your name as *Rob* or *Bob* — whatever you want them to call you. Make sure they get your name right. There's nothing more difficult than correcting a potential prospect who calls you *Bob* when your name is *Rob.* Besides, once you've won them over and they begin sending you referral business, you don't want the referrals asking for the wrong person and letting someone else earn your sales.

The same applies for the names of the people you meet. If a woman says her name is *Judith Carter,* use *Ms. Carter* when you first address her. Don't jump to the familiar *Judy.* That's what a typical salesperson would do, and doing so will cause her to raise her guard against you. Visions of suede shoes, pinkie rings, and gold chains start to dance in her head. Getting familiar too fast is also impolite. Let her decide when you may become more familiar; let her give you the appropriate first name to use.

Once you're involved more deeply in the qualification or presentation stages of selling and you feel some warmth building, it will be more comfortable to use first names with most people. If they haven't given you permission to do so, politely ask for it. With Judith, just ask, *May I call you Judith?* If that's what everyone calls her and she has built some confidence in you, she'll probably say *yes.* Or she may say, *Call me Judy.* You may think that this is an old-fashioned approach, but it's what sells today. People yearn for a time when they were treated with more respect and courtesy.

In a retail setting

Retail salespeople would do much better if they learned to view each contact as a need to get the customer to like them and trust them enough to ask for help rather than immediately pouncing on them with a reflex "May I help you" that gets them no further than a reflex "No, thanks" in response.

Wouldn't you love to have a dollar for every time you've heard, *May I help you?*

Remember to use their name as they give it!

If you are being introduced to a group of people, be careful to use the same level of formality with each member. Don't call Mr. Johnson by his formal name and his associate *Bob* just because you can't remember the associate's last name. That would be more offensive than having to ask again what his name was.

Early in my career, I spent an entire afternoon with a couple, failing to get their names clearly during the initial greeting. The day concluded with them making an offer on a home. When it came time to fill out the paperwork, I asked the husband very warmly and sincerely, "And how do you spell your last name?" He responded, "J-O-N-E-S." Boy, was my face red!

You hear it practically every time you walk into a retail establishment. You may have heard the greeting handled this way: *Hi, I'm Bob. What can I do for you today?* And what's the pat response that this Bob probably hears 99.9% of the time he says those words? *Oh, nothing. We're just looking.*

If something doesn't work 99.9% of the time, wouldn't it make sense to try to come up with a better initial greeting?

If you're in retail sales and that's just why you're reading this segment, good for you! I have some suggestions just for you that will increase your sales and the sales of anyone else in your company you share these suggestions with.

For one thing, when people enter your establishment, *never walk directly toward them.* And, for another, *when you do approach them, don't rush.* Think about a time when you've been approached by a quick-moving, overzealous salesperson, and you had to step back away from them.

You don't want that to happen to you. Let your customers know you're there in case they do have questions. Then get out of the way and let them look around.

What to say instead of "May I help you?"

Try saying,

> *Hello, thanks for coming in. I work here. If you have any questions, please let me know.*

What does this greeting do? It projects a warm, welcome feeling rather than an overwhelmed feeling. You've just invited them to relax, and, when people relax, they'll be more open to making decisions.

Another greeting you might want to try is this:

> *Hello, welcome to Standard Lighting of Arizona. I'm happy you had a chance to drop by today. Feel free to look around. My name is Karen and I'll be right over here if you have any questions.*

Pause momentarily in case they do have questions. Then step away.

When you step away from them, instead of toward them, you distinguish yourself from all the typical salespeople they've ever encountered — and for most customers that's a very good thing. When you leave customers alone, they walk toward what they want. By observing them from a discreet distance, you know exactly what they came in for. When they finally stop in front of something for a moment, that's when you want to move closer to be ready to answer questions. Don't hang over them like a vulture, though. Just be where they can find you when they look around for help.

Recognizing their signals

If they don't look around, but remain by that one item for awhile, then you may walk up and ask a question. Use an involvement question right off the bat because they'll have to answer it with more than a *yes* or a *no . . . and* because you'll learn something that will help you keep the conversation going.

If it's a piece of furniture they're looking at, ask,

> *Will this chair replace an old one, or is it going to be an addition to your furnishings?*

When they answer, you'll know why they're interested and can then begin guiding them to a good decision.

In any place of business where you have a display area or showroom, let your customers look around before you approach them. Being laid-back is much less threatening and far more professional than mowing down your fellow associates and careening toward your potential customer like a runaway freight train the moment she walks in the door.

I know of some places of business, such as automobile dealerships or some furniture stores, that are so large that people usually do need a guide (or at least a map) in order to find their way around. If you work such a setting, you have to take them to the desired type of product. But, again, it's best if you then step away from them and let them relax. When they're ready to talk with you, they can find you quickly but you haven't invaded their space and taken control of their shopping experience.

It's Time to Build Some Common Ground

Now that everyone knows everyone else's name and you've all smiled at each other, you must smoothly transition into establishing common ground. You do that by being observant.

If you just walked into Mr. Johnson's office, and you notice that he has family photos all over the place, you should ask about his family. You don't need to know details now. Just say, *Great looking family,* and let him decide how much to tell you. If you see trophies, you should comment on them. If you can see that he's a fisherman and you're a fisherman, too, then bring up the subject of fishing.

By allowing your prospect to see the human side of you rather than the sales professional side at first, you will help them break through the natural wall of fear that encloses them when typical salespeople confront them.

Mr. Johnson may have been referred to you by someone. If that's the case, mention the mutual acquaintance. That's usually a great starting point. "Good old Jim" may have an excellent talent, great family, or wonderful sense of humor. Those are all nice, noncontroversial topics to cover.

If Ms. Smith has an accent, you may ask where she's from. Perhaps you've traveled there or know people in that part of the country. Be careful here: Ms. Smith may be self-conscious about the accent or tired of people always asking about it, so don't dwell on it.

The following sections cover ways to reach common ground with prospects or existing customers with whom you may not yet feel entirely comfortable.

Keep the conversation light, but move ahead

Don't let this part of rapport-building become too hard for you. If all else fails, bring up something in the local news. Just make sure it's a noncontroversial subject. Try your best not to bring up the weather. They'll know you're struggling for something to talk about or that you're nervous if you start off talking about how hot or cold it is today.

Another good tactic is to give them a sincere compliment. *Sincere* is the key word here. Sincerity takes you everywhere; blatant, insincere flattery gets you nowhere. A stale line like *Gee, Mr. Gargoyle, I'll bet everybody tells you you look just like Warren Beatty* does not qualify as sincere.

Acknowledge their pride

If you happen to be working in a business where you give a lot of home presentations, and the people you're presenting to have a nice home, say this:

> *I want to tell you that I spend a lot of time in the evening in other people's homes and you should be proud of what you've done here. Your home is lovely.*

Look for signs of hobbies or crafts that you can comment on. If a woman is an artist and has her paintings on display, you should say, *You did that? What a great talent to have.* That way you're not lying if you think the painting is really poor. Painting is a great talent. Whether or not your prospect has any is in the eye of the beholder. If your prospect has any hobby they're obviously proud of, give them a sincere compliment about it. People always enjoy hearing compliments.

Avoid controversy

Be cautious that the prospect doesn't tempt you into a conversation about a controversial subject. Some people do that just to test you. Specifically, avoid discussing politics and religion at all costs.

Here's how to get around any topic that may lead you down the wrong path:

> *I'm so busy serving clients, I haven't had time to stay current on that topic. What do you think?*

By tossing the ball back at them, you've dodged what could have been a fatal bullet, *while* you got in a plug for your professional abilities. If they come back at you with a very strong opinion, you'll know to avoid that subject in future meetings. Or you may feel the need to brush up on it if they're deeply involved so you'll have a better understanding of this person before you build a long-term relationship with them.

In any business contact, be certain to never *ever* use any profanity or slang. It doesn't matter if such language is widely used on today's most popular television program; it has no place in the business world. You never know the values of the person you're talking with and don't want to risk offending them. The same goes for off-color, political, ethnic, or sexist jokes. Be sensitive to the values, beliefs, and morals of the person sitting or standing across from you.

Keep pace with your prospect

Another consideration in establishing rapport with people is your rate of talking. Taking time to become aware of your normal speed of talking is extremely valuable. The next step would be to notice the rate of talking of everyone else you encounter. Once you become tuned into it, it happens naturally.

Once you're aware of your speaking rate, you need to know what to do about it. If the person you're trying to persuade talks faster than you do, you need to increase your rate of talking in order to keep their attention. If they speak much more slowly than you do, you should slow down or pause more often in your side of the conversation. Any distortion in your rate of speaking can be deadly. You could lose them if you talk at the rate of a professional auctioneer, or their minds may wander if you're too slow. Try to time your words to their rate of talking.

Let them know you're there to serve

The next step is to set the stage to move into your presentation. You do this by simply letting the prospect know that you're there for the prospect's benefit. By raising the subject of how you can serve them, you get them to focus on the reason why they agreed to this appointment or visit in the first place.

Because you've done a great job in getting your prospect to like you and trust you, now it's time to do what you do best — help them make a decision that's truly good for them!

Make your career a life of service to others and all the good things you desire will come to you.

Chapter 10

Qualifying Your Way to Success

In This Chapter

- Suspense, melodrama, mystery — qualify the ace detective's way
- Qualify the prospect within first
- Do your customers a favor — leave your opinion at home
- Know your prospects' N.E.A.D.S., and *you* will qualify

At this point, you've found your prospect. You've made an initial contact and they've shown a certain level of curiosity about your product, service, or offering. Now, you move to step number three in the selling cycle. You need to determine whether or not they need what you are offering and can really make a decision.

This step in the selling cycle particularly pertains to situations where you don't have a close enough relationship to know whether they need your product or service, and the person needs to make a financial commitment or a personal commitment in order to go ahead.

You may wonder what circumstances would keep someone from being able to make a commitment. Obviously, if it's a financial commitment, they'd have to have the money or some credit to draw upon. If it's a personal commitment, there may be someone else, like a spouse, that they need to check with before going ahead. You need to know their circumstances *before* you go into a full-fledged presentation and try to convince them to go ahead.

Are You Sure They Need What You're Selling?

One of the biggest mistakes people make when they try to convince or persuade others is going into a full-blown presentation before they know that the listener is a qualified decision-maker. There's nothing worse for either of the people involved in a conversation than to be caught up in something that is a total waste of their valuable time. So, for goodness' sake, when you see the word *Receptionist* on a desk, don't give the person behind the sign your whole presentation.

Taking just a few minutes before beginning any presentation to ask four or five simple questions and listen to those answers can save you a lot of time and embarrassment.

Our research has shown that use of this step number three in the selling sequence is the single greatest factor distinguishing those who win most often in their selling presentations from those who don't. Statistics from our surveys of over 250,000 sales professionals shows that the biggest gap between six-figure income earners and those averaging around $25,000 per year is in their skill in qualifying. That statistic alone would make me want to master this area of selling. And all it takes is asking the right questions.

Sales Lessons from a Scruffy TV Detective

How do you get started asking those questions? In some cases, you wait and watch for the perfect opportunity. Other times, you have to create the opportunity. Think of yourself as a detective, a gatherer of information to solve the mystery of your customers' buying needs. It would be simple if all you had to do was come up with a couple of questions and they would always be answered completely and honestly.

But it isn't always that easy. Being able to discover the customer's needs and concerns, as well as successfully incorporate such information into the opening of your presentation, takes a lot of time and practice before you ever walk through the doors of each appointment.

I can think of one "person" — a real character, actually — who exemplifies what effective qualification is all about. In the 1970s this character was quite popular on network television. He resurfaced in the 1990s. See if you can tell who it is by this description.

He drives a battered old car. He walks with a slight limp and has a bad eye. He has poor posture and a 5:00 shadow most of the day. His trenchcoat is always wrinkled and his tie askew. He carries a cigar and a small spiral notebook.

If you watch any television at all, by now you've probably guessed that we're not talking about Lassie. It's Columbo.

I love using the example of Lieutenant Columbo when I cover qualifying tactics and strategies. Columbo does a wonderful job of adjusting his questioning techniques to fit every situation. He also acts as if the person being questioned is better, more important, or smarter than he is.

His demeanor throws his "prospects" off-guard and they often drop their defenses. Their lapses allow him to ask the same question in several different ways. If they come up with a different answer to the rephrased question, he knows that they're not telling the truth or that they know more than they're letting on. Such information is valuable for him in continuing to seek out answers from them.

Columbo uses the following strategies to solve every case.

1. **He always keeps himself out of the limelight.**

   He never presumes to be the top dog — the smartest person in the world. He doesn't enter with a flourish, like Sherlock Holmes might. He lets the situation be the star, explaining it in great detail to the suspects.

2. **He always takes notes.**

   Taking notes is vital, but Columbo doesn't rush to get every word of vital information. Instead, he seems to jot things down casually. His notepad isn't large and threatening. It's small enough to fit in his pocket and rather nondescript. He refers back to this information again and again during his investigation. The information he turns up helps direct his future efforts with each suspect, which in qualifying we call the *prospect* or, more optimistically, the *future client.*

3. **He always makes the people he's questioning feel important.**

   Ever the humble searcher of truth, Columbo always reminds his suspects how accommodating they are to let him impose on their busy schedules. He thanks them profusely for their time and the vital information they provide. No matter how small the tidbit of information, he makes them feel as if it's the single most important key to solving the case.

4. **His questions seem standard and innocent.**

   He rarely comes out and asks a suspect "Did you do it?" Instead, he'll ask what sounds like typical police-type questions about times, people and places in order to gather background information and disarm the suspect.

5. **He listens to both verbal and nonverbal responses to his questions.**

   He notices how people tell him what they have to say, not just noting the words that are used but noting body language. He knows and evaluates not only their posture, but what they're wearing and the surroundings they spend their time in and even the cars they drive.

6. **He questions with building intensity, each succeeding question narrowing upon a single aspect of the preceding question's answer.**

   Rarely do his suspects realize they *are* suspects until they've let their guard down a bit and said something that doesn't jive with a previous answer. They often find themselves having to give "supposin's" to give credence to their errors and still keep their innocent attitudes.

7. **He quickly relieves any tension his questions create.**

   One of his most famous tactics is to change the subject. For example, he asks about a plant like his wife's or acts as if he's finished and begins to leave. This momentarily gets the suspect thinking about something else or answering by reflex. Then, he'll ask another question while they're in the reflex mode and try to get them to hang themselves.

   But then another of his most famous tactics is to return just as the suspects are breathing a sigh of relief and letting their guard down, as if he's forgotten something, to ask just one more question. This usually catches them off guard and they trip themselves up. I love that part!

8. **He always leaves the contact giving the person something to think about and an indication that he'll be in touch.**

   Any good salesperson who doesn't make a sale on the first contact will do whatever he or she can to leave the door open for further discussion with a prospect.

   Of course, with Columbo, letting them know that he'll be in touch is plenty to think about in its own right.

9. **The language he uses throughout his entire questioning process is nonthreatening and sympathetic with their situation.**

   He doesn't create scary images of "going downtown" for a chat. In fact, you'll rarely see Columbo in the police headquarters at all. He knows it's intimidating to his suspects. He also uses lay terms or defines police lingo in words the suspect understands.

Yes, Columbo is a great detective. He always wins through the use of his questions and his ability to think on his feet — just the way you will after you master the use of qualifying questions.

But it's not just detectives and salespeople who benefit from qualifying questions. Qualifying questions pop up in many walks of life and many situations:

- Attorneys use qualifying questions during the deposition of possible witnesses to discover how much the witnesses know about the case.
- Doctors use qualifying questions to diagnose a patient's health status.
- Children qualify their parents' mood before asking for something that might be refused.

Sometimes you'll be able to sit down and analyze the other person's needs as I'll tell you later in this chapter in a way that has you in control of the situation. But there'll be plenty of other times when you'll have to think on your feet and be flexible in your qualifying questions.

Liking to Sell What Your Customers Like to Buy

Many people in selling situations have a problem with their own likes and dislikes. They tend to sell only what they like and mostly to the people they like. You do need to like and believe in what you're selling. But if you're in a career sales position, you will probably have to sell other items in the product line that may not be your favorites. You're qualifying your customers as to what they need, not what you need to sell.

You must always keep what's right for the customer in the forefront of your mind. If you sell only what you like, you also severely limit your income and you leave yourself, at the end of the day, with plenty of things on hand that you don't like. Then what will you do?

Your job is to enthusiastically sell whatever benefits your customers, whoever they may be. During your selling career, you will have to work with some people whom you won't particularly like. (I discuss how to deal with several personality types in Chapter 9.) Remember: If you refuse to work with some people, both you and the customers lose. You lose opportunities to make sales, while the customers lose opportunities to have their needs satisfied. The people you turn down will just get their needs filled by someone else. The moral of the story: Keep your mind and your opportunities open.

Another challenge facing salespeople is having to learn not to prejudge people. Whether we realize it or not, we all make some sort of judgment about people the moment we lay our eyes on them. We judge them based on their physical condition, their clothing, their hairstyles, their postures.

In selling situations, though, acting on preconceptions is a dangerous habit that we must control. If you are committed to becoming a professional, you must force yourself to look at every customer with clear vision. Eliminate those preconceived notions before they start costing you money!

An example from my own experience illustrates why salespeople need to take their customers as they find them.

One Saturday early in my sales career, a couple pulled up outside the real estate office I was working in. They drove a beat-up truck and their clothes suggested that they had been doing heavy labor. Another agent in my office took one look at them and said, *Tom, you can have this one.* He walked away, leaving me to talk with the unkempt couple.

As it turned out, they were looking for a fixer-upper property to invest in. They had made a business out of buying run-down properties and applying their do-it-yourself abilities to turn those properties into desirable homes. They then sold the homes for a tidy profit.

I helped them find their next fixer-upper. A few months later, they came back to me to have me help them invest some of their profits into a luxurious home for themselves. Over the years, I sold them many fixer-uppers — and, as icing on what turned out to be a very satisfying cake, I resold those homes when the couple finished remodeling them. Had I prejudged these folks by their appearance, *I* may have been the one to walk away from what turned out to be a lucrative opportunity.

Try to treat everyone with the respect you would expect to receive were you in their shoes. This may sound suspiciously similar to the Golden Rule — as well it should.

- If you want others to agree with you, you must first be agreeable.
- Don't let anyone's outward appearance affect the way you react to them.
- Always act as if each person you contact is the most important person in your life.

If what you are offering is vitally important to you, your product, service, or idea can be a significant link for you to billions of other people who need what you have to offer.

Telephone qualification: Resist the urge to do too much

Rule #1 about qualifying over the telephone:

> *Be careful that you don't overqualify on the phone.*

If you're in a situation where final decisions are made face-to-face, the most productive use of the phone is for making appointments. (If you're in telemarketing, though, your entire business life revolves around how you present yourself over the telephone.)

Remember: Many products simply cannot be sold over the phone. If that's the case with your product or service, keep the goal of making an appointment in mind during all telephone contacts. That's the purpose of the phone contact — to get an appointment for a face-to-face presentation. What you do sell on the phone is an opportunity to present your offering. So keep your qualifying questions to a minimum when talking on the phone. Ask just enough qualifiers (the N.E.A.D.S. questions) to determine what you need to know to prepare an effective presentation.

Depending on what you're selling, your first meeting might be a fact-finding mission. If that's the case, let them know. Instead of selling your product or service, just sell your need for more information to properly help them.

I recommend that you write a checklist of everything you need to know to determine whether or not your product or service is right for each prospect you meet. *Include all of your qualifying questions in that checklist.* Fill in the answers to the questions that you can comfortably ask over the telephone. Then mark the questions that you will still need to get answers to during your appointment.

Nuts-n-Bolts of Qualifying Prospects

Good qualifying is one of the basics of selling that you cannot overlook or slough off. Don't set yourself up for failure. Work on your style and questions, and then watch your income and your base of happy customers begin to build.

The average salesperson today either lets the consumer totally make the decision as to what they want, or they try to steer the person to what that salesperson likes best. Both of these approaches are wrong. You will recognize steering by the use of these phrases, especially prior to qualifying:

- I know just what you're looking for.
- This is my favorite.
- I have the best thing for you.
- We have the best products.
- This one looks so good in red.

Because of the danger of losing everything if you allow either of these scenarios to develop, I've created an acronym to help you remember key qualification questions. Picture in your mind the word *needs,* but spell it this way — N.E.A.D.S.

Granted, my spelling's a little creative, but that new spelling will help you think of meeting the needs of your customers. The success ratio for your whole company would rise if you could get everyone to say to themselves when they meet a customer, *I am concerned about my customer's NEADS. I will discover my customer's true needs and lead my customers to the right product or service for them.* Satisfying N.E.A.D.S. helps you accomplish more in your business.

You N.E.A.D.S. to hear this

So, really, just what is this weird acronym, N.E.A.D.S.?

The *N* stands for *Now* — as in *What does the customer have now?* Why ask this? *Because average consumers don't make drastic changes in their buying habits.* If you know what they have now, then you have a good idea of the type of people they are — and you have a good idea of what they will want to have in the future.

If past experiences often dictate future decisions — as they undoubtedly do — then you need to explore your customers' past experiences. You need to know what they have now so that, in your mind's eye, you can see the type of buying decisions they will make in the future.

Show me your current vehicle, home, style of dress, or style of jewelry, and I can probably tell you what your next version of each of those products will look like. I'm not prejudging here. I'm simply observing that most people are creatures of habit. People usually don't make drastic changes in their lives unless they've recently won the lottery or received a large inheritance or windfall.

The second letter in N.E.A.D.S. is *E*. As I'm using it here, *E* stands for *Enjoy*. You must know what your customers *enjoy* about what they have *now.* What was the major motivation for getting involved in their existing product or service?

To discover what your customer enjoys, you must structure your questions so as to enable you to discover the customer's past. There's a good chance that what they enjoyed about the product or service in the past, or what they enjoy about what they already have, is exactly what they will want again. That's usually true — unless you can demonstrate a benefit in your product or service that is even better than the one they enjoyed when they purchased their present product or service.

The *A* in N.E.A.D.S. stands for *Alter*, as in, *What would the customer like to alter or improve about what they have now?*

Because it is constant, change is a potent force in business. In some ways, we are all looking for change — more benefit, more satisfaction, more comfort. That normal urge to improve one's present condition is why you want to develop questions to find out what your customers would like to change. What would they like to be different? Once you know your customers' answers to that question, then you can structure your presentations to show your customers how your company can provide the changes they want in their present product or service.

D stands for *Decision*. Specifically, you need to know: *Who will be making the final decision on the sale?*

Many times we meet someone who is looking for a car, a stereo, maybe some furniture, and we salespeople meet only the one person. Is it wise to assume that they will be the decision-maker? No: Never assume anything about your customers. They may be scouting or researching, planning to bring a spouse or parent in later when it's time to make the final decision.

Ask qualifying questions to discover the truth.

> *Will you be the only person driving the car?*
>
> *Who, other than yourself, will be involved in making the final decision?*
>
> *Is there anyone else you usually consult with when making decisions of this type?*

You've probably heard the standard response to a *decision* qualifying question: *I'll have to talk it over with my husband/wife/parents/best friend from college.* Many times the salesperson who has not properly qualified the prospect will go too far in the presentation before finding out that the real decision-maker is not present. You do nothing more than practice your presentation when you present to non-decision-makers.

If you're in network marketing, never *ever* give your business opportunity presentation to potential new distributors without both the husband and wife present. It's the kind of business that requires the spouses' mutual support if it's going to work; if you present when you don't have that mutual support, you're wasting your time. Wouldn't you rather give your best to someone who can truly benefit from your product or service?

Without the S, N.E.A.D.S. would just be N.E.A.D.

Okay, class, we now have examined, with painstaking care and I daresay no small degree of selling insight, 80 percent of that most important of important acronyms in sales, N.E.A.D.S.

Specifically, class, we have reached a point in our inquiries where we have added a new word to our selling lexicons, N.E.A.D. We now know that we N.E.A.D., as it were, to focus on the following areas in order to construct effective qualifying questions:

- What the prospect has **Now.**
- What the prospect **Enjoys** most about it.
- What the prospect would **Alter** about what she has now.
- Who will make the buying **Decision** on the presentation you want to make to the prospect.

But what about *S* — the last letter in N.E.A.D.S.?

What do you think the *S* stands for? Think for just a minute. *Sales?* That's a good guess, but, no, that isn't the word I'm looking for.

Why not? Because, as salespeople, you and I are in the business of creating **solutions.** We are in the solution business. We find out what prospects need, and then we come up with a solution. In most cases, the solution is that they own the benefits of our products or services.

At my seminars, one casual but effective introduction to the qualifying process that I ask people to adapt to their product or service is this:

> *As a representative of (name of your company), it's my job to analyze your needs and do my best to come up with a solution to satisfy those needs so that you can enjoy the benefits you're looking for.*

We serve customers by finding out what they need and then creating the right solution. When we do this, we create a win-win relationship where people want to do business with our company and they get the products or services they need. They give us business and, in turn, we both grow and prosper.

Review a lesson from Columbo that I mentioned at the beginning of the chapter: To save yourself from needlessly repeating questions, make written notes of a client's responses during the qualification sequence. It's okay to refer to your notes in order to remind yourself what questions you already asked and what the client said his needs were. It's easy, especially if you're nervous, to repeat a question you asked earlier.

Inadvertently asking the same question twice (or more) doesn't inspire confidence in the customer about you or your product. Not only do written notes help you during the presentation, but they also help you to remember what you've already covered when you follow up with each person once she's become a regular, happy client. In fact, that's part of how you keep them happy.

And don't forget to ask permission to take notes before you start taking them. Some people get nervous when you start writing down what they tell you; for all you know, they may visualize themselves being grilled in a court of law on what they say to you. If you think you're with someone like that, give them a pad or piece of paper and a pen (preferably with your company name on it), so that they can do the same as you. Being prepared for this situation helps you avoid, or at least to handle, uncomfortable situations.

It's easy to get permission to take notes. All you need to ask is this:

> *I don't have the best memory in the world and I do want to do a good job for you. So would you be offended if, while we chat, I make a few notes?*

Putting it that way gives you an opportunity to admit that you're human and that you're also smart enough to have learned how to overcome that human failing of a poor memory. And even if you happen to have a photographic memory, these little sentences will help put customers at ease and build their confidence in you.

Columbo himself couldn't hope for any more.

Your First Prospect to Qualify: Yourself

The series of questions we'll ask in this section are designed for you to gain a clearer understanding of the need to qualify people early during your contacts with them. If you've ever experienced any of the scenarios we'll cover, then you will benefit tremendously from learning the qualifying questions given in this chapter.

Have you ever . . . ?

I want to make sure you have a clear picture of the need for learning qualifying questions — especially if you're totally new to selling. The scenarios given below have happened to many a novice salesperson. I'm certain you will see the negative situations that can arise from lack of or improper qualification.

If you can answer *yes* to any of the following questions, you're probably reading this book because you've done just enough selling to know that you can do better. Good for you!

- *Have you ever . . .* spent hours explaining your product, service, or concept only to discover that the person to whom you were presenting was not the decision-maker?
- *Have you ever . . .* carefully prepared one copy of your complete presentation, only to find out that your meeting is with a large group or committee? You can grin all you want, but asking them to pass around your single copy just won't cut it.
- *Have you ever . . .* enthusiastically presented your top-of-the-line offering with all the bells and whistles, only to be told by the customer that what they were really looking for was the basic model? (Careful now: If the term *cheapskate* comes to mind, you can't let it slip or show in your eyes.)
- *Have you ever . . .* recommended what you know would be a dynamite product or service for your prospect, only to hear the discouraging words, *Oh, we tried that before and it was a disaster?*

You don't qualify a customer just to make friendly conversation or to break the ice. That's not to say the customer won't feel like you're making friendly conversation when you ask your qualifying questions in a friendly manner, but there must be a definite purpose or plan behind the questions you ask. That purpose is to discover the customer's needs.

If your questions are not geared specifically to gaining information about your prospect's needs or abilities to make a "buying" decision, your customer will have trouble focusing on the business at hand. They may even wonder why you're asking so many questions or exactly what it is you're driving at.

For example, if you're trying to involve your spouse in a discussion necessary to making a decision about how to spend the weekend and you begin by asking what time the kids got home from school today, your beloved spouse won't follow if your second question refers to the weekend. Instead, you'll want to ask more pointed questions throughout the conversation such as what the kids' plans are for the weekend; if your spouse has seen an extended weather report, and so on — all questions that refer to the coming two- or three-day time period available for golf, camping or all sorts of other fun things. Proper qualification sets the stage for just the right presentation.

But before you delve into learning the proper way to qualify potential customers, you must first qualify yourself as to what you are willing to give in order to win with your prospects. You must know your own career expectations, personal needs, and emotional wants.

Questions that qualify you personally

Ask yourself each of the following questions — take the time to think about them. Begin each of the following questions with, *What am I . . .*

What am I . . . Willing to do?

Are you willing to do the things that you know you should do to be successful?

This is perhaps one of the most important questions. A simpler version of this question is *Are you? . . . Are you* willing to study, drill, and practice? *Are you* willing to make all the sacrifices that will be required of you to be successful? *Are you* willing to put yourself in potentially uncomfortable situations?

If you say *Yes* to a long-term commitment in developing your selling skills, you must set up and follow the short-term steps necessary to help you do everything that you know you should do, especially training.

What am I . . . Assured of?

This question is difficult to answer. Can anyone guarantee another's success? No, but I can do the next best thing: I can teach you to guarantee your own success.

If you do what I teach — and you know you should — you can increase your success ratio. Sure, you probably won't be successful every time, but your percentage of success will increase dramatically. When this happens, you'll find the added motivation to examine what needs improving and to do what you know you should — improve your selling skills. At that point, you build a successful selling cycle.

What am I . . . Not able to achieve, and why do I believe this?

Often, when we believe something to be true, it is true. You have certain perceptions of yourself. These self-perceptions have been developed throughout your lifetime by you and all those surrounding you. If you truly believe that there are things impossible for you to achieve, then give up the dream. Don't waste your time pursuing something you don't believe in.

And another little piece of advice: Surround yourself with people who believe in you. No, I don't mean that you should move back in with Mom and Dad. But enthusiasm for what you do is very contagious. Soon you will be on the bandwagon of your own personal support group.

What am I . . . Telling myself every day?

This question is closely related to question #3. You can see this as another *Are you?* question: Are you reinforcing the negative or the positive? Make it the positive, and I'm sure that your results will change for the better. Remember: If you say it, you own it. It's pretty tough to lie to yourself. If you tell yourself you're an intelligent human being and that you can master these strategies in no time, you probably will. On the other hand, if you tell yourself that these strategies are hard to learn, they probably will be. Moral: Be careful what you tell yourself.

What am I . . . Selling?

This is one of the most important questions to ask.

It's obvious that you are trying to involve others in your product or service, but it is also important to help your prospect believe in you and your company as well. If your client does not trust and have confidence in both you and the firm you represent, your product will not have as great an impact on them, even if they also believe it's a good one. Put your own needs behind that of your customers, and you sell yourself as someone who is truly concerned about what's in your customer's best interest.

Now let's see how observant you were.

While you were reading, did you realize that you can put together the boldfaced first letters from the five questions and spell W-A-N-T-S? That is important. You need to determine what your wants are from your career, and then write them down. If you don't know what your wants are, how will you know when you have achieved them? I talk more about your wants and goals in Chapter 16.

Questions that qualify you professionally

After you analyze your personal wants, you need to qualify yourself in the business of selling. Ask yourself the following questions, beginning each question with *Have I . . .*

Have I . . . Searched for and studied all the necessary information about my product, service, or idea?

This is the first step in properly preparing yourself. You could really blow your chances for success if you are lazy at this point in your career. The more time you spend studying your offering, the less worry you experience when you meet your prospect.

It's also a good idea to know your competitor's offering. Knowing your competition helps you feel confident about your product's strengths. Maybe more important, knowing the competition enables you to answer customer objections about your product's possible weaknesses. If you don't know all you can know about what your product or service can do for the customer and how it compares to the competition, you'll never be successful in your negotiations.

Have I . . . Adopted a positive, respectful, and friendly attitude?

We'd all rather do business with people who have these qualities. Any aggressive tendencies should be stifled. Some people think being friendly and positive means rowdy greetings or any of the other slap-on-the-back activities that have created the negative image most people have of salespeople today. But the true professionals are rather low key yet present a friendly, helpful manner.

Have I . . . Learned all the best selling strategies available?

You are well on your way to answering this question positively — just by reading and studying the concepts presented in this book.

But learning the best selling strategies is a continuing process. The time and place to show your mental toughness is in your continuous pursuit of education. You can learn many selling methods and techniques, but always choose your educators wisely. Avoid imitating techniques that will not lead you to success.

Have I . . . Eliminated possible objections through the practice and drill of good selling skills?

You will achieve a smooth, calm manner if you practice these skills until they become second nature to you. Soon people will say, *What a natural in sales.* We know better, don't we?

Have I . . . Sought out all the prospects who can benefit from my product or service?

You can't afford to sit back and wait for customers to come to you. Think of your selling hobby as a constant quest for offering new opportunities to established customers and tried-and-true opportunities to new prospects.

Now look again at the first letter in every question in this list.

Together, what do those first letters spell? *Sales.* If you qualify yourself before you qualify your customers, you will be ready to meet every challenge as a professional salesperson.

Have you asked yourself what you *want* from your *sales* career? If so, now ask yourself if you are prepared to do what you know you should do. If you answered *Yes* to these two questions, you've just qualified yourself to try to move others to buy your product, service, or idea.

Mix these ingredients for success with an abundance of common sense, and you have the makings of a Champion. Here's a great little sentence to remember when you experience any doubts or setbacks in your selling career: *If it is to be, it is up to me.*

Chapter 11

Addressing Customer Concerns

In This Chapter

- The parts of *No* that spell *Oh, maybe*
- Things blessed, things forbidden when you address concerns
- Prescription-strength objection relief through six proven steps

Unless you sell balloons at a parade, few customers will contact you, make an impulse purchase, and go away happy. What really happens is that customers have concerns. What concerns will they have? Questions such as these:

- Will the product or service do what you say it will?
- Will you really be able to make their required delivery date?
- Have they negotiated the best investment?
- Are they making a good decision?

All these little fears creep up on customers when they feel the urge to invest in your product or service or to commit to your idea. It's normal for people to have such concerns when they make any commitment that involves their time or money.

When No Really Means Maybe

Most people new to persuading think that a *No* or a sign of hesitation means *Good-bye, Charlie.* The *seasoned* persuader, however, knows that customers can have good reasons to hesitate. The best reason of all is that they feel themselves leaning toward *Yes.*

Hesitation on the part of a customer or prospective participant thus can mean that they want to slow down the selling process so they can absorb all the information you're giving them. Or hesitation can mean that the customer needs *more* information; in such a case, the customer objects in order to show the salesperson that it's time to back up and resell them on a certain point. Hesitation also can show unseasoned salespeople where they need to hone their presentation skills.

When they hesitate or give you a stall, just think, *they need more information.*

Try it; you'll like it

If you get nervous or afraid when you hear an objection and start beating a hasty retreat for the door, you're leaving empty-handed. And if you try to overcome their objection and they don't like the way you handle it, you're going to be heading for the door anyway, and they'll have it open before you get there!

So why not experiment with ways to address their concerns or handle their objections? The worst that can happen is that you won't get what you want and you'll move on to the next likely candidate. The best that can happen is that your customer sees how competently you handled her concern and that her concern wasn't strong enough to keep her from going ahead with your offering.

Until you learn to expect customer concerns, you won't learn how to handle them. And until you learn how to handle customer concerns, you won't come close to reaching your highest earning potential in sales. So go into every presentation anticipating objections. That way, when you hear them, you won't get thrown by them.

When the fish aren't biting, change your bait

Most persuaders find it hard to influence people who voice no objections and raise no questions. In other words, the most difficult people to persuade are like dead fish: their eyes wiggle every now and then, but they don't respond.

In negotiation situations, you carry the presentation forward by directing and redirecting your course of questions and information based on what the prospects tell you. If they tell you nothing, the communication often stalls. When that happens, you have to guess which direction to follow next. And guessing is very bad. When you guess, you're no longer in control. It's like casting your line with no bait on it.

The people who don't get verbally involved in your presentation likely have no intention of going ahead with your proposition. Those who do bring up challenges for you to address are, at the very least, interested. If they're really tough to convince, they'll probably become your best customers once you do convince them.

So the next time you hear an objection, be glad. Getting objections and getting past them is a necessary step in the selling cycle.

Read their signals

Potential customers tell you three important things when they voice objections or raise concerns during your presentation:

1. They are interested, but they don't want to be thought of as an easy sale.
2. They may be interested, but they aren't clear about what's in it for them.
3. They may not be interested, but they could be if you educate them properly.

All three situations tell you one thing: *the prospect needs more information.* If you've properly qualified them, you'll know what they have now, what they enjoy most about it, what they would alter and that they are the decision-makers (our N.E.A.D.S. formula from Chapter 10). If, armed with that knowledge, you are confident they would benefit from your offering, then item #1 above most likely applies. In that case, you'll want to slow the pace down, encourage questions, and generally get them relaxed and chatting before you ask for a decision to be made.

If they are already asking lots of questions and look somewhat perplexed or doubtful, they don't have a clear picture of what's in it for them. If they don't have previous experience with a similar product and you're educating them from ground zero, this is likely to happen. With these people, you'll have to cover the features and benefits a bit more in depth — asking questions along the way that will help you use the right word pictures in your presentation.

Disinterest because of a lack of information is a little tougher to handle. You must first earn their trust so they'll give you the time you need to educate them. You'll also have to build their curiosity about the product, service or idea so they'll want to know more.

By backing up and clarifying exactly what it is they're objecting to, you know just which direction to take for your next step.

Using the Radio as a Direction-Finder

How do you know which direction to take? You need to tune in a little better to station WII-FM, the station that plays all the hits all day long, but only if the songs fit the traditional customer refrain, *What's in It for Me?* Tuning in to WII-FM helps you learn more about your customers' concerns and helps you help them see how much their involvement with you will improve their lives with your product, service, or idea.

When you tune in better, you also ask the right questions to find out about any past experiences that now stand between you and getting a final agreement. If you properly qualified your people and prepared your presentation according to what you learned, you may realize that they need what you're offering, but they may not yet see the benefit.

Sometimes you can bypass objections

Some objections don't even require an answer. You just need to acknowledge them. You may even have times when you know the prospect wants and needs the product or service you're offering, but he feels a natural inclination to object and you can bypass the objection.

As you can tell, good judgment serves you well here. A word of caution, though: If you are new to persuading others, don't ignore any objection without testing the waters to see how big a concern it truly is. Sometimes just acknowledging the concern is enough. They'll be satisfied that you really are listening, and then they'll move ahead.

Always remember that a concern, once the prospect raises it, may not mean *No way.* It may simply be a way for them to say, *Not this way.* If that's the case, you need to take another path to the same destination.

Condition versus objection

If your customer's objection is *I'm totally broke* and you're selling a luxury item, chances are pretty good that you've just heard a condition — not an objection. There's a big difference between the two.

A *condition* is not an excuse or stall. It's a valid reason that the prospect cannot agree to what you're proposing. If you're trying to exchange your offering for your potential customer's money, the customer has only two valid reasons for not going ahead:

1. They have no money.
2. They have no credit.

If he doesn't have money and doesn't have a way to get money, then just thank him for his time and move on. There are so many potential customers who have no conditions that you have no good reason to beat your head against the wall with those who do have valid conditions.

Always leave people who voice valid conditions on a positive note. You never know what may happen. They may win the lottery in the next 24 hours. Old Aunt Thelma may leave them an inheritance. They could borrow the money from their rich Grandpa. Or, better yet, they could convince Gramps that your offering would make a great birthday or Christmas gift for them.

If they want what you had to offer badly enough, they'll call you. And you can rest assured that their calls won't go to someone else whom they don't have a positive relationship with. Why call a stranger, when you can rely on a salesperson whom they know to be knowledgeable and competent?

They must believe they're trading up

If your prospective clients have money, credit, or both, but they just don't want to part with it now, you haven't convinced them that they'd be better off with the product than they would be with their money.

If an investment you're offering requires the person's time, *No time* is not a valid condition. It's an *objection.* We all have the same 86,400 seconds in every day. How we use them is up to us. If you want someone to invest her time with you, you have to show her enough benefits for her to *want* to spend her time on your offering instead of on what she's already planned.

Trust your instincts

Selling instincts develop through practice and experience. *Selling instincts* refers to that little voice or those inner feelings about what's right and what's not with the selling situation. Everyone has these instincts, but some people's are more developed than others.

To start using your selling instincts, you must carefully listen to your customers' concerns and genuinely put their needs before your own. Then and only then can you trust your own instincts. If you cannot honestly say that your customers' needs come before your own, then you place your own desires before what you instinctively know is right for the customer and your self-concern will show. Your customers will see the dollar signs in your eyes and stop trusting you. And why shouldn't they?

Beat them to their own objections

If you know that your product costs more than others on the market, and if you expect the customer to object to your offering's cost, beat them to it. By being in control and bringing it up when *you* want it brought up, rather than when *they* think the time is right, you can brag about it and turn it into an advantage. If the reason for the higher investment in your product is because it contains only the highest quality ingredients and because of that it makes you feel better, will last longer or perform in a superior manner, that's worth bragging about before your prospect gets busy laying bricks for that wall of defense against the investment.

One of my former students uses this tactic to her tremendous advantage. She markets facsimile machines to small businesses. She's so good at it that sometimes her company has trouble keeping enough inventory in stock to keep up with all the orders she writes.

Her favorite strategy accounts for much of her uncommon sales volume. Rather than wait until a prospective customer asks about a delivery date, she brings up delivery date early in her presentation by saying something like this:

> *Jim, I'm confident that at the end of my presentation you'll want to own my fax machine, as so many of my happiest clients have done. I must say that we're excited about that. You see, if you had decided to get a fax machine from one of our competitors, they probably would have it available immediately.*
>
> *Maybe that's because there's less demand for their machines — I don't know. If you decide on our machine, I'm going to have to ask you to be patient because we're currently in an oversell situation — because everyone seems to want this particular machine. It's popularity speaks for itself, doesn't it?*

Having product that's back-ordered can be a serious challenge if you let it. Bringing it up and bragging about how popular the product is instead puts back-ordering in a different light — a light that many customers will accept.

I'll go over the simple steps of handling known future hesitaters one more time:

1. Bring up the objection or concern before they do.
2. Brag about it.
3. Elaborate on the concern and make it an advantage.

This method has proven successful for many of our students who used to see common challenges as stumbling blocks. Now, they see them as springboards to success.

"I Can Get It Cheaper Somewhere Else"

One of the most common concerns people bring up when you're persuading them to exchange their money for your product or service is *they can get it cheaper somewhere else.* Everyone always wants to believe that. So, again, you need to expect to hear it and be prepared with your answer.

Here's how you should handle that situation:

CLIENT: Tom, I'm sure I can find this product, or one just like it, for a lot less money.

TOM: Well, Jim, I understand your concern. You know, I've learned something over the years. People look for three things when they spend money: the finest quality, the best service, and, of course, the lowest investment.

I've also found that no company can offer all three. They can't offer the finest quality and the best service for the lowest investment. And, I'm curious, for your long-term happiness, which of the three would you be willing to give up? Fine quality? Excellent service? Or the lowest fee?

It's now going to be tough for this client to come back at you and say, *Well, poor quality and crappy service are okay as long as they're cheap.*

Here's another way to handle a concern about money. Your choice between these two methods is going to be a judgment call. When the customer raises the concern, if you think that they have developed a certain belief in you — in your competency — then you may prefer to use this approach:

CLIENT: Tom, I'm sure I can find this product, or one just like it, for a lot less money.

TOM: Jim, I could have chosen to work for any company in the area in my particular industry. After careful research, I chose my company because I wanted to be able to sit with my clients and look them in the eye and say, 'You are doing business with the very highest quality company in the industry.'

> I know you appreciate quality and, because of that, those few extra pennies you'll invest per day to enjoy the finest quality will benefit you in the long-term scheme of things, wouldn't you agree?

With this approach, you enhance the credibility you've already established. In effect, you're telling your client that you're not an amateur. You have a concern for your own reputation and you plan to be around in the business awhile.

Most people use the money concern as a screen to hide a bad past experience or a fear raised by someone else's past experience. It's unfortunate for those of us who are professional, career salespeople, but many people have been hit by take-the-money-and-run salespeople, or they've at least heard of such salespeople.

You always have to remember that fear; you'll have to address it sooner or later in nearly every presentation. What you need to do is give your customers a reason — that is, a benefit *for them* — that will help them rationalize away their fear and allow you to proceed with your presentation.

The Do's and Don'ts of Addressing Concerns

The first Do of addressing concerns is to acknowledge that the other person has legitimate concerns. Dismissing them as unimportant can cause those objections to get completely blown out of proportion. In many cases a simple *I see* or *I understand* is acknowledgment enough. In other cases, you may do well to say, *Let me make a note of that so we can discuss it in-depth after we cover everything,* and then jot it down. Jotting down the concern validates the concern and shows professionalism on your part.

The most important Do of addressing concerns is important:

> *Get the other person to answer his or her own objection.*

That may sound tricky, but here's why it's so important. You're trying to persuade your prospect, so he'll have reservations about anything you do or say. Why? Because anything you say must be good for you, too. Until the customer realizes that you're acting in his best interest, he will doubt you.

Here's something to help you remember that last point:

> *When I say it, they tend to doubt it. When they say it, they tend to think it's true.*

That's why you want to get them to answer their own objections — because they're much more likely to believe themselves than they are to believe you. All you need to do is provide the information that answers their concern and let them draw their own conclusions. You let them persuade themselves.

This technique often works well when you persuade a married couple (children, take note). When one partner objects to something, don't respond immediately. Average persuaders are quick to defend their offering. But there's a better way: *learn to sit tight.* Many times one spouse jumps in with the next comment and you have a 50/50 chance that the originally silent spouse will answer the objection for you. If the second spouse agrees with his or her partner's objection, then you know you'll have to work a little harder to overcome it.

The point is that these two people already have a positive relationship (we hope) and trust each other's judgment. Learning to be quiet while they think it through can cause the objection to evaporate into thin air right before your eyes.

When something important to you is hanging in the balance, it's hard to be patient. During such moments, seconds feel like hours and you can get very uncomfortable. To keep yourself from jumping in too soon, try this trick. Silently count to 30. Or you may want to count the seconds by saying to yourself, *one-thousand-one, one-thousand-two, one-thousand-three,* and so on. Just remember to count to yourself. Some people recite a short poem to themselves. Whatever method you choose, just be careful not to let them see your lips move.

What you never want to do in such times is look at your watch or at a clock in the room. Even a slight glance by you at a timepiece can distract the prospects: they're already looking at you, waiting for your next move. Practice this step until you're comfortable with it.

My first Don't is don't argue or fight with the person you're trying to persuade. That should be an obvious point, but when you're a party to a negotiation, emotions can take over and things can get out of hand. Arguing or fighting an objection or concern also raises a barrier between you and the person you're trying to persuade. You're trying to persuade them to something, not go ten rounds with them. If you keep the perspective that objections are simply requests for further information, you shouldn't have much of a challenge with this Don't.

And Don't minimize a valid concern that a prospect raises. To the person you're persuading, every point they raise is valid. Remember to put yourself in their shoes. How would you react to someone who acts as if your concerns are stupid or unimportant?

Six Steps to Handling Objections

Here are six steps for handling objections or addressing concerns that almost always work in your favor. They also work pretty well in diffusing unusually tense situations, so heed them well.

Step #1: Hear them out

When someone trusts you enough to tell you what's bothering him, do him the courtesy of listening. Don't be quick to address every phrase he utters. Give him time; encourage him to tell you the whole story behind his concern. If you don't get the whole story, you won't know what to do or say to change his feelings. Don't interrupt either, because you may jump in and answer the wrong concern.

Step #2: Feed it back

By rephrasing what his concerns are, you're in effect asking for even more information. You want to be certain that he's aired it all so that no other concerns crop up after you've handled this one. You're saying to him, *Go ahead. Lay it all on me. Get it off your chest.* In doing this, you're asking him to trust you.

Step #3: Question it

This step is where subtlety and tact come into play. If a guy objects to the fact that you are asking Block Watchers to wear a reflective vest while out walking the neighborhood, don't say, *What's wrong with it?* Instead, gently ask, *Wearing the vest makes you uncomfortable?* If it does, he'll tell you why. Maybe he's shy. If so, you have to build his confidence in the respect the uniform generates and in the authority it lends to him as a participant.

Step #4: Answer it

Once you're confident that you have the whole story behind his concern, you can answer that concern with confidence.

Step #5: Confirm your answer

Once you've answered the objection, it's important that you confirm that he heard and accepted your answer. If you don't complete this step, the other person very likely will raise that objection again.

You can confirm your answers simply by completing your answer with a statement such as, *That answers that concern, doesn't it, Bob?* If he agrees with you that, your comment answered his concern, then you're one step closer to persuading him. If he isn't satisfied with your answer, now is the time to know — not later when you try to get his final decision to go ahead.

Step #6: By the way . . .

Know those three words. They're three of the most useful words in any attempt to persuade or convince another person.

You use the phrase to change gears — to move on to the next topic. Don't just keep talking. Take a conscious, purposeful step back into your presentation. If it's appropriate, turn the page in your presentation binder or booklet. Point to something other than whatever generated the objection. Take some sort of action that signals to the other person that you're forging ahead.

These six steps, if you learn them and apply them properly, will take you a long way toward achieving your goal of selling others even when they raise objections or concerns.

To give you a better feel for how these steps work, here's an example:

CUSTOMER: It costs too much.

Hear them out.

SALESPERSON: And try to bypass objections until the end of your presentation.

Feed it back.

Today, most things do. Can you tell me about how much too much you think it is?

CUSTOMER: Around $1,000.

Question the importance.

SALESPERSON: So your real hesitation is just this $1,000, is that right?

CUSTOMER: I guess so.

Answer it.

SALESPERSON: I can certainly appreciate your feelings.

But I think we ought to keep that $1,000 in the proper perspective. Over the years, most of my happiest clients received true enjoyment/value from this product for at least five years. This fact really makes that $1,000 only $200 per year, doesn't it?

CUSTOMER: Yes, it does.

SALESPERSON: If you're like most people, you'll receive the benefits of this product for 52 weeks per year, which means that $1,000 breaks down to about $3.85 per week. Then, of course — and this may sound ridiculous — but it finally boils down to about 55 cents per day.

Do you think you should avoid enjoying all the benefits we've discussed for 55 cents per day?

CUSTOMER: Well, when you put it that way, it does sound a little silly.

Confirm the answer.

SALESPERSON: So that settles that, doesn't it?

CUSTOMER: I guess it does.

By the way . . . (time to change gears)

SALESPERSON: By the way, I'm looking forward to serving your company for many years, so don't worry. We're going to bend over backwards to make you happy.

Sometimes you'll hear more than one objection or concern. If you start running through all six steps with each objection you hear, you can spend a lifetime trying to persuade these people. Experience helps you tell which concerns you need to address and which you may be able to bypass.

The Lady Doth Protest Too Much

If a prospect bombards you with objections, you may want to ask a few questions to get them to express their real final objection. If people protest too much, they're either not interested and don't have the guts to tell you so, or they're hiding the real reason they aren't going ahead. For some people, liking your offering but being unable to afford it is hard to admit. So, instead of admitting that they're strapped, they come up with a hundred other reasons why your product, service, or idea isn't right for them.

Eventually, you may need to say something like this:

> *Mrs. Johnson, obviously you have quite a few concerns about our product. May I ask, what will you base your final decision on, the overall benefits to your family or the financial aspects of this transaction?*

There you are, nice, warm, and friendly, asking as is your right, for the real objection to your product or service. You cannot move beyond this step in the selling cycle until you identify and handle that real final objection.

Eliminating your fears about handling objections is as easy as learning the steps to follow when you handle them. Objections are a way to slow things down, a request for more information or clarification. They are not doors slamming in your face. As with anything new, you'll be a little uncomfortable at first, but if you can remember to use the steps in order, you'll increase the *yes* quotient in your life right away.

Chapter 12
Getting to the Ultimate Agreement

In This Chapter

- The joy of consummation
- Coming right out and asking for it
- Taking down the objections
- Confirming interest in the consummation
- Consummate not only with joy, but with empathy

This is the fun part, the moment when you tie it all together, the moment when what your client needs and what you're selling become as one.

Selling uses the term consummation, from the Latin *consummatio,* to describe this moment. Like most words, *consummate* can mean different things, some of them far more risqué than I know you would ever permit to cross *your* mind. For that reason, we'll begin this chapter by defining this most crucial of terms.

Consummation is the Big Moment, the great What It's All About of our profession.

If you've adopted this book's philosophy of selling, you know that in effect you work on consummating the sale from the moment you first contact any prospect. That's a given. But unless you hone your *instincts* for consummating into finished *skills,* you're just winging it.

The bottom line with this most bottom of all lines in selling is this: *If you want the sale, sooner or later you need to ask for it.* After you get past your own version of first-timer's jitters and you've done it a few times, I'm confident you'll agree that this most essential aspect of selling is downright *fun.*

Sometimes All You Need to Do Is Ask

Often when a selling or persuasion situation arises, the person in the position of persuader gets an uncomfortable feeling if they have to go beyond throwing the offering out there. If the person on the receiving end of the idea, product, or service doesn't quickly see the value and jump right in to own it or participate in some way, the persuader starts to lose confidence.

This wavering of confidence then weakens the salesperson's desire to consummate the transaction. In other words, the persuader doesn't ask for the order, call for a decision, or otherwise try to get a commitment.

No ask, no sale

You always learn interesting things when you ask a variety of people the same question. Tom Hopkins International, Inc., conducted a little survey and asked people who were not persuaded to buy why they didn't go ahead with whatever it was. Interestingly enough, the most common answer was that (drum roll, please) *they were never asked.*

They were contacted, a product or service was demonstrated to them, and their questions (or objections or concerns) were answered. In some cases, they were convinced of the value of the offering and probably would have gone ahead, but nothing happened. The persuader or salesperson didn't ask them to make a commitment or to part with their money, so they didn't.

Don't ever let that be the reason someone doesn't go along with you. In the rest of this chapter, I'm going to explain when to ask for a decision to be made and give you many ways of doing it.

When and how to ask

Sometimes people in persuasion situations wait so long to ask for the sale that the right time to ask passes them by. To get past this timing challenge, learn to take their buying temperature. You do this by asking an ownership question. If they answer such a question enthusiastically in the affirmative, they're probably ready to go ahead. But if such a question brings up another concern or hesitation, then they're probably not ripe yet to make a commitment.

An ownership question is something like this:

> *Not to be assumptive, but if everything we've discussed here makes sense, how soon would you want to begin benefiting from your new computer system?*

Because you're asking an assumptive question, soften it by beginning with *Not to be assumptive.* The same goes for a personal question. Begin with *Not to be personal, but . . .* Sure, you're being personal; however, by stating it that way, you've shown respect for their privacy and it gives them an option not to answer if they are uncomfortable. We never want to purposely make a customer uncomfortable, but there will be selling situations in which we need to ask questions of a personal nature.

Another good opening if you're not sure what their reaction will be at this point in your presentation is, *Would you be offended if I asked . . .* When they say *No,* go ahead and ask your question. Demonstrating that you're sensitive to their feelings at this point in the transaction goes a long way toward winning them over in the end.

Tom's Tales: Stories to Close a Sale

Everyone loves a good story, and the best stories are those that make the listeners think that the events of the story can happen to them. Good stories draw the listener in, making them able to see and feel from the perspectives of the key players in the story. They become emotionally tied to someone or to some event in the story.

Where do the stories come from? Most stories come from your real-life experiences or the experiences of the people around you. And what you say to bring about a positive consummation to your sales process is nothing more than a story. You tell stories about others who have needs, interests, or desires similar to those of your current client. The stories you use should help your clients see that they aren't the only ones who have faced a decision like this about your product or service.

Sales stories help people to overcome fear, procrastination, or both in making ownership decisions. In the world of sales, these stories have been called *closes* for as long as I can remember — but, in most cases, they're just good *stories.*

I'll give you a few examples of such stories. After you read each example, write down what you think that story is meant to overcome: fear, procrastination, or both. As a by-product, these stories may also give a feeling of confidence to help the prospect make the decision when you want it: *now.*

For the examples, I'll demonstrate the strategies using a particular product or service. Please understand that the strategies will work for nearly any product, service, or idea.

Tom's Tale #1: Benjamin Franklin

This strategy was developed by the great Benjamin Franklin to consummate many decisions and has been used successfully by millions of people for years. Everyone can understand its effectiveness because it's so simple, basic, and easy to understand that it rarely fails to get the point across.

Here's an example of how to use this story with Kevin and Karen Smith in a real estate office:

TOM: (a.k.a. your humble narrator and real estate salesperson)

Do you think that the home on Third Street might be the best decision for your family?

KEVIN: (hesitant, noncommittal)

Well, Tom, you know that home is a pretty big investment. I don't know that I'm ready to make a decision on this right now.

I've asked a lot of questions up to this point, and now I'm ready to put the answers to work for me to close the sale. I can see that he and Karen really don't want to make the final decision. They're impressed with the home. They need to get the family moved quickly. The numbers work out. But they're trying to avoid committing to the home. In other words, they are behaving like typical buyers. This is a perfect opportunity for the Benjamin Franklin decision-making process.

TOM: (level, determined to help Kevin and Karen to make the decision they want to make, to help them make the best decision for them)

Could it possibly be, Karen and Kevin, that the problem is that you haven't had a chance to weigh the facts involved?

KEVIN: (nodding, open to reason)

Yeah, I don't think we've really gotten to the heart of this thing yet.

TOM: (a veritable master of the tie-down questioning technique covered in Chapter 2 of that dynamite new book, *Selling For Dummies*)

Well, a decision is only as good as the facts on which it's based, don't you agree?

KAREN: (she, too, seeing the wisdom of Tom's reasoning)

I think that's probably true.

TOM: (reflective and sincere)

You know, it's interesting. Awhile back I was reminded of a man we Americans have long considered one of our wisest men — Benjamin Franklin. What Ben used to do when he was uncertain about making a decision was to take a sheet of paper and draw a line right down the middle. On one side of the page he would write all the reasons in favor of the decision, while on the other he would write all the reasons against the decision. Then he would simply add up the reasons on each side, and see which decision was the best.

It's a funny thing. One day I decided to try Ben's system, not only in my professional life, but in my personal life, as well. Pretty soon, my whole family was using it to make all kinds of decisions. Would it be okay with you if we tried it now just to get a feel for the facts of your decision?

The important thing here is to keep going with the flow of the conversation. Once you master the material, you'll know how to weave it into any conversation.

TOM: Ben Franklin said that if a decision was the right thing to do, he wanted to be sure to go ahead with it.

If it was wrong, he wanted to be sure to avoid it. So why don't we analyze the decision and "get down to the heart of it," as you put it?

KEVIN AND KAREN: (as one voice)

Okay, yeah, let's do that.

TOM: Great. So the reasons **for** the decision go on one side, and all those **against** the decision go on the other side. Then you can add up the columns and the right decision should be clear. We have time, don't we? It'll take us just a couple of minutes.

KEVIN: Yeah, okay.

I have a long list of things they like about the home because I've made notes on every positive comment they've made since we drove into the neighborhood. If they run out of positives off the tops of their heads, I'll remind them of those on my list.

TOM: (waits a beat for Kevin's agreement, draws a line down the center of the page he holds in front of him)

Okay, let's start it off here. Let's think of the reasons favoring the decision. You agree that the home has all the features you were looking for, isn't that right?

KAREN: Yes, it does.

TOM: And we've already established that with the right financing you could actually have a smaller monthly investment than what you have on the home you're in now.

KEVIN AND KAREN: (as one voice)

Right.

TOM: You said you wanted to be close to the elementary school and this home is just three blocks away. That's certainly a plus, don't you think?

KEVIN AND KAREN: Absolutely.

TOM: Let's go on.

You thought the professional landscaping in the backyard was impressive.

KAREN: (looking at Tom but seeing the future)

Yeah, the kids would have a lot of fun in that yard.

TOM: Wouldn't they? Let's write that down. And what about the outside of the home? When we first pulled up, Karen, remember how you got so excited?

KAREN: It really is a beautiful home.

TOM: (counting the positives)

Let's see; that's five. Can you think of any others?

KEVIN: Well, we really liked the extras in the newly remodeled kitchen.

TOM: All right. We'll put that down.

KEVIN: I like all the big trees on the property.

TOM: Okay. We'll put that down, too.

KAREN: Oh! We both liked the sunken bathtub in the master bedroom.

TOM: Great. Is there anything else you can think of?

Set a goal for between six and ten items on the plus side. If you haven't reached ten at this point, refer to your notes and remind them of other items to add to this column. When you make note of each item, do it with a check mark.

But don't write down their actual reasons. You're just tracking how many there are now. If you start writing each one out, this strategy takes longer and the prospects start weighing each reason against the others. When your goal of ten reasons for the decision has been reached, continue this way:

TOM: (objective, fair)

Now, how many reasons can you come up with on the negative side?

KEVIN: (heavy sigh)

Well, let's see. The down payment is a concern. It's almost all we've saved.

TOM: Okay, what else?

KEVIN: We were really interested in finding a home that had solar heating.

TOM: Those are both valid points, Kevin. Can you come up with any others?

After a pause, it's obvious that Karen and Kevin aren't coming up with any more concerns. They've just told me, bottom line, exactly what will keep them from owning this particular home. I don't even have to answer those objections at this point, because what I'm looking for is a clear desire to own this particular property. Once that decision is made, we'll work on the financial details of how they can own this home, so I say:

TOM: All right. Why don't we just add these up?

I show them the list and together we count aloud. Afterward I announce the results: 10 Yeas, 2 Nays.

TOM: Karen, Kevin, don't you think the answer is rather obvious?

The 8 most important words in the art of consummation

Whenever you ask a consummation question, shut up!

I expect to wait through a long silence now. The key here is to shut my mouth and not do or say anything that takes away from my request for a decision. One of three things will happen:

- Kevin and Karen will try to stall, to put off making the decision by asking for more time or asking a question to change the subject.
- Kevin and Karen will decide to go ahead.
- Kevin and Karen will give me an objection.

Just as I expected, a silence pervades the room for some time while they think this over. Finally Kevin replies with a stall.

Tom's Tale #2: Getting past a vague stall to a concrete final objection

KEVIN: Tom, I'll tell you something. We're the kind of people who really need to think it over.

I hope you can see how this method, delivered with real warmth and sincerity, will be so very valuable to your career. This is how all selling situations should be handled: in a relaxed, friendly, gentle, and professional manner. It's not only what you say, but how you say it, that creates a successful sales environment.

But sometimes even the warmest presentation, delivered with genuine care for the customer's needs, can be met with, *We're the kind of people who really need to think it over.* And always remember that the *I want to think it over* line is a stall. We all use it, so why shouldn't we expect to hear it from others when *we're* on the persuading side of things?

So how do you handle a situation where the prospect absolutely insists on *thinking it over?* With these same two prospects, I'd continue like this:

TOM: That's fine, Kevin. Obviously, you wouldn't take the time to think it over unless you were seriously interested, would you?

KEVIN: (reassuring, but committed to The Stall)

Oh, we're interested. We just really need to think about this before we decide.

TOM: Since you are interested, may I assume that you will give it very careful consideration?

KAREN: Of course we will.

TOM: Kevin, you're not telling me this just to get rid of me, are you?

KEVIN: (polite, but committed to The Stall)

No. I'm not trying to get rid of you. We like the house, but we have to think it over.

TOM: (trying to keep communication open)

Just to clarify my thinking, what is it about the house that you want to think over? Is it the value of the home? The neighborhood?

Ask about the benefits of the home that you know they liked. Every time they say no, they are that much closer to *yes,* aren't they? Kevin and Karen have answered *no* to every benefit, so what is it that they want to think over? In most cases, the decision comes down to money. Either the home is too expensive, the prospects won't be comfortable with the large initial investment, or they may be worried about their credit and getting qualified for the loan.

TOM: Well, could it be the financing or even the initial investment that you want to think over?

KAREN: (as at a life raft)

Yes. We might have another baby and I'm not sure if we should make a financial commitment like this right now.

Tom's Tale #3: Handling "It costs too much"

Use this consummation technique when you isolate a money objection as the obstacle to final agreement. It helps both you and the customer see the big dollars they're afraid of in much smaller, easier-to-handle numbers.

To show you this technique at work, I'll stay with Karen and Kevin in the real estate office:

KAREN: Tom, I just feel that this home costs too much.

TOM: (ever in search of specific obstacles to *yes*)

Today most things seem to. Can you tell me about how much too much you feel it is?

Salespeople tend to look at the total investment when we hear *It costs too much.* This is trouble. Instead, go for the *difference.* If someone plans to spend $20,000 for a car, and the car they are looking at is $22,000, the problem isn't $22,000: it's $2,000.

KAREN: We really wanted to spend around $110,000, and I don't feel that we can go as high as $115,000.

TOM: So, Karen and Kevin, what we are really talking about is $5,000, aren't we?

KEVIN: $5,000. Right. That's exactly what I'm concerned about.

Tom's Tale #4: Reduction to the ridiculous

Now that you know exactly what amount of money they are concerned about, you can work with them to help them see how they can handle the amount and have what they really want — the product or service.

Hand them your calculator. This is a good way to get them involved as you work out the finances.

TOM: (asking what Karen already knows, a technique covered in Chapter 2 of that dynamite new book, *Selling For Dummies*)

Karen, do you think it would be safe to assume that this would be your dream home and you could be happy here for a long time, assuming everything else was right?

KAREN: (Tom's words having summed up her dream of Ownership — the Future — their Life)

Probably. I think it would be a great place to raise the kids.

TOM: Okay, so let's just say that you're going to live in this beautiful home for 20 years. Would you say that's about right?

KEVIN
AND
KAREN: Twenty years . . . Yeah, that'd be about right.

TOM: Let's divide that $5,000 by 20 years, okay? We get $250, don't we?

KEVIN: Yes.

TOM: And would you say that you would actually be in the home 50 weeks a year, allowing for two weeks of vacation each year, of course?

KEVIN: (agreeable)

That sounds about right.

TOM: Dividing our $250 per year by 50 weeks. That makes the difference in the investment $5.00 per week. So now we have 7 days in each of those weeks, and when we divide $5 by 7, what do we get?

KAREN: (catching an early glimpse of the Ridiculous)

71 cents . . .

Crunch numbers when you crunch numbers

Champions always do their selling math with a calculator. No matter how confident you are in your mathematical abilities, always use a calculator. Know your formulas and figures so that you can quickly provide any numerical information that your prospect might request.

A prospect who sees you punch numbers into your calculator — or one who runs the figures himself — probably won't question the figures. But if you start furiously scratching numbers on paper with a pencil, the prospect gets uncomfortable sitting and watching you have all the fun with numbers. Even worse, if you rattle figures off the top of your head, your prospects may doubt you. Instead of paying attention to your presentation, they will be looking over your shoulder to double-check your math.

Not using a calculator will raise doubts about not only your mathematical abilities, but if you're this careless with figures, where else will you be careless? You don't want to do anything at this stage of the relationship to make them start wondering if they should be working with you at all. You want them entirely focused on the math at hand as you show them how they really can afford the product they want so badly.

Tom's Tale #5: The oblique comparison

Here you will help them rationalize having the home simply by sacrificing, for now, some small luxury that they would certainly give up in order to have a much larger gain.

TOM: (giving them something to compare it to)

Kevin, do you and your family drink much soda?

KEVIN: Sure. You know how kids are. We probably go through at least one sixpack a day.

TOM: How much are sodas these days?

KAREN: Around $2.00 a sixpack.

TOM: Karen, Kevin, wouldn't you agree that the benefits and the enjoyment you will get out of this wonderful home are worth 71 cents a day? Do you think that we should let 71 cents stand in the way of all the family memories you will make there, for less than it costs your family to have three sodas per day?

KEVIN: When you look at it that way, I guess it doesn't seem to be such a significant amount.

TOM: Then we've agreed, haven't we? Now, let's get to work to get you out of your existing house and into this **beautiful home** by the **holidays** so you and your family can begin **building memories** right away. By the way, would the 10th, or the 12th, be the best closing date for both of you?

Notice the words that I boldfaced? These key words will create pleasant pictures in these buyers' minds. For the sake of this example, assume that Kevin and Karen said they wanted to be in the home by November 1st. That gives you the license to address the upcoming holidays, a time of year that almost always creates warm feelings in buyers.

This scenario demonstrates how easy it is to flow from one consummation to another. It's important that you know as many consummation stories as there are objections. Create your own consummation stories and tailor them to your product or service. The important thing is to be prepared.

Tom's Tale #6: Similar situation

What better way to ease your prospects' fears than a story of another couple who had all the same concerns and indecisions, but who still decided to buy and now are glad they did?

> *John, Jennifer, I know you're hesitant about the financial commitment of buying a home when you have your first baby on the way. You know, I had another family looking for the perfect home just about a year ago. We searched and searched and they just couldn't decide on a home.*
>
> *One day we looked at a beautiful home and they got very excited about it. I asked them if they thought that this was the home for them and they agreed that it was a great house. I also asked if they wanted to begin the process of owning that great home. Bob thought we should go ahead, but Kathy was afraid that the home might be a bit larger than they really needed. She thought they could get by in a smaller home and she wasn't sure that she wanted to move before their baby came.*
>
> *Well, they decided to go ahead and were amazed at how much space the baby things took up. After they moved in, Bob and Kathy were so glad that they decided to invest in the bigger home when they did.*
>
> *Now, you'd like to be all settled in at your new home before your baby comes, wouldn't you?*

I hope you can see how important it is to develop and know multiple consummation stories.

Tom's Tale #7: Competitive edge

Competitive edge stories don't need to be elaborate. They just need to remind commercial prospects that they are in business, and that they have competitors. So, because you're not telling them anything they don't already know, what's the appeal in competitive edge stories? In a word, survival.

A little competitive edge "story" like this, for example, would work well:

> YOU: Mr. Parker, remember that many of your competitors are facing the same challenges today that you are. Isn't it interesting that, when an entire industry is fighting the same forces, some compa

nies do a better job of meeting those challenges than others? My entire objective here today has been to help provide you with a competitive edge. Gaining a competitive edge, no matter how large or small, makes good business sense, doesn't it?

These stories are not meant to talk anybody into anything they don't want or need. Their sole purpose is to help people make decisions that they want to make. Remember: Your prospects would not invest their valuable time talking with you about your product or service if they didn't want it.

Prospects are just like us: We all need help making decisions. Think about it. How many things have you been talked into owning that you really didn't want? Probably not very many. Few people get talked into buying something they don't really want. If it's a major purchase, it's usually difficult to sell your prospects even if they *do* want it.

Problems arise when an unscrupulous salesperson lies about what a product is and what it will do. Through deceit, such a salesperson violates the buyer's trust and the buyer ends up owning something other than what she thought she was getting. The jails are full of salespeople who have done things like this. They let greed get in the way of their service to customers. Such an approach to selling is directly opposite of the kind of selling I advocate. If you put service to your customer ahead of money, you will always come out on top.

Do I consider consummation questions, assumptive statements, and "salestime" stories to be in the best interest of my customers? Based on my experience, my answer is an unequivocal *yes.* I've done a lot of selling, and I always took my customers' interests to heart. I knew that they would get the truth from me, as well as great service. I would not be able to guarantee them truth-in-selling and excellent service when they went elsewhere.

All along, from my early days in selling to today, I've tried to help every consumer have a positive image of the sales industry. I knew that positive image would be there if I gave my customers professional service, and I've always been one to provide it. That's why I worked harder than many of my associates to consummate sales that I knew were in the best interest of my customers. This obviously would not include selling them anything they didn't want. However, if all things were right, I would do everything I could to help them get over the hills of fear and procrastination.

If you properly qualify people, you'll know whether or not they truly have a need or desire for your product or service. If their lives will be better for owning your offering, you should do your best to persuade them into having it.

In consummation, the end is really at the beginning

Consummating the sale starts at the *beginning* of the transaction, when you first make contact with your customers.

If you are weak on original contact, on qualifying, on handling objections, on presentations, or on any other area of the sales process, or if you are generally weak in asking pertinent questions, I don't care how great a salesperson you think you are, you are costing your prospect, yourself, and your company a lot of money, time, and aggravation. No one consummates every sale, but just think of how much better you can become when you put your best effort into it.

A perfect ending needs a perfect beginning.

Now a question for you: Drawing on your own experience, have you appreciated the professionals who have helped you make buying decisions? Have you been happy enough to recommend those people to others? Of course you have! We all have.

To become a champion salesperson, you should set a goal to become someone people will not hesitate to recommend. Become someone people seek out as an expert in your field.

Consummation Questions and Statements

You now know what the consummation of a sale is all about, and you know that it doesn't need to be complicated, either. In fact, consummating a sale can be even less complicated than the seven stories I just showed you. Here are some examples of simple questions and statements you can ask to consummate a sale without the assistance of a full-blown story.

Basic Oral Consummation

To use this question, first define the needs you can fill, and then ask a question:

> *You had said that you start your new job on the 21st. Would the 15th or the 18th be the best date for you to pick up your new suit?*

An example of an oral consummation statement is this:

> *John, Mary, I'm excited to help you take a major step toward financial independence. We can do that with your approval right here.*

If you know everything is right and that all the cards are on the table, go ahead and ask for the order. Don't keep selling. That's one of the biggest mistakes novice salespeople make. They don't always recognize when they can close. They simply keep talking, redemonstrate the product, or even change the subject searching for a reason to continue in the company of their prospects. I guess they think if they get an invitation to spend the night on the prospects' couch it means they like them well enough to buy from them in the morning. If they're not ready to go ahead, they aren't going to throw you out on your ear. In most cases, they'll say something that will give you an opportunity to have further discussion and try closing again.

In your typical selling situation, prospects have at least five ways of avoiding making decisions. If you, as a salesperson, only know one or two ways to close, you'll run out of closing material before they run out of "no-sale" material.

Basic Written Consummation

This is an effective consummation if you use order forms.

Walk in with a leather binder. Have an order form under a cardboard protector. Such an arrangement allows you to flip to it instantly when the time is right.

PROSPECT: Does it come in blonde wood?

SALESPERSON: Is blonde the best color accent for your furniture?

PROSPECT: Yes. I think that would look fantastic.

SALESPERSON: Let me make a note of that.

Now you write down the prospect's preference on the order form. (Be careful, though. Some people panic when they see you filling out a form.)

PROSPECT: What are you doing? I haven't agreed to anything yet.

SALESPERSON: Mrs. Palmer, I like to organize my thoughts to keep everything in order. I do that on the paperwork so I don't forget anything.

If it suits your product or service to do so, add particularly anything that could cost you time or money. Then continue with the sale.

Go into every consummation sequence by asking a *reflex question,* a question they can answer without thinking. You should have earned the right to use their first name by the time you reach the point in the sales cycle where you can comfortably ask for specific information to write on your form. If you're not sure if you've earned that right, you probably haven't. Never jump into the familiarity of using that first name unless you're certain it's okay with them.

YOU: Mary, do you have a middle initial?

PROSPECT: It's K.

If you're dealing with a corporate executive, a good reflex question is to ask for the company's complete name and address. If the executive hands you their card and lets you copy all the information, then congratulations to you for moving ahead.

Always use a legal pad and your paperwork for making notes — and always let the prospect stop you from writing your notes. Having them stop you doesn't hurt you. It helps you. Your desire to take good notes shows the prospect that you are a professional salesperson who knows how to get things done. Keep filling out that order form. By the time you finish your presentation, the form will be almost completely filled out. In most cases, the forward momentum you've developed while completing the form will be enough to get it approved. If the prospect gets used to seeing you write on the order form, you're almost home.

The problem many salespeople have is that they don't start writing soon enough. You should begin writing on your paperwork when you begin your qualification questions. If you feel better using a qualifying form that you custom-make for your product or service, then go ahead and do so. But make sure you explain to the customer that you're asking for this information only to help them make a better decision.

Sharp Angle

There will be times when your prospect will in essence throw down the gauntlet and challenge you to give them exactly what they want. The key here is to accept the challenge, but with the understanding that if you can come through, you win by getting the sale and they win by owning the product or service just the way they want it. It's called "Sharp Angling" them into ownership.

Sometimes a prospect asks you an assumptive question of his own, a question that assumes that he will buy your product or service. What to do? Answer with a question that shows that in his own mind he has bought your product or service — if, that is, he answers according to his original question's assumption.

MR. STEWART: If I decide I want this boat, can you handle delivery by Memorial Weekend?

YOU: If I can guarantee delivery by Memorial Weekend, I bet you can guarantee me that you will be prepared to have a great time enjoying the holiday on your new boat, can't you?

In this example of Sharp Angling, you're still guiding your prospect, Mr. Stewart, toward what he wants to do: to buy a boat.

MR. STEWART: If I decided to go with this boat, I'd want delivery by May 15. Can you handle that?

The average salesperson would be tempted to jump in and say *yes,* whether or not she could "handle that." Pay close attention to how a professional takes advantage of this same opportunity.

YOU: If I could guarantee delivery by May 15, are you prepared to approve the paperwork today?

Or, if you really don't know if you can make delivery on that date, you may want to respond this way:

YOU: If I could guarantee delivery by May 15, and I am not certain yet that I can, are you prepared to approve the paperwork today?

Then you remain silent until Mr. Stewart answers.

To use the Sharp-Angle method, your prospect must first express a demand or desire that you can meet. (Although my example here uses delivery, you can Sharp-Angle many other demands or needs besides delivery.) For you to use your prospect's own demand as your way to get to *yes,* always remember that Sharp-Angling involves two pivotal points:

- You must know what benefits you can deliver.
- You must know when the delivery can be made.

Be aware that Sharp Angling can be hazardous to your selling health: A dangerous part of the Sharp-Angle is that you may be tempted to apply it before you've gathered enough qualification information or before you've built enough rapport. I recommend that you do not use the Sharp Angle too early in the selling process. It could easily be a case of too much too soon. If you

Sharp-Angle too soon, you may offend some people because the method is not smooth and can be interpreted as overly aggressive. But if the prospect's thinking and the rapport are right, the Sharp Angle is a wonderful way to get agreement early in the sales process.

The following exchange shows you how to time your use of the Sharp Angle:

PROSPECT: Can you get it for me in red?

YOU: Are you ready to go ahead today if I can?

PROSPECT: Yes.

or

I might be, but first I need a lot more information.

Before you ask *Will you go ahead if I can?,* you must be absolutely sure that you can deliver your product. It won't do much good if you say you can deliver if you can't. One of the reasons trained salespeople outsell average salespeople is that the professionals know more about their products and what their companies can deliver.

How do you get this information? The answer depends on your product, the company, and your attitude. Salespeople often make enemies in the production department and on the shipping dock by promising clients things the company can't deliver. When the client gets angry over a missed delivery date, the production department or the shipping dock usually takes the blame. Know what your company can deliver. And always thank the people in your company who help you get your job done, especially if fulfillment requires extra effort on their part in order for you to keep your sale.

Higher Authority

Every happy client is a potential higher authority for another prospect. This consummation method is very effective if you know it thoroughly and set it up correctly. No matter what your product or service, all you need to do is adapt the wording to your own style of selling.

The higher authority must be exactly that — someone who is respected by and known to the prospect. The prospect doesn't have to know the higher authority personally, but she must know of the higher authority's existence and position. If you sell industrial equipment, you want a prominent decision-maker at a well-known company; if you sell advertising, you want a high-profile businessperson.

Here are the steps for using this close successfully:

1. **Select your higher authority figure.**

   You should constantly be on the lookout for higher authority figures.

   As an example, let's say that you're the sales-record-smasher for Builtgreat Computer Systems. A prominent businessman in the area invested in a computer system for his company, Marketshare Inc., and is very pleased with the system's performance and increased productivity. This businessman, George Steele, is an ideal higher authority figure for anyone interested in your computers.

2. **Recruit your higher authority figure.**

   On one of your visits to Marketshare Inc., after they have had plenty of time to know the system inside and out, you ask George Steele if he'd be willing to share his knowledge of your product with other businesspeople.

   George agrees because you've done a solid sales and service job for him on a good product, and you've assured him that you'll only call when you need help with an occasional prospect who may be in a similar situation. In other words, you promise not to bother him if you're working on selling a two-computer system to a small business. A small gift of appreciation for Mr. Steele would probably be in order. After all, he listens to WII-FM, too.

3. **Schedule your higher authority figure for the sales situation.**

   You're out to update the computer system at Southwest Advertising with your newest system. Mary Phillips is the decision-maker there. While planning your appointment with Mary, you decide that you may need the higher authority figure confirmation, so you call George Steele to determine if he'll be available to take a phone call while you're with Mary Phillips. With George's cooperation, you complete your plans for a powerful presentation to Mary at Southwest.

4. **Use the higher authority figure confirmation effectively.**

   You know that Mary will have concerns about your system similar to those that George Steele had. Will the software that makes your systems superior be the right one to increase productivity for Southwest? Is your service department as good as you say it is? In planning your presentation, you know that Mary will have specific technical questions.

   The primary purpose of your interview with Mary Phillips is to isolate the specific technical and other reservations that she has about your equipment and company. Once you clarify these questions for her, and once you agree that these are all reasons why she questions the idea of installing your system now, you're ready to bring in a higher authority.

It's vital to make the list of reasons specific, and to get Mary's agreement that they are all the reservations she has. Write them out on a piece of paper. After you clarify and write down the causes of Mary's reservations, you're ready to appeal to a higher authority.

YOU: Do you know George Steele of Marketshare Inc.?

MARY: No, but I know of the company.

YOU: George is the owner, and he's a client of mine. Mary, so that I can relieve your mind of some of the questions you may have about the system or our services, would you be offended if we called George and asked him your questions? You see, he had the same concerns you did before he invested in our system.

When George is on the phone, tell him, *I'm here at Southwest Advertising with Mary Phillips and she has some questions about Builtgreat.* Then hand the phone to Mary and let her take it from there. She has the list of questions in front of her, so she'll miss none of her objections when she talks to George.

5. **Close after the call.**

   Once George Steele has discussed the technicalities and reassured Mary that the Builtgreat computers are performing well in his office, Mary's objections have vanished. When the phone call ends, you're in a position to smile and ask, *By the way, what delivery date is most convenient for you, the 1st or the 10th?*

   If something should keep George Steele from taking Mary's call, even though you set it up with him in advance, you may not be able to consummate the sale today. Try to set up a specific recontact time for when you can be present with Mary, or try to arrange a conference call.

   Take a copy of Mary's objections and hot buttons with you to the recontact so that, at the start of the recontact, you can get back to where you left off. Remember to do a brief recap with Mary before you get George on the line.

Some salespeople turn away from the higher authority confirmation because they think that all competitors hate each other and won't cooperate. There are exceptions, of course, but as a rule most people at competing companies are friendly with each other. They respect each other, and there is always the possibility that they will look for another job in their industry someday and will be able to use good connections at several companies. If you do happen to run into a case of bad blood between competitors, simply back off.

Don't settle for just one higher authority because you can wear out any one person with overuse. When you do your job with the utmost professionalism, most clients will be happy to help you out: it's an ego boost for them to be considered a higher authority.

Confirmation questions

Confirmation questions are just special questions. When answered, they tell you that the prospect has reached a high level of interest and that they are willing to go further. When you ask a confirmation question, you're looking for answers that give you positive stimulus.

Here are three confirmations:

The Alternate Advance

This strategy involves giving your prospect two choices. Either one advances the sale. It's so much better than just giving them one suggestion that they can flat out say *no* to. Giving them choices helps them focus better on what would be best for them and that's what you really want, isn't it?

YOU: Ms. Hall, which delivery date would be best for you, the 8th or the 13th?

MS. HALL: I'd need to have it in my warehouse by the 10th.

What's happened? As long as you can meet that delivery date, she owns it. Stay on course in your consummation sequence and you're all set. If she's uncertain, she'll raise an objection here or try to change the subject.

Here's another example of the alternate advance:

YOU: Jim, would you be the one trained on the use of the new system, or would you want someone else to be involved?

When Jim tells you whom to train, you know that he's going ahead.

Erroneous Conclusion

A Champion listens throughout the presentation for anything that she can use later for an *erroneous conclusion* test close. The erroneous conclusion is an intentional error made to test how serious the prospect is about going ahead. If they don't correct you, you may have missed some information along the way that would have told you they weren't serious. If they do correct you, their buying temperature is heating up. As we explained back toward the beginning of this chapter, in a test consummation, all you want to do is test their buying temperature — to see if it's warm enough to go ahead.

For example, you're in a home and selling home improvements there. During your demonstration, the wife tells her husband,

> *Honey, my mother is coming in July. If we decide what we want today, we ought to have it finished by then.*

Many salespeople would ignore that remark or regard it as an interruption. But the professional hears it and remembers it. Later, the salesperson might smile at the wife and say:

SALESPERSON: I can see that you're kind of excited about this addition. Now, your mother is coming in August, is she?

PROSPECT: No, in July.

SALESPERSON: So the first week in June would be the best time to get started?

PROSPECT: Yes.

SALESPERSON: Let me make a note of that.

You can use the erroneous conclusion test close on size, color, windows, almost anything. The wife might have said:

PROSPECT: I think I'd like a bay window on the south wall.

Later, you can use that line for an erroneous conclusion test:

SALESPERSON: Let's see. You said you wanted the bay window on the east wall. . . .

PROSPECT: No! I want it on the south wall.

SALESPERSON: Yes, that's right. Let me make a note of that.

Put that information on your paperwork, too. If you make a mistake and they correct you, they may be agreeing to move forward by letting you write down the correction.

The purpose of this method is not to tell a lie or trick the customer. I would never teach that. It's simply a test for you to determine if the prospect is sincere in moving ahead. They wouldn't correct you if they weren't. If you are at all uncomfortable with this method, don't use it.

Porcupine

I discussed this strategy earlier in Chapter 2, "Questioning Your Way to Success." There I tell you that the Porcupine method works well for gathering information. Aside from being a good information-gatherer, it's also a terrific confirmation question.

Look at a car dealership example:

A young woman is walking through your car lot looking at convertibles. Suddenly she stops, points at a car, and says:

PROSPECT: This is the convertible I'm interested in. Do you have it in red?

The average salesperson would answer her this way:

SALESPERSON: If we don't have it in red, I can call around and get one for you in a hurry.

When a salesperson gives an answer like that, are they looking to help themselves, or the customer? It's a pushy statement. The real power in selling is in pulling with questions.

Unlike the average salesperson, the *professional* salesperson answers this way:

SALESPERSON: Would you like it in Red-Hot Red or Cranberry Red?

or

Red is one of the most popular colors in this model. If I can locate one for you in red, would you be ready to go ahead with the approvals now?

What's she going to say? She's already told you that she's interested in the convertible and she wants it in red. She'll most likely choose one color or the other and you can note that on your paperwork. You're now one step closer to getting her autograph on that dotted line and having her drive happily away in her new Red-Hot Red convertible.

Consummate with Empathy

Empathy is *an intimate understanding of the feelings, thoughts, and motives of another.* That's why empathy is of prime importance in professional selling. Empathy is putting yourself into the prospect's shoes. It's knowing and feeling what your prospect is feeling. It's knowing exactly how to proceed depending on the information the prospect has given you.

Until you develop empathy for your customers, until you develop the skill of calling for and getting a favorable agreement that we call *consummation,* you probably won't make it in selling. The customer should sense that you understand and care about helping them solve their problems, not that you are just looking for a sale.

As a professional salesperson, you must truly believe that you can satisfy the prospect's needs. You must see the benefits, features, and limitations of your product or service from your prospect's view; you must weigh things on the prospect's scale of values, not your own; you must realize what is important to the prospect. Your prospect must always be the star of the show.

Focusing on your prospect enables you to answer the crucial question in any selling situation: *When should you consummate the sale?*

There's a certain electricity in the air when the prospect is ready to go ahead, but here are some positive buying signs to watch for:

- **The prospects have been moving along at a smooth pace, and suddenly they slow the pace way down.** They're making their final analysis or rationalizing the decision.
- **They speed up the pace.** They're excited to move ahead.
- **Suddenly, they start asking lots of questions.** Like anyone else, they ask questions only about things that interest them.
- **They ask questions about general terms of purchase before they settle on one particular model.** Some people immediately start asking questions about initial investment, delivery, and so on. They feel safe doing this because they know you can't sell them everything. If they ask these questions after you know exactly what they want, it's positive stimulus.

Go for a test consummation after you get positive stimulus. If you think that your customers are ready to consummate the sale, try a test question to make sure you are reading the stimulus correctly. As you get more experience in selling, you will become more proficient at reading body language and other buying signals. This skill can be good and bad for you.

Some people start relying so much on positive readings that they short-cut other vital steps such as qualifying or demonstration. When you shortchange the overall selling cycle, it's hard to go back and restore the steps you skipped. Invariably, short-cutting steps causes you to lose many sales. Although it is important to become better at knowing when to consummate the sale, each prospect should get your full presentation to make sure you don't come up short at the end. *Then* you can move ahead with the consummation.

When you ask a question from which you expect an answer confirming that the prospects want to go ahead with the purchase, you want one of two things to happen:

- The prospect gives you a *yes* or an answer that indirectly confirms their desire to go ahead with the sale.

  or

- The prospect gives you an objection or asks for more information to enable them to make a decision.

If you start talking before they answer, you lose control of the negotiations. And you gain nothing. You have neither a confirmation to go ahead nor an objection; you wasted your attempt to consummate the sale.

Would you like delivery on the 15th or the 30th? They pause to think when would be the best time to have the product delivered. You get uncomfortable with the silence and think, *They must be thinking they don't want it.* Then you panic and say, *Okay, how about if I give you another 5% off?* — when the total investment wasn't what the prospect was considering in the first place. That's why you always wait for them to respond before you speak, after asking your consummation question, and why it is so important to keep quiet after you ask your final consummation question. If you have a big mouth, this would be the time to put your foot in it — literally — to keep yourself quiet.

If you start looking around or fidgeting, you distract the customer and let them know how uncomfortable you are. Neither of these scenarios helps you move toward a successful consummation. Try to focus your stress in a way that they will not see or recognize it as a nervous action. For example, recite the ABCs backward to yourself, or wiggle your toes — they can't see that, either. Your stress-release can be that simple.

I had a real challenge mastering this business of not speaking first. I didn't even know what I was doing wrong until an instructor of mine shouted *shut up* at the audience at a seminar I once attended.

The first time I kept quiet, I was prepared for the prospect's reaction. I expected her to sit there quietly. What I wasn't prepared for was the intensity of my own feelings. The silence that followed my final consummation question felt like being buried under a mountain, one stone at a time. I sat there. My insides churned. I bit the inside of my lip, suddenly conscious of every nerve ending in my body.

Finally, the prospect looked me straight in the eye and said *Yes.* After that first time, I never again had much trouble sitting through the silence after asking my consummation question.

Part IV
Building a Business

The 5th Wave By Rich Tennant

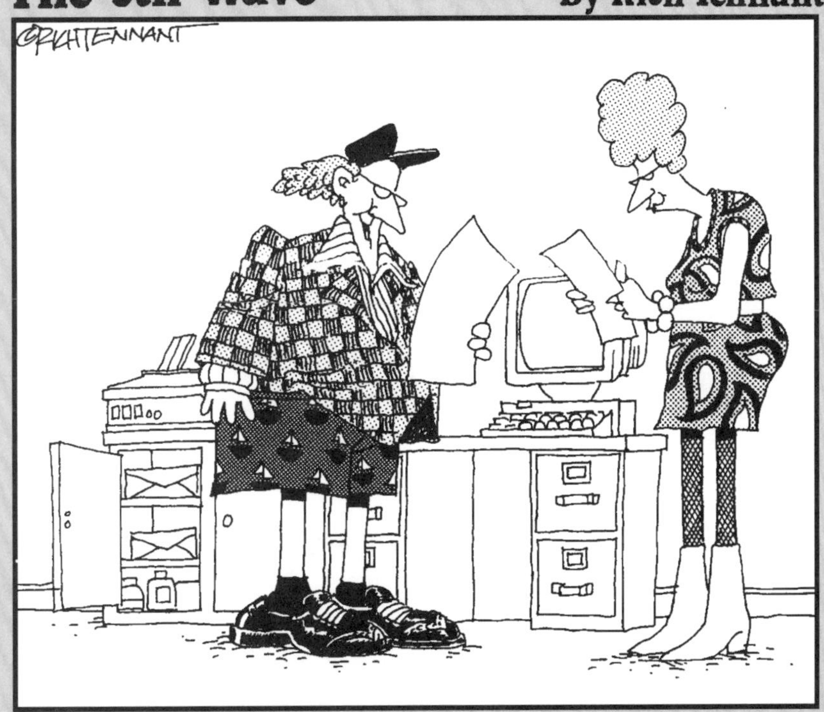

"Don't you agree that a little style goes a long way in making a memorable sales presentation?"

In this part...

If your goal is to build a long-term business or to take your career to great heights, this part is for you. This is where I'll talk about building relationships, not just businesses.

Chapter 13

Tapping into the Strongest Advertising — Your Present Clients

In This Chapter

- How to know a referral when you see one
- How to find a referral when you want one
- Seven downright potent steps to better referrals
- How to set a time and a place for meeting referrals

For many seasoned salespeople, referrals are a major source of new business. Clients who contact you on an existing client's recommendation are usually more inclined than cold-call clients to own your product, service, or idea. Why? Because they already have a positive feeling about you and your offering — and the source of their positive feeling is someone they already know and trust. Prequalified, referred leads are slam dunks: they've already bought you because the person who referred you to them already thinks you're a true pro. With referrals, you enjoy tremendous credibility going in.

Studies show a 60 percent closing ratio with qualified referrals. Compare that impressive figure to a closing ratio of 10 percent with nonqualified nonreferrals, and you get a good idea of how much harder salespeople have to work on cold calls. Don't get left out in the cold. If you can learn to be successful at getting referral business, it just doesn't make sense to give all of those choice customers to your competitors.

Salespeople universally agree that referrals are easier to convince. But some salespeople think it's impossible to control referral business and refuse to give referral methods much attention. Such salespeople take the attitude that attaining referrals is just a haphazard, sometimes-it-happens-and-sometimes-it-doesn't way to prospect. Don't buy into such thinking for a second. Professional salespeople consistently benefit from referral business, so consistently, in fact, that they shoot holes in this theory every day.

As a matter of fact, effective ways to benefit from referral business are what this chapter is all about; this chapter helps you produce a much greater number of leads through practicing a proven, highly effective referral system. The system you're about to learn may not work 100 percent of the time, but even if it works only 50 percent of the time it will generate many more selling situations with clients who look forward to learning about you and your offering.

As with any other sales technique, method is not the only factor to consider when you try to get referrals. Salespeople must show referrals the same positive attitude, the same high energy level, the same respectful manner, and the same quality presentation that they show for cold calls. Remember: Referrals are only partially sold on you or your product. Yet they are willing to give you the opportunity to convince them of your offering's benefits to them.

If you're successful, referrals just keep on coming. Before you know it, you'll create an endless chain of happily involved clients who want to do whatever they can to contribute to your success. Customers love to think that they are partially responsible for your success, and it certainly doesn't hurt to encourage their continued participation and interest in promoting your career.

Whence, When, and How Referrals Arise

With qualified referrals providing you a closing ratio of a whopping 60 percent, you can't afford not to know how to identify and obtain such a substantial increase in your sales. But what if getting referrals isn't all that important to your specific selling situation? You still need to know about referrals: referrals make for good relationships when you freely give them to people in related industries who do thrive on referral business.

One way or the other, then, whether as a source of prospects for your own business or as general PR, referrals play a key part in your success in sales. That's why it's surprising that so many people take part in referral-building activities without recognizing the opportunities.

If only they had read a good overview that would help them recognize referrals when they see them — an overview just like the one you're on the verge of reading right now, for example.

Where do you get referrals?

Referrals are like flies, they're always buzzing around you, but unless they land in your soup, you don't always notice them. The key to success in getting referrals is to become like flypaper and catch all referrals that fly(?) by.

Family and friends

Perhaps the easiest and most accessible referrals are those given to you by family and friends. If you are of the mindset that you don't want to *burden* those close to you by getting them involved in your offering, then you'd better rethink just what it is you are selling. After all, if you really believe in your offering, wouldn't you want the people close to you to enjoy its benefits, too? By assuming that your offering will burden others, you may be cheating them out of all the enjoyment that your offering could give them.

Networking

Networking at business conferences, clubs, professional organizations, and religious gatherings is a way to increase your number of referrals. But the gatherings don't have to be formal affairs. Getting referrals can be as simple as mentioning to others what you do or something exciting that has happened during your busy week of selling. When you're excited, other people will be, too. People are attracted to energetic conversation and happy dispositions — so be a people magnet.

If you're having a particularly great week, share it with the world. Let them enjoy your success! If your week has been particularly trying or difficult, ask for the advice of the people you respect. That can be a way of getting others interested in your business offerings, too. The next time they see you, they'll want to hear your appreciation of the positive affects their advice had for you.

So what have you done in such cases? Through your willingness to share your concerns and victories, you have involved others in your career: other people now have a vested interest in your future success.

Happy customers

Make sure that your sales and service are beyond reproach because negative news spreads like fire through dried country meadows. Slip up just once, even just a little bit, and where it was once comfortable to visit your clients and their associates, it becomes awkward, maybe so much so that you avoid old clients altogether if a bad reputation precedes you.

Satisfied customers tell at least three people about their experience with you. Dissatisfied customers tell at least 11 people. Negative stories generate more sympathy than positive stories do. Don't fan the flames of discontent.

Avoid promising the moon and stars within a two-day delivery period unless you can also twitch your nose like Samantha on *Bewitched* and make it happen. It's so easy to get carried away and tell the client what they want to hear, even when you know your information is inaccurate. In the long run, not only will you lose the disillusioned client, but you also can kiss good-bye all the wonderful referral opportunities they could have steered your way.

If you leave your customer's office with a sale but no referrals, you have unfinished business to attend to — kind of like having a great dinner, but leaving before dessert. It's never too late to get referrals later on during the service of your new clients, but when you leave empty-handed you also deprive your customers.

It's true! What's the first thing you want to do when you shop nonstop for days and then eventually, finally, find a great bargain? You want to tell people about it! What's the first thing you want to do when you buy a beautiful new car? Show people! What's the first thing you want to do when someone comments on what a terrific new whatchamacallit you have? Let them know where they can get one just like it for a great price!

Don't cheat your customers out of all their fun by not giving them the referral tools they need to help others help you.

Other salespeople in your field

It isn't necessary or productive to think of other salespeople in the same or related fields as your enemies. Believe it or not, it's much more profitable to think of them as a possible source for referral business.

If your relationship with other salespeople is based on mutual respect, you'll find other salespeople sending clients your way. Perhaps their company is smaller than yours and unequipped to handle clients beyond such-and-such magnitude. Bingo! They send the Big Clients to you. Or maybe a contact insists on having a feature that your competitor's product does not have — and another prospective client trundles down the turnpike headed right your way.

Of course, it is only common courtesy to return the favor. It's not unusual for salespeople at car dealerships or insurance agencies to recommend another salesperson who is better suited to meet a particular customer's needs. These people are professionals who have the needs of the client at heart and know they would do them a disservice by handling them ineffectively. They also know the value of giving good "customer" service to their fellow salespeople.

Public speaking engagements or teaching appointments

These are great opportunities for referral business, especially if you're the professional chosen to give the presentation or to teach others. When this happens, you're automatically considered the expert in your field. To earn the reputation you've been awarded, you'd better be prepared and handle your presentation well. Compare it to giving your best sales presentation to an audience of 50 or more potential clients all at once. Pretty important, isn't it? I recommend this strategy only to those who can carry it off effectively. Too many people get carried away with the moment of stardom and forget that they're there to build their business, not to audition as a replacement for David Letterman.

I once went to a conference where the speaker provided cards on which participants wrote their names and those of others to contact who would also benefit from attending the conference. Each referral was put on a different card along with comments on why the participants believed that their referrals would enjoy and learn from the conference.

The speaker encouraged us to fill out as many cards as we liked. We then put the cards into a large barrel. Each day of the conference, a member of the speaker's entourage pulled a card from the barrel to see who would win weekend getaways, free admission to advanced seminars, audio- or videocassettes, or books that were being sold at the conference.

At the end of the conference, the speaker had the makings of another conference. What a system!

When do you get referrals?

It's simple! You get referrals *when you ask for them.*

You'd be surprised how many salespeople feel awkward asking for referrals. How do such salespeople "solve" the problem of their awkwardness? They avoid the referral part of the selling situation altogether — and in the process cost themselves and their companies big bucks.

Or some salespeople try to get referrals by asking, *Can you think of anyone else who might be interested?* And, the clients can think of no one who might benefit from the salesperson's offering. Such a salesperson concludes that asking for referral business didn't really work for him.

In reality, it wasn't that it was impossible for these two groups of salespeople to get referrals, but that *it was impossible to get referrals using the methods they were using.* Rather than analyze their methods and try something different, they stopped asking for referrals altogether.

So, specifically now, when *do* you get referrals?

You prepare to get referrals the moment you make contact with someone. From the first words they utter, you should look for areas in which you can help the client isolate names and faces that they can give you later (the names, that is, not the faces). Always listen carefully, not just to what will help the present client, but also to what will help the present client's referrals — your future clients — who may also need your services.

Good referral business comes from customers with whom you have a good relationship. This doesn't necessarily mean that they own your offering. For example, you may have built a good relationship with a customer who for some reason is unable to own your product at this time. If you've kept in close contact and done a good job in building rapport with the customer, though, he more than likely would be only too willing to steer you toward a business associate who can benefit from your product or service. All you have to do is ask.

Although any time is a good time to get referrals, there is one specific time when your chances of getting referrals are better than most. Just after you have successfully closed a sale and the customer is excited about owning your offering, they are usually more than happy to give you referrals, names of other people who need what they now own. Just after the sale is a time when enthusiasm is high and resistance is low.

But don't just plunge in and say, *Do you know anyone else who might want my whatchamacallit?* If you ask in this way, your client probably won't be able to come up with a name. They're too distracted by their new purchase. You have to *prepare* them in the art of giving good referrals.

Seven Steps to Getting Referrals

This easy seven-step process to obtaining referrals will give you so much more success in developing your referral business that you will make it an automatic part of every selling situation. Begin by setting a goal for how many referrals you want from each contact. Start with one and work your way up to where you know the steps so well and they flow so naturally that you'll get at least three with every contact you make.

Get to know these seven steps to getting referrals. The better you know them, the better you'll mine the rich lode of referrals that's just waiting for you in your current clientele.

1. Isolate referrals' faces for your customers.
2. Write referrals' names on cards.
3. Ask qualifying questions about the referrals.
4. Ask for the referrals' addresses.
5. Get the referrals' addresses from the phone book (if the customer doesn't know the addresses).
6. Ask the customer to call and set your appointment with the referrals.
7. Ask if you can use the customer's name when you contact the referral (if the customer shows nervousness or refuses to call).

I'll break down each step and closely examine this referral system so that you can make it an integral part of your successful selling plan.

Step #1: Isolate faces

When you ask for referrals, you have to give them a group of faces to focus on. It is impossible for them to center on one or two faces when their thoughts are bouncing off the wall with their new offering. That means that it's your job to get them focused again. You can refocus your customers by using a method like the one shown in the following hypothetical situation:

SALESPERSON:	Bill, I can see you're excited with your new car, aren't you?
BILL:	Oh, it's sweet. I can't wait to drive it off the lot!
SALESPERSON:	You were a tough negotiator, Bill. I guess it feels good to know that you received a significant savings on the car, too, doesn't it?
BILL:	Yeah! I didn't expect to be able to afford a car this nice!
SALESPERSON:	So tell me, Bill, where do you plan to drive your new car this first week?
BILL:	Well, I'll be going back and forth to work, of course. And I play baseball in a city league every Thursday night. I can't wait to drive up in my new car.
SALESPERSON:	I wish I could be there to see the faces of your co-workers and teammates as well as yours. Bill, is there anyone at your workplace or on your baseball team who is in the market for a new car?

That's what I mean when I advise you to isolate the faces of referrals for your clients. By mentioning work and baseball, the customer focused in on those people he is closest to and with whom he'll be in contact that very week . . . *while* his excitement over his car is still fresh.

Step #2: Write names on cards

When Bill has thought of several people at work and on the team who are in the market for a car, take out a few 3-x-5 index cards and write down their names. Be sure to ask Bill how to spell the names. Keep the cards out so you can make notes of the information Bill gives you. You'll need those notes to qualify the referrals.

Step #3: Ask qualifying questions

While Bill is busy answering questions about the referrals, you should jot down notes to help you remember specific things about them. Here's some information you may want to know when you contact the referrals from this specific example:

- What kind of car do they drive now?
- Would they be the primary drivers of the car?
- How many are in their family? (You need to know what size of car they need.)
- What did they say when you told them you were looking for a new car?

When you get in touch with the referrals, it'll be easy to begin a conversation with them based on the information you already have about them based on Bill's answers to these questions. When you've taken a few notes, hand the index cards to Bill and move on to step #4.

Step #4: Ask for the address and phone number

This step's more difficult because the customer may not know the referral's address offhand.

But don't let that deter you. Don't just settle for the name. There may be several people with the same name in the phone book when you try to look it up later. It is important that you know how to contact the referral.

Step #5: If address is unknown, get the phone book

If your present customer is willing to give you the referral's address but doesn't know the address, reach for the phone book and politely ask the customer if she would be good enough to help you out and look up the address in the phone book.

Your request could be as natural as the one in the following conversation:

SALESPERSON: I don't know about you, Bill, but this has been thirsty work. What would you like to drink, a soda? Or would you prefer coffee?

BILL: Coke's fine with me.

SALESPERSON: Tell you what. While I run to get us some Cokes, would you mind looking up addresses in the phone book so we can get this done?

Ask a question such as this when you hand the customer the phone book, and then leave the room to get the Cokes. At this point, you've all but "closed" on how to contact the referral.

Step #6: Ask your customer to call and set the appointment

This is where we separate the men from the boys, so to speak. This is the step where most novice people balk. They won't even try it. What's important to understand is that this question is simply setting the stage for Step #7. Few people will be comfortable calling to set an appointment for you. What happens, though, is that they'll be so relieved that you offer them Step #7 that they'll jump on it. If you had gone directly from Step #5 to Step #7, you may not have gotten the same response. There is a method to my madness here. Let me show you how this works.

SALESPERSON: Thanks so much for the referrals, Bill. You know, since I won't get to see your excitement when you show off your new car, would you mind calling Jim and sharing your good news with him? Then we can work on arranging a time for me to meet with him.

If your customer is fine with that, then good: start dialing. But if they hesitate and act uncomfortable, take the pressure off immediately.

Step #7: If they act nervous or refuse to call, ask to use their name when you make contact

Some people may not know the referral all that well, or they may feel uncomfortable making the call. If this is the case, let them know you understand their hesitation, but ask if you could bother them for one more favor. Ask for their permission to use their name when you contact the people they referred you to. Most people will be relieved to be let off the hot-seat and be more than happy to give you permission to use their name.

Setting Appointments with Referrals

I discuss referral appointments more in Chapter 14 where I cover assorted follow-up techniques. For now, though, I need to reinforce a few methods for setting referral appointments I just talked about.

One method was to encourage the customer to make the appointment call right after the sale when you're both enthusiastic about the transaction. This is the "get 'em while they're hot" strategy. Although this situation is ideal, if your customer is in a hurry or you sense that he or she is not comfortable with the idea of setting the appointment for you, you should move on to the next step at once. Ask if you can use the customer's name when you make the contact.

When you call someone and you already have an "in" with a close personal friend or respected business associate, you have common ground. You also have the benefit of knowing some pertinent information that could be relevant to getting the appointment.

Before you call such a referral, review the information you wrote on the index card and decide how you will set the stage for this selling situation. If you properly qualified the referral, you know enough about the prospective customer to ask some additional questions to get her involved and interested in your offering.

Through testimonials from your mutual business associate or friend, you are able to inform the referred client what they thought was most attractive or appealing about your offering. Chances are good that your referral will be just as interested in those same special features as his friend or associate was. If she's not interested, keep asking questions until you discover what about your offering does interest her the most.

The following conversation with a referral could have happened just as easy in the earlier selling situation with Bill-the-car-buyer:

SALESPERSON: Hello, Tom, my name is Allen and I work at B & B Motors. I just helped Bill Robinson get his dream car, a new 300Z, and I promised him I would call you and let you know about the special offerings we're having on our Nissans this week. He just bought a beauty and told me you two had been talking together about needing a new car. Tell me, Tom, what are you looking for in a new car?

TOM: Well, I'm not really ready to buy yet. I've just been looking around.

SALESPERSON: What have you seen so far that you like the best?

TOM: Well, what I like and what I can afford are two different things.

SALESPERSON: I hear you. Bill said the same thing. That's why he wanted me to call you and let you know about our special promotion that's going on now. You know, you aren't too far from our dealership. I work late tonight, so I'm available around 6:00 o'clock this evening. I know Bill said you shared his love for fast sports cars. Is that right?

TOM: Yes. But the ones I've seen are so expensive. I think I'm just gonna wait a while.

SALESPERSON: I'll tell you what. Why don't you come on over after work and we'll sit down and you can explain to me your situation. Because of the success of the promotion, our dealership is serving munchies in our lobby in appreciation of our loyal customers. So don't eat first. You can munch out here while we talk. Is 6:00 good for you, or would 6:30 be more convenient?

TOM: Actually, 6:00 is better for me.

SALESPERSON: Great, I'll see you then. Just come to the front desk and ask for Allen Brice.

Not only did this salesperson use the qualifying questions from his referral card; he further qualified Tom by asking more questions. It was more likely that the salesperson would get the appointment because Tom knew that Bill had had a similar car and perhaps some financial concerns — and he knew that he was able to work out a way for Bill to own his dream car. The salesperson's ability to help Tom's friend Bill encouraged Tom to find out if the same would be possible for his situation.

What do you think the chances were of getting the appointment if the salesperson had been making a random cold call? You're right — also known as the "slim-to-none" category.

Will You Get Referral Appointments Every Time?

Of course not. Just like you won't get a sale every time. But you should always try to get referrals, even when you don't persuade or convince the original prospect to get involved with your product or service. Now may not be the right time for them, but that doesn't mean that they don't know anyone else who may be ripe for getting involved with the product, service, or idea you represent.

Many times you can get an appointment with someone referred to you, but an appointment with the referral requires more time and persistent follow-up. People who are referred to you don't have a relationship with you. You need to build it. You have to keep your face and name in their heads and in front of their faces all the time.

I'll grant you that that's not the easiest thing to do when you're busy trying to service old clients and to contact leads you've received from other sources. Often, the ability to get the referral appointment depends on the success of your follow-up program — if, of course, you use one at all. It's disheartening to go through all the work to get referrals, only to lose them because you lack an organized follow-up system.

In Chapter 14, I show you how getting referrals and making appointments are closely linked with practicing proper and creative follow-up methods. When you follow up on those who offered the referrals, they're happy to refer you again when the situation arises. When you follow up on the referrals themselves, you give yourself greater opportunities to increase your profitability. How? By improving your closing ratios through cultivating an effective referral business.

You may not get an appointment with every referral. But then you don't need to in order for referrals to become a highly productive way for you to find new business.

Chapter 14

Following up and Keeping in Touch

In This Chapter

- List after list after list of things you need to know about follow-up
- Like — a list of times when you really, really *need* to follow up
- Like — a list of ways to warm your clients' hearts *when* you follow up
- Like — a list of proven follow-up techniques
- Like — a list of prewritten, uncopyrighted, perfectly stealable follow-up *Thank you* notes
- Like — a list of ways to guarantee more productive follow-up
- Like — is that enough already, or what?

Once you start collecting all these referrals and building your client base, what do you do with them? You put your talents to work to get an appointment with the people who you already know need your offering.

You do this through effective follow-up on your new leads. Even though you have an in with the referred customer, you still have to invest time and energy to get the appointment and sell your offering. But the odds are on your side. Studies show that experienced salespeople spend half of the time selling a referred, qualified lead that they spend selling a nonreferred, nonqualified lead — with the results being a much higher closing ratio.

But hold on — referral business is only one aspect of follow-up that a good salesperson pursues. Practicing *con*sistent and *per*sistent follow-up has been proven to be one of the most important factors in successful selling. That's why it's to your advantage to develop an organized, systematic approach to follow-up while individualizing your chosen methods with your own creative flair.

When to Follow Up, What They Want When You Do

In today's market, more and more professional salespeople are practicing aggressive, thorough follow-up methods that even a few years ago would have been considered unnecessary on some of their marginal inquiries, that is, people don't represent a sale. If your desire is to compete with the big boys and girls, you must make follow-up an important part of your regular selling routine.

Five situations are apropos

It's important to distinguish between the types of follow-up you should make so you handle each prospect appropriately. It also helps to designate how much time you'll commit to following up with each prospect. Obviously, professionals follow up every lead because even the briefest contact or smallest sale can lead to a whole new list of potential referrals for new business.

You must make five types of contact to be a professional at persuasion:

1. Follow-up with referral contacts
2. Follow-up to service the people who are already happily involved with your offering

   You need to contact these people as part of the professional service you provide to them in appreciation of their continued loyalty to you, to your company, and to your offering.
3. Follow-up to inform clients of new-and-improved versions of your offering, reminding them when it is time to consider updating the product or service you may have interested them in several months or years ago
4. Follow-up to get with hard-to-reach prospects who require several contacts to make them one of your clients
5. Follow-up to thank those people who have stuck with you through thick and thin and have been instrumental in helping you to develop your sales career through their long-term patronage

These five groups are your foundation of business. Keeping in touch with them will build your future.

Ten customer concerns are vital

To adopt effective methods of follow-up, the beginner in sales must know the concerns that customers have about service and follow-up. It's only by learning to understand their needs that you can best serve them.

Here's a list, in descending priority, of customers' most important concerns about the selling and servicing of their accounts:

1. Receiving a call that a salesperson promised to make
2. Knowing contact numbers and the best available times to keep in touch with the sales and service people
3. Having the ability to talk to somebody in authority
4. Knowing that the salesperson and the salesperson's company appreciate their business
5. Spending minimal time on hold in order to speak to a real person
6. Being kept informed of ways to keep costs down and productivity up
7. Being informed promptly of potential challenges and quick action on their resolutions
8. Receiving acknowledgment of recognized challenges and accepted responsibility for errors
9. Being addressed politely and receiving personal attention
10. Being given realistic and honest information as it applies to delivery or problem-solving issues

By making follow-up and service a regular part of your day, you can efficiently address all of these customer concerns and maintain an edge over your competitor who may not be as determined to follow up as you are. When you provide excellent service and follow-up with your customers and prospects, you earn the reward of serving the lion's share of all the clients who need your offering.

Four Effective Ways to Follow Up

You already know the need to follow up before and after the sale. Now go one more step. Recognize the most *effective* ways to follow up and when you should use them.

Those two recognitions are the first steps to developing a follow-up program that carries your personal flair. After all, you can expect the best of the best in sales to practice follow-up. That means that you have to be that much better by occasionally creating a more memorable situation or a more thorough, *con*sistent, and *per*sistent follow-up program.

Some of the methods of follow-up that this section presents are common but highly effective ways to keep in touch with your clients. Just as I hope you will do, I've gone a step farther, though, to show you some creative follow-up techniques that you can easily apply to almost any offering.

If you want the customer to remember you and your offering, then you must offer them a memorable experience. If you see follow-up as boring, tedious repetition, you can expect your clients to feel the same way: bored and tired of your constant contacts.

You must *create* a need in your customers or prospects. And believe this: The need you create in your customers is directly proportionate to the enthusiasm and creativity you put into your follow-up program. So make sure that your methods of follow-up — and the messages you give through them — add up to a rewarding and memorable experience for your customers.

Follow-up by phone

Phone follow-up is perhaps the most common, least expensive — and most difficult method of follow-up to turn into a memorable experience. Why? Just look at all the ways your customers can miss you.

The potential client can avoid your calls by using screening devices such as answering machines, secretaries or voice mail. If that's the case, you have to get creative to instill enough curiosity in them to make them want to talk with you. Let's face it, though, most people are just flat out very busy and what you're offering may not be the most important thing in their day — even though it is to you.

Reaching the decision-maker by telephone can be difficult if you aren't creative in your efforts. For example, when you try to reach that high-powered executive on the phone, you probably have to go through a company receptionist, a private secretary, and sometimes even a business partner before you get to the money player. But the real frustration comes only when, at the end of this gauntlet, you discover that you've gone through it all just so the decision-maker can advise you to leave a message on her voice mail or pager!

If you aren't prepared with a creative and tempting message, how often do you think the important decision-makers will return your call as it lines up with the dozens of other sales calls they receive on a daily basis?

Now do you see the value in giving your follow-up your own little flair?

To make your phone calls memorable, prepare a message that will get their attention and pique their curiosity. The people at the top are always looking for ways to improve profitability and productivity to carve out a greater percentage of market share. If you believe that your offering will help them, give them a teaser in the message that will make them want to put your name at the first of their callback list.

A message such as this one, for example, will help you cut through the clutter and connect you with the people in charge:

MESSAGES: I'm sorry you missed my call, but you may still have an opportunity to find out how to increase quality production while decreasing company expenditures in labor and stored inventory.

Look for the informational packet that will be sent to you on May 22. Expect a call back from me, Eric Post, to discuss how you and your company will benefit from our new offer. Or, for immediate information, call me tomorrow morning before 11:00, at 555-0000.

One short phone message such as this one accomplishes several objectives:

1. **It peaks** (to say nothing of piques) **the customer's interest by teasing her with possibilities of how to do her job more efficiently.**

   And did you notice the more subtle ego stroke in the sample message? If not, then *you* need to read item #2. Please proceed to item #2 . . . now.

2. **It tells the executive that you can provide individual as well as company benefits.**

   That's a good habit to get into, whether your offer of individual benefits occurs during follow-up or you incorporate it right into the fabric of your presentation. Stroke the ego of a high-powered executive and show her how she will look good to the corporate elite, and she will be that much more willing to own your offering.

   And there's one other important aspect of this phone message . . .

3. **It gives the customer a specific time to call if she wants to hear more.**

   By being specific, you can schedule your time to remain in your office to receive returned calls. This follow-up technique helps you avoid playing the annoying game of telephone-tag with people you really need to reach.

   If the customer is too busy (or has not been tempted enough) to return your call at the suggested time, you've at least given yourself the opportunity to contact them via direct mail.

And guess what follows the mailing? You got it — another phone call!

Follow-up by direct mail

This is another common method of follow-up, but your mailings can be anything but ordinary. As with phone follow-up, with direct mail, too, you should personalize your program to make it memorable for the customer or prospect.

For example, you can include premiums with your mailings. *Premiums* are offerings that benefit customers when they respond to a mailing. Premiums may include a special promotional discount on your offering or a coupon to use the services included in your mailed package.

Sometimes a mailing includes nothing but a premium. When the premium is the only thing in a mailing, the follow-up's "only" purpose is to build goodwill with your customers. If you use this method of follow-up, let the customer know that you will call them in a few days for their feedback. Your notice about the upcoming call gives you *another* opening to contact them with effective follow-up. It's a win-win situation. Your customer feels valued and you can expect a warm welcome when you contact them in hopes of keeping or receiving their business.

Another personal touch you can give to direct mailings is to include *For Your Information* (*FYI*) materials with a message of how your customers can benefit from them. Such materials may not have anything to do with your personal offering, but they will let your clients know that you were thinking of them.

What are FYI materials? Maybe you recently came across a press release relating to your client's field of expertise; if you did, let your client know about it. Sending the release may be of no direct, immediate benefit to you except as it informs your customers of events that may profit them. But that's precisely why you can benefit from watching out for FYIs that will benefit the people with whom you do business.

The more spontaneous your FYIs are, the more effective they will be. Instead of having your secretary type a formal cover letter for your FYIs, just jot a little handwritten note and attach it to the mailed material. Your note can be as simple as a few lines to let them know that you were thinking about them. Don't forget to include your business card with the note and maybe a little teaser to get them to call.

Follow-up by warm-and-fuzzy

Everybody likes to be appreciated, and I think we can agree that there's precious little positive stroking in this world. So use your follow-up system to let your customers know that you appreciate their business and all the referrals they've sent your way. Warm-and-fuzzy follow-up comes in a form that should become a permanent part of your sales repertoire ASAP — as in sometime yesterday. That form: the deceptively modest thank-you note.

I learned the value and power of thank you notes early in life. When we Hopkins kids were young, our parents occasionally went out with friends for dinner. As most kids do, I often tried to stay awake until my parents came home. On those times when I did manage to stay awake, invariably I saw my mother sit down at her little desk in the hallway as soon as she got home and begin to write.

One time I got up and asked her what she was doing. Her answer came straight out of Emily Post:

> *We had such a wonderful time with our dear friends this evening that I want to jot them a note to thank them for their friendship and the wonderful dinner.*

My mother's simple act of gratitude, expressed to people who already knew that she and my father appreciated and enjoyed their friendship, helped to keep my parents' friendships strong for their entire lifetimes.

Because I understood that building relationships is what selling is all about, I began early in my career to send thank you notes to people. I set a goal to send ten thank you notes every day. That goal meant that I had to meet and get the names of at least ten people every day. I sent thank you notes to people I met briefly, people I showed properties to, people I talked with on the telephone, and people I actually helped to own new homes. I became a thank you note fool.

To this day, on a plane on the way home after a seminar I write thank you notes to students, to my staff, and to the wonderful people I meet at hotels and in taxicabs. And do you know what happens when I go back to those cities? They remember me. They remember that I cared enough to thank them for a job well done or for sharing their time with me.

I believe so strongly in the power of thank you notes that you can find one in the back of every seminar workbook I print. And, if you look real hard, you probably can find my thank you note to you somewhere in the pages of this very book.

I go out of my way to make it easy for my students to get started with the "thank you note" habit by giving them the exact wording they can use for at least ten instances in which thank you notes are appropriate. I give them to you now.

1. ***Thank You* for telephone contact.**

   Thank you for talking with me on the telephone. In today's business world, time is precious. You can rest assured that I will always respect the time you invest as we discuss the possibility of a mutually beneficial business opportunity.

2. ***Thank You* for in-person contact.**

   Thank you for taking time to meet with me. It was a pleasure meeting you, and my thanks are for the time we shared. We have been fortunate to serve many happy clients, and it is my wish to someday be able to serve you. If you have any questions, please don't hesitate to call.

3. ***Thank You* after a demonstration or presentation.**

   Thank you for giving me the opportunity to discuss with you our potential association for the mutual benefit of our firms. We believe that quality, blended with excellent service, is the foundation for a successful business.

4. ***Thank You* after a purchase.**

   Thank you for giving me the opportunity to offer you our finest service. We are confident that you will be happy with this investment toward future growth. My goal now is to offer excellent follow-up service so that you will have no reservation about referring to me others who have needs similar to yours.

5. ***Thank You* for a referral.**

   Thank you for your kind referral. You can rest assured that anyone you refer to me will receive the highest degree of professional service possible.

6. ***Thank You* after final refusal.**

   Thank you for taking time to consider letting me serve you. It is with sincere regrets that your immediate plans do not include making the investment at this time. However, if you need further information or have any questions, please feel free to call. I will keep you posted on new developments and changes that may benefit you.

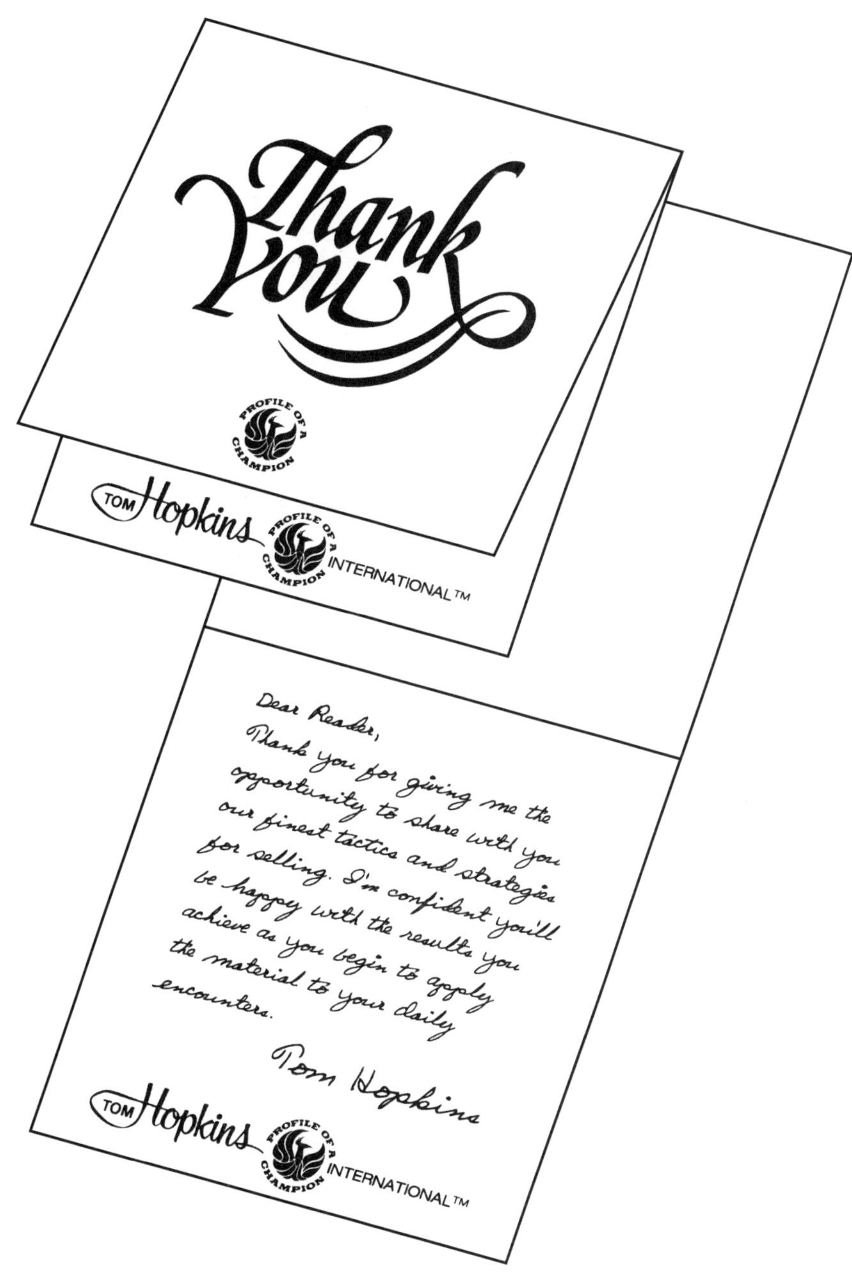
Thank You
PROFILE OF A CHAMPION
TOM Hopkins PROFILE OF A CHAMPION INTERNATIONAL™
Dear Reader,
Thank you for giving me the opportunity to share with you our finest tactics and strategies for selling. I'm confident you'll be happy with the results you achieve as you begin to apply the material to your daily encounters.
Tom Hopkins
TOM Hopkins PROFILE OF A CHAMPION INTERNATIONAL™

7. ***Thank You* after they buy from someone else.**

   Thank you for taking your time to analyze my services. I regret being unable at this time to help you appreciate the benefits that we can provide you. We keep constantly informed of new developments and changes in our industry, though, so I will keep in touch with you in the hope that, in the years ahead, we will be able to do business.

8. ***Thank You* after they buy from someone else but offer you referrals.**

   Thank you for your gracious offer to give me referrals. As we discussed, I am enclosing three of my business cards, and I thank you in advance for placing them in the hands of three of your friends, acquaintances, or relatives whom I might serve. I will keep in touch and be willing to render my services as needed.

9. ***Thank You* to anyone who gives you service.**

   Thank you for your continued and professional service. It is gratifying to meet someone dedicated to doing a good job. I sincerely appreciate your efforts. If my company or I can serve you in any way, please do not hesitate to call.

10. ***Thank You* on an anniversary.**

    With warm regards, I send this note to say hello and, again, thanks for your patronage. We are continually changing and improving our products and service. If you would like an update on our latest advancements, please give me a call.

As you can see, you have many reasons to say, *Thank you.* A thank you note or two to the right person at the right time can go a long way toward building your success.

How? Suppose receptionists or assistants who think they don't get enough recognition do get recognition from you. Will they remember? Of course, they will. Will they feel good about you? Yes. Will they be more receptive to your calls and questions? Probably. You can never go wrong by thanking someone.

If you don't know whether a certain thank you gift is appropriate, ask someone else their opinion even if you have to consult Miss Manners, Emily Post, or Dear Abby. And do note this sidenote, too: Many gifts to customers are tax-deductible to your business. Ask your accountant about this. Your thank you gift could be a *triple*-win for you.

Maybe you just want to thank a prospective customer for her time or give a word of encouragement to a client who was interested but who could not take advantage of your offering because of insurmountable conditions. Let such prospects know that you won't forget about them, that you will keep looking for ways to increase their business so that you can look forward to serving them in the future.

Do you say thank you or send a medal?

If someone has gone *way* out of his or her way to help you, and if you think they deserve a little gift or an extra-special thank you and a thank you is appropriate, then by all means send that person a thank you pronto. This isn't for every time someone does something for you, but for those times when you know that someone has put a lot of his or her effort, time, and energy into something for you. This is for those times that someone has gone "above and beyond the call of duty" for you. Acknowledge that effort and that person. The last thing you want is to become known around that office or by that person as "why, that ungrateful so and so."

If a customer likes classical music, consider sending her a set of tickets to a symphony performance. You may want to send movie tickets to a secretary or assistant. You can thank clients with a round of golf at their favorite course or with lunch for the secretary and her guest to show your gratitude for her extra effort to arrange the appointment that you worked on for a month.

As strange as this may sound, you may even want to send an appreciative follow-up to negative prospects for pointing out potential challenges that you have since been able to correct. Now that would surprise them, wouldn't it? Talk about a memorable follow-up!

Follow-up by networking

Top-producing salespeople have found ways to follow up that are both effective and creative. It may not be too effective to ask your competitors for their methods of follow-up. But other salespeople in your company may be doing creative things that they would be more than willing to share with you.

At your next sales meeting, make a point of discussing different methods of follow-up. This is called networking right at home within your own ranks of salespeople. And don't forget to follow up your discussion on follow-up!

Before you toss all those collected business cards from all those business meetings into the circular file or tuck them away in a file you'll never see again, take the time to go through the cards and write a note about how much you enjoyed the person's input or conversation at the business meeting. If you've been thorough enough to jot down a word or two on the back of each card to remind you of your conversation, you'll have something specific to address when you do your networking follow-up.

So how well do prospects respond to follow-up?

The way that your prospects respond to your follow-up depends entirely on the effectiveness and efficiency of the method of follow-up you use. If you use follow-up with flair, you can expect higher percentages of response from your prospects. Of course, it also depends on whether you've chosen prospects who can benefit from owning your product or service.

Don't get discouraged if some prospects don't respond at all. Sometimes, no matter how good your follow-up, you get zip, zero, zilch for your efforts. If you take the goose egg more times than not, it may be time to evaluate your methods of follow-up and start putting another kind of zip into your messages.

It takes time to tell which methods work best for you and which types of clients respond to one method of follow-up rather than another. So be patient. Don't give up if, after your first few attempts at follow-up, you get disappointing results. Instead, keep seeking ways to improve your follow-up program. Contact other professional salespeople who are willing to listen and look at your follow-up and offer advice.

Good follow-up techniques can sometimes take as long to master as good selling techniques.

You'd be surprised how many people have such a positive response to this type of follow-up; many go out of their way to contact you with future needs! If you follow up shortly after you attend the business breakfast or networking event, you'll more easily recall what everybody said. And another tip: It's also helpful to keep a copy of your correspondence attached to the prospect's card so you can remember them when they call.

Three Ways to Maximize Results from Follow-up

Maximizing results is a great goal to have in handling any contact, not just a follow-up. To do so requires efficiency, having a well-laid plan and good records. In this section we cover just those aspects of follow-up.

In the beginning, impose order

Follow-up sounds so simple when somebody advises you to send a letter or two or to just pick up the phone and make a call, but establishing an effective follow-up system is much more than that. An effective follow-up plan requires you to master and implement the Rule of Six.

The Rule of Six simply states a rule of selling that can increase your sales volume manyfold:

> *In order to make the sale, you should contact prospects six times within a 12-month period.*

Think of all the contacts and prospects you have — now multiply that number by six. When you look at it that way, it's easy to see how some salespeople get overwhelmed with follow-up. In fact, many Champion salespeople hire assistants whose main function is to do prompt and effective follow-up.

This is often not the case for the beginner in sales. The beginner must work extra-hard to provide prompt follow-up to referrals, prospective clients, loyal customers who now own your offering, networking possibilities, and just about everybody you come into contact with during a normal business day — as if there is such a thing as a normal business day!

If follow-up is to be effective, and because it is a constant in the selling process, you must organize your follow-up time and program to ensure that your business stays productive. You have many options for setting up your follow-up system. As I mentioned before, you can use something as simple as a 3-×-5 index card, or your business may require you to use a more sophisticated filing program.

In today's world of high-tech equipment, it may be easiest for you to keep all your follow-up on a program designed to store the maximum amount of information in the minimum amount of space. By setting up a database specially designed for follow-up, you can save time and energy that you can devote to face-to-face selling.

Whatever way you choose to organize your time and the follow-up information you collect, your method should enable you to systematically and periodically keep in touch with all your contacts.

As you schedule your follow-up time, keep your customers informed of the best times to contact you. Be sure that you are accessible at the times you tell them to call. Just by being there, you eliminate telephone tag or the nagging fear that the call you've waited for all week will come when you're out on an appointment.

Let your customers know your working schedule (as much as possible), and they'll appreciate being able to reach you when you say you'll be available. They'll reward you with a warm greeting on the phone or in person when they contact you. Keeping your announced office hours is just another way to let them see how efficiently you run your business and, likewise, how efficiently you would service their needs.

Gauging your nuisance quotient

One of the most important tidbits of sales wisdom is to *avoid harassing your customer.* Sometimes it's hard to know when keeping in touch with your client has crossed the line to downright bothering them. You defeat the entire purpose of follow-up if you fail to recognize the signs of annoyance a customer may be sending your way. If they hang up on you, that's a pretty good sign that you've failed to recognize their annoyance. How many hang-ups do you get on a given day?

Be sensitive to your clients' needs. Don't call them on a Friday before a holiday and try to sell them your new offering over the phone. This is not follow-up; it's irritation. Similarly, don't call at lunchtime or right when the prospect should be going home and expect a long, drawn-out conversation with her undivided attention. Her mind is set on beating a path to the door, not on listening to your offering.

Keep your follow-up short and sweet and do it at times most convenient for your prospects' schedules. Sometimes interruptions are unavoidable, but when too many interruptions occur, give your customers the opportunity to get back with you at a time better suited to their busy schedules.

If, after all the follow-up, you still get a *No* from a client, leave the contact or meeting on a positive note. If you know that their answer was not based on your poor performance, it may still be possible to get a referral from them or do future business with them when their situation changes.

Be polite! Find out when they expect their situation to change and ask their permission to call back again. They may be receptive to hear what you have to say a few short months down the road when they *are* ready to own your offering. If you leave them with a positive feeling and continue to build rapport through constant and persistent follow-up, the only thing stopping them from owning your offering is time — and that, too, shall pass.

If your customer admits that he has bought from your competitor, don't you think you need to discover why he chose your competitor over you? If this situation arises, don't get angry with your prospective customer. Instead, make him feel important by asking him if you can take up just a few more moments of his time to get his advice on how you can improve your sales skills.

If you've invested a lot of time in such a customer, there's a good chance that he will feel obligated to meet with you. These meetings can be the best learning experiences you have. Not only will you find out what you may need to improve, but you will gain new insight into your competitor's offering or into what your competitor says about you and your company. Think of these times as invaluable opportunities to become a better salesperson.

Oh, and don't forget to take this opportunity to follow up with a thanks to the customer for his advice.

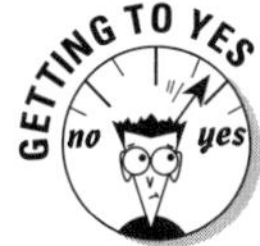

If you're diligent in following up with customers who choose not to own your offering, you may just sneak them away from your competitor the next time they get the itch to own. By keeping in touch with them even better than the salesperson with whom they chose to do business does, you will make the customer wish that they had done business with you. Let them see your organization and care for their well-being through your effective follow-up — and when they need a new-and-improved version of what they now own, they'll probably think of you first.

It's okay to be disappointed and to let your clients know you're sorry not to have the opportunity to do business with them. Let them know that you're not giving up and that you still hope to win their trust. And, for the customers you obtained because of your effective follow-up, you need to remain just as *con*sistent and *per*sistent in the service you provide. Make sure they know that you're concerned about meeting their needs and that you put their needs before your own.

Dear Diary: Follow-up really likes me!

Keep thorough notes on all your follow-ups and the success you have with your current follow-up methods. When you do something great that gets excellent response, write it down in your success journal. Be specific and detailed, and describe the selling situation in which you implemented the successful follow-up method. The more information you record, the more likely you are to repeat the experience.

When customers tell you what you need to work on, put those comments into your success journals, too. Remember: If you take all this time to write down what you do well *and* what you need to improve on, then you should take the time to review your journal periodically and evaluate whatever changes you make.

Sometimes you may need to solicit the help of another professional salesperson in your office to hold you accountable for making the changes you know you need to make and to help you implement such changes constantly. When your colleague sees you kicking back and relaxing, she should have your permission to give you a gentle wake-up call, a reminder of what you said you wanted to do to improve your sales results.

Be a fanatic in follow-up! Even if you haven't hit upon the most creative or memorable way to follow up, practicing follow-up with zeal is better than doing nothing at all. Allow yourself mistakes and time to organize and maintain your chosen follow-up schedule. Expect gradual increases in the number of *yeses* you get. Be diligent about follow-up with your prospects, your customers, and yourself. Above all, think of follow-up as your way to travel the path of sales success.

Part V
You Won't Always Win

"I SENSE YOU'RE IN A HURRY, SO I'LL BE BRIEF."

In this part...

Rejection is a part of life. This part will help you handle the rejections and show you how each rejection actually means more success for you. It also helps you to best use your time and focus on the big picture.

Chapter 15

Handling Failure and Rejection

In This Chapter

- Motivators by the half-dozen
- Demotivators do damage
- Wresting success from failure

No person yet has walked the earth who didn't experience rejection. It just hasn't happened. You're *bound* to experience rejection; it's as inevitable as death and taxes. What will separate you from all those who let themselves get sidetracked by rejection is your attitude toward it.

As you gain more experience in persuading, convincing, or selling others, you also create a protective shell that protects you from the slings and arrows of outrageous rejection. If you don't jump out there and take some of those arrows, you won't learn how to protect yourself, you'll take rejection personally, and you may end up depressing yourself right out of the persuasion business.

The best thing to do is to appreciate the benefits you receive as a result of practicing more sophisticated selling techniques, and to keep learning more about your product, service, or idea so as to offer your clients the most for their investment.

Doesn't sound too difficult, does it? In theory it sounds like a definite winner, but in practice it's hard to continue on the most productive track when rejection and failure rear their ugly heads.

So what is the best weapon to fight those inadequate feelings created by failure and rejection? *Enthusiasm!* It doesn't seem possible that one measly little word like enthusiasm, a word everyone has heard so many times, can make the difference between being a highly successful Champion in sales and an ineffective struggler who refuses to call new prospects or even leave the office for an appointment.

If you're just going through the motions of selling but doing so with little or no enthusiasm for the job, you'll be terribly disappointed with your results on payday. That's what payday is, you know. Your income in selling is in direct proportion to the amount of service you give others. Little service = little income. Lots of service = lots of income.

You won't have much success in serving others unless you are enthusiastic about what you do. As a matter of fact, if enthusiasm isn't present in every selling contact you make, you may as well save yourself and your prospects the time and trouble of showing up at all. You would have been just as productive staying home in your jammies and slippers because clients won't want to get involved with you any more than you want to get them involved.

Dwindling enthusiasm isn't the only concern of professional persuaders, but it is the forerunner of many more difficulties that may short circuit your career. To see what makes enthusiasm such a rare commodity in many sales situations, you need to examine where enthusiasm comes from and why it so easily gives up the ghost to depression and inactivity.

If people knew the secret of why enthusiasm wanes and depression creeps through the back door, it would be easy to see the enemy approach and prepare for its descent on our livelihoods. The hard part about battling the depression experienced because of failure and rejection is that it sneaks in disguised as a friend to bring us comfort, relaxation, or even fun, and we don't recognize depression for what it is: a total thief of our motivation to succeed.

Instead of focusing on why depression happens, I focus on how to overcome such feelings. Keep reading, and you'll see what motivates people and what can be done to increase your own levels of enthusiasm.

Six Motivators

Why do we do what we do? Philosophers, psychologists and psychiatrists have had a field day with that question for hundreds of years. Their constant asking of that question has provided a short list of the most common reasons we give for doing whatever it is we do. Review the list so you can determine what your primary motivator is and how to use that knowledge to spur you on to even greater success.

Money

Many professional salespeople admit to being motivated to sell because they enjoy lighting up the faces of the people they help to benefit from their offering. Few but the candid and outspoken, however, ever say that money motivates them to sell.

Give yourself permission right now to admit that money is a big motivator. It's okay to be money-conscious — as long as the money you make is in direct proportion to the service you give your clients. If that's not the case with you, your money will soon disappear, as will your motivation to strive toward greater achievements in sales.

Money can be one of your motivators, or even your primary motivator, but it cannot be the be-all and end-all of all your sales transactions. Many top producers look at the amount of money they make as a reflection of the excellent service and high sales standards they develop over the years in their industries. When Champion salespeople notice a decline in income, they look to improve service and product knowledge instead of wasting time being depressed about how a drop in income could have happened to them.

Security

Many people say they work to have security. What exactly does that mean? Security is a false motivator. There are no guarantees in life itself, much less in sales; thus, there is no such thing as security.

In fact, you are only as secure as your ability to handle insecurity. Webster says that *security* is *freedom from danger, freedom from fear and anxiety, or freedom from want or deprivation.* If that's the case, then none of us has ever been totally secure. I don't care how successful you are; you have experienced fear and want somewhere along the way. Fear and want can even *motivate* you to achieve. So it isn't the state of being free of these feelings that contributes to security, but rather how we deal with the insecurities that confront us.

The key to getting what you want may be the ability to give up what you have.

Look at this a little closer. If you are bound and determined that you will never take a chance to further your career, then you may as well get out of sales right now because taking risks is what selling is all about. If you can't give up what you have, then keep it; resign yourself to the knowledge that you will never go much farther up the ladder of success.

Most famous and powerful people who have acquired a great deal of security or money have also lost as much (if not more) than they have made. The difference between them and the average worker is that they were willing to take the chance in order to become all that they could be, while the average worker is not willing to take the necessary risks.

Great salespeople follow the same pattern. Be willing to give up what you have for what you can attain — *be a risk-taker.* You may wonder how you ever find security! Actually, with whatever semblance of security you ever find will come the knowledge that you create your own destiny. Your success and security are determined primarily by your ability to overcome the setbacks that your career in sales hands you. And, believe me, in sales you'll have plenty of time to test your ability to be a risk-taker.

Achievement

No person lives who doesn't want to achieve something. Some strive only for modest goals, while others shoot for the moon, but all are in gear to achieve. It is human nature to want to achieve. Few people are born who wander aimlessly through life without at the very least the desire to achieve the basic needs of food and shelter.

All people believe that they should get what they deserve, and, sad, but true, many of us feel we are deserving of greatness whether we work for it or not. In those moments when we're brutally honest with ourselves, I think most of us will admit, we usually get what we deserve.

You may wonder about people who choose to do little or nothing with their lives. Don't be quick to call them failures. Even they are achieving their goals — goals of nonachievement.

Achievement isn't always measured monetarily. Instead, you can measure it by the influence and power one wields, or by the humanitarian efforts given to those in need. Achievement means different things to different people. When you think about it, even the nonachiever has achieved what they set out to do — nothing.

Recognition

For most us, the need for recognition begins in childhood. Think about it. When you were five or six, you probably stood on your head, played dress-up, or did other clever little-kid things that adults thought were adorable just so that you would get attention. Some children have even been known to eat bugs or destroy things, all for the sake of recognition.

Not only do we have a need for recognition, but we also like to be the ones to do the recognizing. Look at much of the media today. It doesn't seem to matter if the recognition is negative or positive; the results are similar. Isn't it ironic how most people recognize the evil but well-publicized face of Charles Manson more quickly than they do the face of someone who has *positively* changed history, someone like Neil Armstrong?

Recognition is a tricky business!

Acceptance from others

Others' acceptance is a dangerous motivator.

You must realize that the day you rise above the masses as a top producer is the same day that others stop trying to climb up to your level. Do you know what they do instead? They try to pull you down to their level. There's a lot of truth in the old adage: *It's lonely at the top!*

When was the last time you heard people say or do things to bring a person down who is already down in the dumps? It just doesn't happen that way. You can always find someone to tell you, *Oh that won't work!* or to say, *Well, that may have worked for them, but do you really believe that you can carry it off?*

The search comes when you try to surround yourself with positive people who support you in your efforts toward a successful career. Why not make it your philosophy to keep company with people who have similar goals and desires as yours. Try to get the acceptance of the people who you know are good for you — and try to get the dismissal of the people who are not. When you think about it, how many people in your lifetime have you accepted advice from who are more messed up than you? Stay away from the negative people: they only pull your opportunities down the tubes with them.

Self-acceptance

When you accept yourself and are happy with the person you are, you experience a freedom you never thought possible. You are free to do things your own way or not to do them at all. You are free to enjoy life and all the wonders it has to offer. You are free of the damaging effects of rejection and failure.

Sounds pretty ideal, doesn't it? The difficult thing about having self-acceptance is that in order for it to become a reality, you must first have all the other motivators in place:

- You cannot accept yourself if you have no acceptance from others; you cannot accept yourself if you do not receive positive recognition for the good you do.
- You cannot get recognition if you have achieved nothing.
- You cannot attempt the things you want to achieve without first having a sense of security in your ability to do so.

And what exactly is *achieving success,* anyway? We're taught to measure our success by how much money we have, so self-acceptance runs neck-and-neck with the amount of money we accumulate.

When you truly accept yourself, you can do what you want to do and not what you think you must do. Life is much sweeter, and wonderful things and people seem to gravitate toward you. Like people, all motivators are interrelated. You are not in this alone, so what you do or don't do may profoundly affect many others in your sphere of influence.

Remember that the next time you're tempted to do something which you instinctively know is not the best thing for you to do. Whichever way you look at it, you are not alone in this universe and the rippling effect is alive and well, especially in the sales industry.

Why Don't We Get Equal Shares of Motivation?

If motivators are what make you move forward toward successful sales careers and demotivators cause you to stop dead in your tracks or even go backward, why wouldn't everyone just do the things that motivate them? Believe it or not, it's because the average human being is more demotivated than motivated. Negativity is kind of like gravity — a powerful force that can hold you back and requires tremendous effort to overcome.

As important as it is to know what motivates you to succeed, it is just as beneficial to recognize the danger signals that will bring your career to a halt. Here are four of the most powerful demotivators that stop people from achieving.

Loss of security

Do you know how many people are afraid to give up their security or money? When you begin your new career in sales, you often have to spend money to make money. Think of it as a business investment, an investment in your future.

Even large corporations spend money on training their sales force and creating goodwill with prospective clients, so what makes you think you're any different? To build your business, you must invest time and money. You have to sacrifice your fear of losing your security.

Self-doubt

Self-doubt is a big demotivator in selling. I can hear what some of your family members probably said the day you told them you were going into sales: *What? Are you crazy?* or *Selling . . . It's feast or famine!* or *Can you get me stuff wholesale?*

They have yet to discover what you and I already know: Selling is one of the few things left that when you overcome self-doubts and learn the strategies of selling you become one of the most secure people around.

Most beginners in sales busy themselves with the unnecessary question of *What did I do wrong?* when they do not succeed in their selling attempts. The difference between Champions and novices is that Champions ask themselves a different question: *What did I do* right*?*

Once again, it's just a different way to look at things. Once the Champion examines what was right about the sale, it's easy to keep doing what was right over and over again. The professional in sales has learned this important lesson:

> *The only way you ever learn what to do right in selling is by doing it wrong, keeping your enthusiasm, learning what to do, overcoming that pain, and just keep on keeping on!*

The only way to overcome self-doubts is to face them, look them in the eye, and stare them down by doing the exact opposite of what they make you feel like doing. Don't give in to your self-doubts.

Fear of failure

A great many people are so afraid of failing that they just quit trying. *There's* a surefire way to never experience failure — never attempt anything! Of course, you won't experience any successes, either, so you throw out the baby with the bathwater. You will never *not* close the sale if you never meet the client. If you were to stay home in bed all day long, you are guaranteed never to fail.

Not a very good trade? Instead, I recommend that you live by this principle:

> *Do what you fear the most and you control your fear.*

If you're afraid of one of the required aspects of selling, such as phoning for appointments, you're going to need to face it down if you truly want to succeed in sales. Almost anything you do that you once feared doing turns out to be much easier to do than you thought. The process gets easier each time you make yourself do what you fear until, one day, you forget how badly you feared what you feared so much only a few months before.

Control your fears, and you will receive such gratification that soon you will burn with anticipation to do what you once dreaded. Bungee jumping anyone?

The pain in change

Change is a fierce opponent of progress. You've probably often heard statements such as these:

We've always done it this way.

You'll get used to it — it's just my way of doing things.

We prefer to stay with the standard procedure.

Workers really don't favor the old ways, though. Instead, what they really favor is resisting the pain in change. If they only knew for certain that the potential benefits in making change far outweigh the pains, their resistance would quickly dissipate.

The hardest thing for most salespeople to do is to prospect. Wouldn't it be wonderful to just hang around the lobby or the office and wait for people to come through the doors begging for your product? Dream on!

If you can

- push yourself to make your calls
- get out of the office
- meet with the people who need to hear about your offering
- and call back the difficult clients you sometimes wish you'd never heard of

If you can take all of those steps, then you are on the road to sales success. You don't have to depend on or blame your company when business is bad. You are responsible for your own success or failure, whatever the case may be — so take charge.

By the way, doing what you don't want to do is what you are paid the most to do. You really have to *want* to change. It's still necessary to be satisfied with yourself today, but if you want more tomorrow, then you must be willing to put up with the pain of change. It takes 21 days to effect change according to Dr. Maxwell Maltz, former plastic surgeon and developer of psycho-cybernetics.

For example, it will take about 21 days of concentrating and studying the material in this book for this material to become a part of you. That's the painful part. No pain, no gain.

Champions' Anti-Failure Formula

What's the first word your mother and father taught you when you were a baby?

No!

Ah, those were the days, now weren't they? And why do you suppose this was the first word you learned? Obviously, because your parents wanted to protect you from painful experiences.

The eternal conflict between motivators and demotivators

Motivators and demotivators are powerful opposing forces that work to contradict themselves in your selling situations. If you are unable to maintain a high level of enthusiasm, you demotivate and enter your danger zone. When you are in this place, one of two things happens: either you become withdrawn or you become hostile. Not a pretty picture, is it?

On the other hand, when you are motivated, happily striving for security, recognition, and the other motivators, you are more likely to be in your comfort zone and encouraged to keep performing, reaching ever higher levels of achievement.

Of course, discomfort could be a catalyst to get you moving since our main goal in life remains to be comfortable. However, once the momentum builds, your enthusiasm will carry you to a new comfortable level of performance.

Keep in mind that many of the people you meet as prospective clients will be in their danger zones when you meet them simply because they are having to meet with salespeople. It's a common fear that we covered in Chapter 5. You can easily identify their attitudes by one of the same two things that can affect you: withdrawal or hostility. Your job as an experienced salesperson is to take your clients *from* their danger zone and help them *into* their comfort zone. Such a transfer is mutually beneficial: you cannot close the sale if they are in their danger zone, and they are incapable of production if they are too preoccupied with negative feelings.

Turning these negative situations into positive ones is what makes selling so exciting. It's really a kick to enter the office of a hostile or withdrawn executive and leave him or her an hour later with a smile on his or her face and a positive attitude with which to face the rest of the day. What an experience!

But all you knew as a child was that *no* kept you from getting what you wanted. So, as you grew older and kept hearing *no,* you didn't give up quite as easily as when you were a baby. No ("no" pun intended), you caught onto this persuasion stuff early on when you realized that *No* doesn't necessarily mean *No! Absolutely not! Never! No way!* and you tried to cajole your parents to see things differently — even if it involved holding your breath and turning several lovely shades of blue.

It's the same way in your selling career. When you begin in sales and you hear *No,* you think it's the end of the discussion. Some beginning salespeople even relate stories of how they never got completely through their prepared presentation because the moment the client said *No* the salespeople slid out the door quicker than a pat of butter on hot pancakes.

As they matured in sales, though, their stories changed. *No* took on different meanings. *No* came to mean many things besides a plain old final everyday *No.* These salespeople began to realize that *No* could mean

- Slow down!

Or

- Explain that part a little more.

Or

- You haven't presented the feature I'm most interested in yet.

Or

- You need to ask more questions about my likes and dislikes.

Or

- I don't want to part with that much money right now.

These salespeople realized — as one of their first steps toward professionalism — that they could overcome *all* those things instead of having to slip out the back door with their tail tucked between their legs.

Now, about this Champions' anti-failure formula: use it only when you know you have no chance to get to *Yes* during your meeting. If you follow this formula, you will be able to look at every *No* you receive as money in your pocket.

Here's the formula. Suppose that you earn $100 for the closing of a sale.

1 Sale =  *=$100*

Of course, as a Champion you operate on sales ratios. You should know your ratio of sales per contact and strive daily to improve your ratios. For the sake of this formula, let's say that, for every 10 contacts you make, you receive 1 sale.

10 Contacts = 1 Sale

That means that nine of ten people say *No.* If one person says *Yes* and you receive $100 for that *Yes,* how much then is each *No* worth? Right — $10. Every rejection you get brings you that much closer to that $100.

So what does that knowledge do for you? If you concentrate on it, you will see every *No* as a moneymaker instead of getting down on yourself when the prospect gives you a *No.* Instead of getting angry or feeling as though you've wasted an hour of your day, think of a *No* as just being handed $10 and just getting one step closer to your goal.

Here's another way to look at it: If you work with a client who has said *No* many times, but you persist in your attempts for a *Yes,* then you may sit through $200 to $300 dollars worth of No's in that one meeting when it results in a long-term sales relationship. Just keep asking. Don't fear rejection. Welcome the admiration they will have for you when they realize that you hung in there to the end.

Five Attitudes toward Failure

OK, so to be totally realistic, admit here and now that you will experience nonsuccess at least once or twice a day when you're new. How you handle that experience will determine how far and how fast you'll start seeing sales or persuasion success. There are five strategies I've been teaching students for many years, based upon the works of one of my teachers and fellow speaker, Art Mortell.

1. I never see failure as failure, but only as a learning experience.

When you demonstrate your product to a disinterested party, when you are rejected by a prospect, or when you thought you had your offering sold and the transaction falls through, you can react in one of two ways:

1. You can get angry and unproductive.
2. You can get serious about investigating the reasons for the failure.

I recommend option #2. When you discover what went wrong, you can avoid those pitfalls next time.

Look at the tremendous negatives Thomas Edison overcame when he invented the light bulb. It took over 1,000 failed experiments before he succeeded. But, because of Edison's persistence, today we have the light bulb, an invention that has changed our quality of life.

Can you imagine receiving a big fat *No* to what you want to achieve — more than 1,000 times — and still persisting? What fortitude! The priceless part of the story of the light bulb, though, is Edison's comments in response to questions about how he felt after experiencing all that failure:

> *I did not fail a thousand times. I only learned a thousand ways that it wouldn't work.*

You see? It's all in the way you look at things.

2. I never see failure as failure, but only as the negative feedback I need in order to change my direction.

What a delightful way to look at rejection! Because that's really all that negative feedback is: feedback to get you on course again. When a client never gives you any negative feedback and loves everything presented in your offering yet still decides not to own, you have nowhere to turn. It's almost impossible to close a client like that.

It helps if you think of yourself as a torpedo being guided by a machine that feeds you negative information only to keep you on course. If you veer to the left, the machine says *No* and guides you back to point A. Through a series of *No* corrections, the torpedo makes it to its proper destination.

But what if the torpedo's feelings got hurt from all this negative input and entered its danger zone? What are the two things that occur when you enter into your danger zone? Withdrawal or hostility.

So what would happen if the torpedo decided it couldn't take any more rejection and returned back home? *Bam* to the mother ship.

Or what if the torpedo took the rejection personally and decided to take it out on the closest target? An innocent victim gets hurt.

If you take negatives personally, not only will you not reach your destination, but others around you will share in your untimely explosions. That's why some salespeople lose it right in the midst of their officemates and why some just stop showing up at the office and stay in bed all day feeling sorry for themselves. When the torpedoes hit the wrong target everybody loses!

3. I never see failure as failure, but only as the opportunity to develop my sense of humor.

Can you remember having an absolutely disastrous meeting with a prospect? At the time, you wanted to crawl in a hole and never see daylight again. But what did you find yourself doing about two weeks down the road? Sure enough, after a little time to heal, you tell the story to your peers, embellishing it to provide special effects, and everyone gets a good laugh.

What you have to learn to do is to laugh sooner. Laughter is a powerful tool in healing hurt feelings and wounded pride. As a matter of fact, when you share your humorous stories with other salespeople, you learn that similar things have happened to them. Misery loves company, you know!

4. I never see failure as failure, but only as the opportunity to practice my techniques and perfect my performance.

What happens when you do everything you were supposed to do and the client *still* doesn't decide to own your offering? What have they given you? That's right! They've given you an opportunity to practice and perfect your selling skills.

5. I never see failure as failure, but only as the game I must play to win.

Selling is a percentage game — a game of numbers. The person who sees more people and faces more rejection also makes more money. So, even if you haven't gambled before, you begin to do just that when you get into the game of sales.

Develop these five attitudes toward failure and you'll begin to have more fun with your selling situations than you ever have before. In learning from all of your experiences and playing the numbers, you'll begin refining your skills and having more success, too.

In life, it is not the number of times you fail that count, but the number of times you succeed.

The Champion's Creed

I have one more suggestion for you as a way to keep your attitude up when things are down. I call it my Champion's Creed. I dubbed my students as Champions many years ago because they were striving to reach that status in their selling careers by attending my seminars and learning the techniques I used to become successful in sales. This creed was created for them and since you're striving to learn or improve your selling skills, now it's for you, too. Here goes:

I'm not judged by the number of times I fail but by the number of times I succeed.

And the number of times I succeed is in direct proportion to the number of times I can fail and keep trying.

This is so true and if you focus on your successes through your success journal and sales records you'll have an easier time recovering from every non-success you encounter.

Chapter 16

Setting Goals Keeps You Focused

In This Chapter

- Five (count 'em) five ways to set effective goals
- An order to commit yourself to your success
- What may be the first contract you won't mind binding yourself to
- Authentic participation from our live studio audience
- One law that gets the best of Murphy's poor little law, hands down

Success should be something you don't just kinda-sorta want to reach, but something you *must* reach. Those who acheive the most burn with a "have to" not a "want to."

If you have no concrete goals and you've been succeeding in spite of yourself, just think of how much more success you would enjoy if you set your sights on a definite path and had a specific timeframe in which you expect to reach your destination. If you're a newcomer to sales, and you think you don't need to set goals — think again. The sooner you map a course of success, the more likely you are to reach what you want.

Even though you don't need to set goals in order to reach some level of selling success, most professionals who fail to set goals reach a peak in their selling skills and lack either the motivation or the direction to go beyond it. They never move upward to a higher selling status.

What they don't know — and what you *should* know — is that goals give you three distinct benefits that help you succeed:

- Goals keep you on track.
- Goals let you know when and what to celebrate.
- Goals give you a focused plan to sell by.

And, if nothing else, goals let others know what they have to shoot for to keep up with your standards of selling.

You've Got to Set Effective Goals

Give yourself the time and privacy you need in order to think out what would make you happy, about what would motivate you to sell with the big boys and girls. Obviously, you had some vague notions of success in mind when you first considered selling. Now you need to turn those notions into specific, vivid pictures that entice you when you feel like packing it all in and running away to a deserted isle somewhere in the Pacific to lay on the beach all day watching your toenails grow.

Avoid knocking yourself out and ending up setting no goals out of fear that the goals you set will be wrong. So what if they are? Are the Goals Police going to come to your front door and ask to do a goals audit? I don't think so! Goals are maps, but sometimes maps change and include unfinished roads or roads that you must detour around while improvement is underway.

But setting goals that you may need to change later is better than not setting any goals at all. When you're in the beginning stages of goal-setting, you need to remember two things:

1. **The goal must be better than your best — but believable.**

   Don't set a goal that you don't think you can reach. The trick to setting goals is to make them high enough to push you to strong levels of performance, yet reasonable enough that you can envision reaching them. If you set goals you don't think you can reach, then you most likely won't pay the price to reach them when the going gets tough.

   Another aspect that weakens your resolve to achieve is when you talk yourself into achievement, yet you still aren't quite convinced that achieving your goals is a possibility. When others try to dissuade you or feed you negatives, your belief system and ability to focus on your goals can start to lose strength like an air-filled balloon with a slow leak. You get deflated and don't continue to act on the achievement of those goals. Eventually the desire for your goals will flicker and fade away. You feel strong until someone says *No way,* and then little seeds of doubt start growing until you're convinced that you chose the wrong path. All that really happens is that your own insecurities prohibit you from achieving anything, including happiness.

   So set believable goals and stick to your guns. Don't be tossed around by others who think they know more than you do about what's best for you.

2. **Set goals based on productivity, not on production.**

   If you set goals based on the money you want to make, you're setting yourself up for failure. It's better to set productivity goals; they'll guide you on how many people you must contact in a week or how many calls you must make. Productivity precedes production anyway, so if you set production goals you're jumping the gun. Actively pursue your productivity goals and increased production will result.

Keeping these two rules of goal setting in mind will help you to form and stay committed to what is important in your life.

Time yourself — by years, by decades

Begin with long-term goals and work backwards. Your long-term goals are probably the hardest to set anyway, so if you set those first you accomplish the tough stuff right up front.

Long-term goals should be 20-year projections. Granted, if you're 75, your 20-year goal may be just to plant both feet on the ground each morning. In all seriousness, it's hard to picture what you want your life to be like 20 years from today. Knowing full well that those goals may change, though, you should *set them anyway.*

Three areas you may want to consider when you set your long-term goals are personal accomplishments, status symbols, and net worth.

And three other ideas to keep in mind are the three main phases of the goals you set for yourself. The breathtakingly imaginative names of these three phases are

- Long-term goals
- Medium-range goals
- Short-term goals

Each phase offers its own special set of concerns.

Long-term goals. When you set long-term goals, be specific. Instead of saying,

> *In 20 years I want to live in a large house and be financially independent.*

you should say,

> *In 20 years, in June of 2015, I want to live in a large beachfront house by the Pacific Ocean, on property that covers about 50,000 square feet, and I want to own it free and clear with $1,000,000,000 in the bank.*

Get the picture? Your long-range goals don't have to be this grand, but they do need to be this specific.

Medium-range goals. When you finish setting your long-term goals, cut them in half and set medium-range goals for about 10 years down the road. Compare your 10-year goals to your 20-year goals, and then determine the activity you need to keep to make those goals a reality. Next, divide your 10-year goals into 5-year goals, and so on, and so on. When you get to your short-term one-year goals, divide them into months, weeks, and even days. Your medium-range goals will be your largest and perhaps fuzziest area, the goals you'll probably have to adjust the most frequently.

Be specific to be terrific

As my example above indicated, it's vital that you be specific when writing your goals. The mind is a goal-seeking device. If you don't have a perfectly clear idea of what you want, how can your mind start seeking it?

As an example, I'll use a computer. If you enter into your computer something as vague as *Find the letter that I talked about Aunt Mary's operation in,* how quickly and easily would it be to find that document? Your computer would probably come back to you with "No file found." You weren't clear enough about what it was to seek.

The computer, like your mind, is a slave to your desires, but can only operate within a certain set of very specific parameters. Proper goal setting involves using the most specific parameters you can come up with so your mind can go to work for you.

Short-term goals. Surprise, surprise: Your short-term goals will demand most of your attention.

For best results with short-term goals, never set them for any longer than 90 days. Short-term goals for anything longer than 90 days aren't immediate enough to create a sense of emergency. And another good thing to do: Immediately after you set short-term goals, start taking steps to reach them. That way, they take root as real, not-to-be-denied entities in your mind — not tomorrow, not next week, but as soon as you make them.

For example, if one of your short-term goals is to buy a Cadillac, then go down and order one that you can pick up in 90 days. That will light a fire under you, don't you think? Talk about making it a reality!

You can also use this last goal-setting strategy to test your belief in your goals. If you feel too pressured to reach a goal right after you set it, then you're not sure you can reach your goals. You see, if your belief were real, ordering the car would just excite you to get actively involved in its achievement.

Set a well-balanced diet of goals

It's important to set personal as well as career goals to keep your life well-balanced. If all your goals are business goals, you'll have trouble taking time out for family and friends because you'll always be pushing toward the next career goal.

Although I encourage you to pursue your business goals with fervor, I also encourage you not to pursue them at the expense of family, friends, or time out for yourself. If you do, you risk becoming so one-track-minded that you will eliminate the human qualities you need in order to succeed in sales. Nobody wants to do business with someone who is too busy to understand and care about their needs. Setting personal goals gives you life both in and after business.

Enlist the spouse, the kids, the in-laws, the pet, the . . .

Let your family help you set your goals. If you do, they'll more likely understand when, say, you have to spend a late night working or invest in a two-day training seminar — in Hawaii, while the family is shoveling snow off the porch in Minneapolis. Your family is more willing to share in your sacrifices if you let them share in the celebration of achieving your goals, as well.

Another benefit from involving the entire family is that they hold you accountable for your part of the goal and will do what it takes to motivate you. Have you ever thought that sleeping an extra few hours is just what you need, only to have your spouse encourage you to get up and get busy earning your share of that trip that you both set as a mutual short-term goal? You knew you should get up, but your immediate desire for sleep clouded your judgment. How do you think you'd feel, and what message would you send to your spouse, by showing him or her that sleeping is more important to you than working to achieve shared goals?

Put your goals in writing

Now that you've set goals and allowed your family to share in the process, it's time to make your final commitment to your goals by putting them in writing. This is the single, most vital step in goal setting. Writing down your goals makes them something you can grab onto. The day you write down your goals is the day you commit yourself to reaching them. Until they're in writing, they're merely wishes and dreams. And after you write them down, your mind will start seeking out whatever it will take to make them a reality, then it's time to practice *In Your Face* goals viewing.

In Your Face goals viewing is an art. For maximum effect, put your list of goals where you can look at them often. When you'd rather nap, remind yourself how important it is to get your behind out of bed and do what you know you have to do to succeed. Each time you accomplish a step toward achievement, visibly scratch a line through that step.

That's the basic formula for proper *In Your Face* goals viewing (and you thought this book didn't come with any extras, didn't you?). *In Your Face* is great if you need a tangible reminder of how far you've come toward your goals. What's better, *In Your Face* encourages you to complete the effort. No matter how tough it gets, who wants to put their foot on a banana peel when they're right at the brink of reaching their goals?

Commit yourself to succeed

The harder you work toward a goal, the sweeter the taste of success. Don't think for a second that your road to success won't be painful at times. If you don't experience at least a little bit of stretching to achieve your goals, you probably haven't set them high enough to challenge you. And if your goals *aren't* high enough, then they may be holding you back, making you content to reach levels that are no big deal for you.

When the road gets rocky, dig in your heels and get so single-minded that nothing can distract you from your goals. The people who persevere today produce tomorrow. It's not natural for us to give up immediate gratification or to postpone what would satisfy us today for a promise of greater things to come down the road; in today's instant-gratification society, long-term gains are almost unheard of. Don't sell yourself short by settling for what you know will bring you only temporary satisfaction. If you settle for less than your goals, that's exactly what you end up with — less.

If you're determined and enthusiastic about your goals, you won't settle or waiver. Your resolve helps you keep a vivid picture in your mind of what you want to happen and how you will make it happen. If your imagination isn't vivid enough, cut out pictures or write detailed descriptions of your goals so that you can refer to them when you get distracted. The more reminders you force yourself to bump into, the more determined you are — and the more determined you are, the more goals you will achieve.

An effective tool to help you reach your goals is a binding contract in which you commit to reaching your goals. Such contracts are hard to recognize in the wild, but if you see something that looks like the *Proposal and Agreement* in the nearby sidebar, you're probably face to face with a bona fide self-contract.

Take all of your goals *extremely* seriously, no matter how small each goal. Reward yourself and congratulate yourself for starting the habit of planning your life. You will reap unbelievable rewards.

If you want your life to change, then *you* have to change it or you are going to stay pretty much the same as you are. So set some goals that turn you on and get your life into gear. All you have to do is make the effort to do it. You can change and become or do anything you want. Just want!

Proposal and Agreement

It may seem silly to talk to yourself in the mirror, but think about it for a minute: If someone looks you in the eye when he or she makes a statement, it makes you have more faith in what that person is saying. There's an element of belief, trust, and confidence with eye contact. That's why I recommend using a mirror. It's easy to make plans in your head and even write them down, but when you have to look yourself in the eye and say them you'll see whether or not you're confident enough in your ability to achieve them. If you see doubt in your eyes, you'll know you need to modify the goal and make it more believable.

Binding Contract of Commitment with the Person in the Mirror

________________19________

Name____________________________

The undersigned proposes to furnish all materials and perform all labor necessary to complete the following goal:

____

____

____

____

____

I hereby swear to start today to reach out and do more with my life and achieve the greatness that I know lies within me, which is waiting to be brought out.

From this day forward, I will not deny myself any longer. Today is the day when I finally get the guts to do what I know I must do and quit taking the easy way out. I will pay the price that is necessary to reach this goal because I know the pain of not fulfilling myself is greater than the pain of doing any job, no matter how hard the job may be.

I understand that I will reach my life's plan by reaching one goal at a time, each smaller goal putting me one step closer to my greater future. I understand that each contract I fulfill always puts me one step closer to what I want out of life, and I will not have to settle for what others give me or for just earning a living. I have the power to change my life.

____

Signature of Commitment

As I endorse this contract, I understand that my future is in my hands only and I can look to no one else for its fulfillment.

Acceptance

I, as agent for the face in the mirror, on the completion of this goal congratulate you for proving once again that you can do anything that you want and be anything that you want. You also can get anything you want as long as you know what it is.

You have taken one more step toward being the person you dream of. You may take pride in knowing that you have the backbone to plan and reach a goal.

You are now one step closer to your major goal. As you know, major goals are just a string of successful small goals that lead you to the top.

____

Agent for the Face in the Mirror

Date Fulfilled ____________________ 19_______

Terms and Conditions

1. Any goal you ever include in this contract, no matter how small, must be treated with great respect because the achievement of goals builds your character and self-image.
2. This contract must be filled out in full and dated with starting and completion dates.
3. Your goal must be precise and explicit. It must paint a very clear picture of what you want and when you want it.
4. In front of the mirror every day, you must read all of your contracts that you have not completed, and you must read them with great conviction so as to imbed your goals into your subconscious mind.
5. When a you reach a goal, you must sign as agent for *The Face in the Mirror* and then write, in large red letters on the face of the contract, *This contract fulfilled.* You must save all fulfilled contracts and keep them in order by date completed, so that you may see a pattern of growth.
6. You must remember that you can be as great as anyone, but you also must remember that you have a plan. Each goal in your plan, no matter how small, must become part of your larger plan; when it does, it may then help you to turn your beautiful dreams into a fantastic, rewarding life.
7. Do not make conflicting goals, such as *I will spend more time at home* and *I will double my sales,* for they may not work together and may cause frustration in your life.
8. Your goals must entice you so intensely that they ignite your soul and make you burn with enthusiasm.
9. You cannot reach a destination if you do not know how to get there. Each goal becomes a stopping point or starting point on the road map of your life, which in turn becomes the blueprint for your every success. If you don't have a blueprint, then, how are you going to build your life?

Goals review

Follow these four steps in goal-achieving, and you'll be on the straight-and-narrow road to reaching your goals:

1. Goals must be in writing.
2. Goals must be vividly imagined.
3. Goals must be ardently desired.
4. Goals must be sincerely committed to.

If you have all four of these things in place with your goals and you review them daily, you will soon find yourself making great headway toward their achievement. You will be focused both consciously and subconsciously on seeking out the means to your chosen end.

Results to Expect When You Practice Goal-Setting

To accomplish anything in life, it helps if you have some idea of what you want as the results of your actions. That's called setting a goal.

Really now, what's the goal of goal-setting?

That's a fair question. Obviously, setting goals is not the only answer for the many challenges that can plague a selling career. But they do help to provide a strong start on the road to success.

One challenge that setting and working toward goals does help you overcome is procrastination. There's nothing like having clearly defined goals to keep you busy. They will inspire you so much that there may be times when you don't want to take breaks to eat or sleep, but don't let that happen. The journey to success isn't much fun if you trash your body along the way.

With goals in place, suddenly you're motivated as never before. You have a map or blueprint for successful selling, you have others holding you accountable for doing what you promised, and you have daily tasks that keep you from spending most of your day chit-chatting with your officemates.

To reach your goals, you have to get after it every hour of every day. For every hour you waste by being unproductive, you must work that much harder to make it up if you're to attain your goals. Your purpose isn't just about what you want anymore; it's about the promises you made to your family and peers —

and to yourself — about what you plan to do this year. You don't want to let others down, so get out there and actively participate in the goals you wrote and pictured.

Okay, so what do you do when you achieve your goals?

The funny thing about achieving your goals is that as you get close to achieving them and you look back, the struggle to achieve them doesn't seem as difficult as you had originally thought. Time has a way of blurring the gory details of the grind.

As an example, think back now to what you were doing five years ago. Now think forward five years. Which seems longer? If you're like most people, the future always seems to loom out there longer because we don't know everything that will happen and how our lives will take shape.

Once you get in the habit of setting goals, you'll find yourself looking toward the next set of goals before you close on those you're about to achieve. That's good. Remember, success is the journey, not the arriving. We don't want to plan when we'll be done with goals. There's a real advantage to always keeping your eyes on the future and the opportunities it can bring your way. Soon you get so caught up in the goal-setting process that achieving your goals becomes reward enough.

One of the first things you want to do when you achieve your goals is to celebrate your success. When you celebrate, involve everyone you involved in the setting and accomplishing of your goals. And, when you celebrate, keep these pointers in mind:

- **Celebrate in proportion to your achievement.**

  For example, don't give yourself a trip to Hawaii for calling 100 people in one month. 100 calls in a month is no biggie, and you know it.

- **Ready yourself for a letdown after you achieve a difficult goal.**

  It's okay to indulge the natural tendency for a letdown, but don't allow the letdown to run too long. The longer you remain inactive, the harder it is to get yourself revved up again. Play awhile, but then head back to work. If you sell something that you enjoy, your work is just an extension of your hobbies anyway.

The next thing you want to do is set new goals. Keep records of all your successes. When they start piling up, you'll want to do whatever it takes to add to that file. Remember the difficulties you overcame while you accomplished each preceding goal; mentally reward yourself for your successes. When you do set the next goal, push yourself just a tad more. Always stretch yourself; that's what keeps you growing in sales. If everything's too easy, you get bored. Selling stops being a hobby and looks more and more like a job.

Most people in sales like the challenges that selling presents and are more than willing to meet the demands of a goal that brings great rewards. Remember: *The harder the goal is to achieve, the more value you find in its achievement.* In fact, don't wait until you close on one goal before you set your next one. Have your new goal already in place so that you're ready to work the necessary steps to make you succeed again.

The Law of Expectation

Most of us have experienced the phenomena of fulfilled expectations, but we tend to shrug off fulfilled expectations as coincidences instead of planned, envisioned events.

The Law of Expectation states otherwise:

> *When you think something will happen, and you feel strongly about it, you will bring about its happening.*

I think this is where the phrase *mind over matter* came from. The Law of Expectation works with simple things, as well as with matters as complicated as achieving your 20-year goals.

For example, one evening a friend of mine left home to take a walk. All she took with her were the keys to her apartment (and, of course, the clothes on her back and the shoes on her feet). She had been out for about an hour and was returning home right around dark when she felt a grate beneath her feet. No sooner did she feel the grate than the thought crossed her mind that if she dropped her keys into the grate she would not be able to get back into her apartment because her husband was away on a three-day business trip.

What do you suppose happened? You got it! The keys fell into the grate and left my friend with the dilemma of finding the best way to break into her own apartment.

Now because my friend learns from every situation, even the negative ones, after the whole ordeal she sat down to record what her experience had taught her. One of the things she learned was the power of your thoughts.

But she learned something else just as important. When she finally broke into her apartment, she realized just how easy the task really was. The next day she went to the hardware store and bought various goodies that, after she installed them, made it difficult if not impossible for someone to break in to her apartment. She had avoided a dangerous situation by being open to learn from what began as a negative experience.

So be your own fortune-teller. Predict your own success by *making* your goals happen. The more you believe in your own success, the more you will do to turn your goals into realities. *Success is no accident!* You plan it, you work on it, you monitor it, and you adjust it to enable yourself to enjoy a productive and prosperous life.

That's why it's so hard to take when people look at the success you've spent years accomplishing and see you as an overnight wonder. Some people even try to tell you how lucky you are to have the things you have. Well, I say you create your own luck. You control your own destiny. Lady Luck has little to do with your success, and she shouldn't get the credit for your achievements.

Chapter 17

Time Planning — Moving You Forward

In This Chapter

- Ways to plan and save time so that you have even more time to plan to save time
- New insights into the space-time continuum or, How uncluttering your work space saves you time
- A not-so-short discourse on the gentle art of timesurfing
- Ways to know and avoid ten common time traps
- Time-saving arrival of high-tech

Time is our most valuable resource. Until you realize that, you will continue to wonder where all your time goes.

If you still doubt the importance of time in our world, just take a look around you. Have you walked through a grocery store lately? The package labels that used to read New and Improved now say Instant or Microwaveable. When you look at cooking directions on frozen foods, the microwave instructions now come before those for the conventional oven.

The frozen food aisle itself used to be a small freezer case in the back of the store with just a few frozen vegetables or juices in it. Most grocers now devote nearly a third of their floor space to the frozen food aisle, and they usually locate that aisle in the middle of the store for shoppers' convenience. In other words, grocers do their part to help shoppers save time.

Mail order, TV, and computerized shopping have claimed a large chunk of the retail market. Why? Because it's much easier for busy people to thumb through a catalog or make a few phone calls than to trek from store to store sorting through hundreds of racks for what they want.

Everyone is searching for more time. The value of time has increased dramatically in recent years. Time's stock has risen so high because of an adaptation of the law of supply and demand: The busier you become, the more time you need. Ask anyone to name one thing that would make his or her life easier, and the overwhelming response would be more time. And if you had more time to do the things you need to do, there's a good chance that you would generate more income to do the things you want to do.

Average people often spend their time foolishly doing unproductive busywork — and then wonder where their day went and why they accomplished so little. The key word there is *spent:* they *spent* their time instead of *investing* it. The difference makes all the difference.

Spending Time versus Investing Time

Spending and *investing* connote very different ideas. When you *spend* money, you may think of the loss of money rather than the benefits you'll enjoy from whatever it was you spent your money on. On the other hand, *invest* signifies a payment from which you will derive a return; you don't focus on the momentary loss of money, but rather on the gain of the product or service that you will receive. When you spend your time instead of investing it, you focus on lost time rather than on personal gain. It all goes back to how you value time.

If you've never put a dollar value on your time before, do it now. To determine what your time is worth, take your hourly rate and follow this simple equation:

$$\frac{\text{Gross Income}}{\text{Total Annual Working Hours}} = \text{Hourly Rate}$$

To see the value of this equation, suppose that your annual income is $30,000. That means that the value of each hour in your work week is $14.42. In straight-commision sales, if you spend just one hour each day of each workweek on unproductive activity, you spend about $3,749 a year on nothing. And that's exactly what you have to show for your wasted time, too — nothing. By choosing not to manage your time, you can waste 12 percent of your annual income or more. This amount doesn't even account for all the future business you lost because you spent time instead of investing it. If you're a regular, full-time employee, that $3,749 is money your employer might as well drop off the roof for all the productivity he gets for it.

In sales or persuasion situations, you often don't see immediate financial payoff from the time you invest. When I was selling real estate, for example, I invested my time in prospecting, demonstrating property, and getting agreements approved, but I saw no return until the transaction was completed and my broker had the check. The final transaction commonly occurred weeks, and in some cases months, after my actual investment of time.

During the period between my invested time and my financial reward, I sometimes lost sight of my goals — but that's normal in selling. The longer the period between selling and payoff, the harder it is to stay focused on investing your time wisely. When you invest time in the people you're trying to persuade, it's normal to think of the returns on your investment. I don't know of any new salesperson who doesn't take out his or her calculator and figure the percentage they get on a sale as soon as they're out of sight of the client. After all, helping others is a career choice that pays very well.

Time Management or Self-Management?

Management of time is really management of self. Don't believe me? Stop and think about it for a minute.

When did you last control time? Can you stop time or even slow it down? No way. Can you negotiate with time? If you've figured out how, then you should be writing a book instead of reading one.

No one has more time to invest than anyone else, yet some people succeed more often than you do, and they do it without controlling time. It's impossible to control time, but, like other people who have learned how to succeed often, you *can* control how you invest your time.

If your particular situation calls for a healthy dose of road time, you can choose to use that time to listen to motivational or educational tapes. In doing so, you turn your expenditures of time into investments in your professional education.

Another way to manage yourself when you have to spend time traveling is to cluster your appointments. By organizing your presentations or customer service appointments by geographical area, you can save a *lot* of travel time. If your travel time is primarily inner-city, you may want to schedule it so that you don't get stuck in rush-hour traffic. Taking sidestreets and backroads may lead you to new opportunities. Invest time in planning your time, and you'll think of dozens of ways to manage yourself more efficiently.

If you think that people who practice time-management strategies are fanatical workaholics who leave no time for personal relaxation, you're mistaken. Just the opposite is the case. In operating more efficiently, they create more time for personal endeavors.

Make Time to Plan to Plan Time

A common complaint from people who do not practice effective time management is that they do not have time to plan their time. You often hear this common complaint:

> *How can I take that time out of my busy day to plan, when I never have a spare moment?*

If you don't make time for planning and self-improvement, you may as well plan to earn the same income you earn today for the rest of your life. It's a fact: by taking the time to plan, you will save *as much as* 20 to 30 times the time that you expend in the planning process.

When I plan, I categorize the things I choose to spend — or I mean *invest* — time on into three areas:

1. Immediate
2. Secondary
3. Relatively unimportant

Even though these are the three main categories, emergency situations should be part of any time-management strategy, too. Emergencies are rare, but it's wise to build flexibility into your schedule to allow for them.

Planning immediate activities

Immediate activities are *only* those activities that you must complete today. If you clutter your mind with things that should be secondary activities, you can neglect your immediate activities or not give them the full attention they require.

Ask yourself these questions to determine the immediacy of your activities:

- If I can achieve only three or four activities today, which ones should they be?
- Which activities will yield the largest rewards?
- Which activities would complicate my tomorrow if I do not achieve them today?
- Which of these activities can I delegate to someone else in order to leave myself more time to generate more business or enhance my personal relationships?

Example: If yard work is not your hobby or a form of relaxation for you, pay someone else to do it for you while you do something more productive with that time.

- Which activities, if I postpone them, would damage my relationships with others?

You should have your immediate activities in front of you at all times. If you can't see what you need to accomplish today because you've buried your immediate activities under other less-important work, those activities can get lost in the shuffle — and you can lose sight of your goals.

Planning secondary activities

It's usually easier to identify this group of activities. Some may be almost-but-not-quite immediate activities; put them at the top of your secondary activity list. As you do for immediate activities, prioritize here, too.

It's important that you place secondary papers or other items in their designated location. By that I don't mean that you should put them on top of your desk where they can distract you. Put them in a desk drawer or a letter tray that can be moved to your credenza or even put on the floor if needed. Don't let yourself get preoccupied with piles of paperwork. Paperwork overload causes stress and confuses you about what really needs immediate attention. A simple rule: Pick up paperwork only once! Decide its importance and deal with it. Don't read it and put it in a pile to be looked at again later. If it's birdcage liner, take it home for "Petey-Boy" and let him ponder over it.

Planning relatively unimportant activities

You may be surprised by how hard this list of activities is to identify. I tend to think everything needs my attention; if it didn't, it wouldn't come my way.

But such thinking simply isn't true. Other people pass many unimportant activities to you to take care of, activities that have a funny habit of working themselves out if you just give them a little time. By putting them in your relatively unimportant category, you may never have to spend time on these chores when you should be investing time on your immediate activities.

What do I mean by *relatively unimportant activities?* Stuff like this: How many times has an associate come to you for help with a problem, only to reveal that it wasn't your assistance they wanted, after all? They just wanted you to take on the problem as yours. What begins as a favor thus ends up being a real chore. Their worries become your worries while they're off having a relaxed two-hour lunch, knowing you'll handle it.

Although I am not suggesting that you never help an associate, I *am* cautioning you about taking on work that should be someone else's responsibility. If you help an associate, make sure that you get compensated, either financially or by an exchange of help on one of your projects. And here's one further word of caution: Get *your* work done first. Establish reasonable rules with your peers about work-related assistance. Doing so helps prevent hard feelings later.

Every day, many relatively unimportant events happen, but somehow they seem more urgent than they really are. What to do? Learn how to recognize a time trap when you see one. Later in the chapter, I'll tell you how to identify ten common time traps and how you can avoid them.

Planning for emergencies

Planning your time efficiently can prevent emergencies, but you should invest a few moments thinking of an alternate approach to your most important activities should an emergency arise.

For example, if you have children, you know that they get sick, hurt, or forget to tell you about vital events you need to attend. If you have a whole day of report-writing to get done and you get one of those *Mrs. Slack, Mary Beth has just thrown up at school, how soon can you pick her up?* calls, do you have a backup person, such as Grandma who would be willing to care for your daughter — at least until you can get there yourself? If not, see what you can do about getting that someone in place. Your next step would be to notify the people at work that you're leaving in 15 minutes so they can get what they absolutely need from you. Save all of your report data off to disk, grab your laptop, daily planner, and head for the door.

Is there someone else at work who lives near you whom you can hitch a ride with those mornings when your car won't start? Or, if there's a bus route close by, do you have a schedule handy? Is there a taxicab number in your address book? Better yet, do you have a cellular phone to call for help if you have a flat out in the middle of nowhere? If not, you'd better keep a pair of tennies in the car for that long walk to the pay phone.

Planning ahead and being prepared like good little Boy and Girl Scouts will keep you from panicking and completely trashing your schedule, and that of others, when emergencies do arise.

How Organizing Work Space Saves You Time

One of the main causes of wasted time and lost income is disorganized office space. Believe it or not, clearing your desk also helps to clear your mind. When your mind is clear, you're more able to focus on one task at a time. And all you can accomplish is one thing at a time, anyway.

So where do you start? Try these three steps.

1. **Keep only immediate activities on your desk.**

   Keep everything else out of sight. But keep everything you need for accomplishing the immediate tasks somewhere near you so you don't waste steps running hither and yon.

2. **Take charge of your time.**

   If you suffer innumerable interruptions, close your door. If you don't have a door, try ear plugs or a headset attached to a cassette player to isolate yourself. As a last resort, consider posting a snarling Doberman near your desk!

   Develop your ability to focus on your work. Let your coworkers or family know that sometimes they simply cannot interrupt you.

   In general, make yourself less accessible. If you need to, set up a specific time of day for your associates to freely walk into your office; make all other times off-limits. If they drop by at a bad time, don't be afraid to look at your watch and say, *I'd love to catch up with you, but let's do it at 3:00.* If what they have to tell you is important enough, they'll be happy to schedule the time. If it's not that important, they'll beg off, and you will have saved yourself some time.

3. **If necessary, remove the phone from your desk.**

   If the phone is not a necessary tool of your immediate business, remove it from your desk. Put it on a table behind you or even on the floor if you must — but get it out of your sight.

   Not every phone call is an emergency. When the other party gets off the subject, or when the other party stays on the subject but is longwinded, try these techniques:

   - When you initiate the call, tell them, *I have three things to cover with you.* If they start to get you sidetracked, you then have the right to bring them back to one of your three topics. If the other party initiates the call and you don't have a lot of time to give them, let them know their call is important, but that you were just heading out the door. Get the basic information they need to relay and make an appointment to call them back. Unless it's an irate customer who has a total stoppage of an assembly line because of your equipment, most people will be willing to accept a callback. If they can't wait, it's an emergency and you'll have to handle it.

- Call the long-winded party just before lunchtime or just before they go home for the day. If that's not possible, start your call by saying, *I'm really pressed for time, but I just wanted to let you know something,* or *I'm on my way to an appointment, but I wanted to touch base with you.*

If you don't learn to take control in these situations, you'll be forever at the mercy of others. And they will hardly ever have your best interests in mind.

Time for a commercial break: For more help with time management, seek out a copy of *Time Management For Dummies* at your local bookstore. It's filled with more great ideas.

Timesurfing the Wave of the Future

I learned a lot about timesurfing a couple decades ago with Alan Lakein, but I'm going to tell you how I've used it to become a Champion in sales. This is time management for people in selling, with the tips and techniques for salespeople.

Just as you separate work tasks into three categories, so you need to separate your personal life into three areas in order to effectively organize your time. You need to

- Investigate your yesterday
- Analyze your today
- Discover your tomorrow

In other words, timesurf. Here's how you do it.

Investigate your past

Take some time to write down what you do with each of the 168 hours in your typical week. If you're like many self-management beginners, you probably have habits that are serious time-wasters; you can easily eliminate them once you become aware of them. Try to be as honest and thorough as possible.

Also, keep a daily log for at least 21 days of your typical routine in order to establish an accurate record of habits you may need to change. The best way to keep such a log is to design a customized time sheet. Don't make it so elaborate that you won't complete it every day. Just jot down the time you spend moving through your daily routine: three hours running errands, five minutes looking for a purchase agreement, half a day scouring around for a misplaced phone message, and so on.

After completing this time log for 21 days, you'll be amazed at how much time you cannot account for and how much time you waste on relatively unimportant activities. Few people know how they spend their time. Time is like money. You know you start the week with $50 in your wallet. On Wednesday, you've got only $7; where did that $43 go? It's a struggle to reenact your spending week. The same goes with time; unless you account for it daily, it's gone with the wind.

Get tough with yourself. Do this audit for 21 days. After you complete each sheet, be sure to tally your total hours spent on each category. Keep all your sheets and evaluate them at the end of three weeks. Above all, be honest when you record the time you spend on each activity.

Analyze your today

When you analyze, you break a whole into its component parts, and that's exactly what you need to do to your today.

By the time you reach this stage, you've learned from your time log how you spent your last 21 days. You've identified yesterday's time-wasters. Now you're ready to take apart your today, examine how you can improve it, and put together a new and improved today.

Here's a hint: If you use the word *productivity* when you refer to time planning, time planning won't be such a mystery to you. People frequently come up to me or write to me and say, *Tom, I just can't plan my time* or *I just can't seem to keep up with everything I need to do.*

Invariably, I give such people a saying that someone gave me when I first started out in sales, a saying that made a huge impact on my career and my success. It also made a lot of further discussion on the subject of time management unnecessary for me. It goes like this:

> *I must do the most productive thing possible at every given moment.*

I have been teaching that saying for over 20 years, but I'm afraid that it's so simple that many people don't understand it.

No matter what I'm doing, I ask myself, *Is this the most productive thing I can do at this time?* You need to do a few simple things to answer that question:

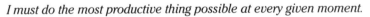

- Keep a list of important tasks
- Keep an appointment calendar
- Know what your time is worth

To increase your productivity, you must figure out, by doing the most productive thing at each moment, how to increase the value of each hour. If that sounds simple, it's because it is simple. You do that by constantly asking yourself this question: "Is what I'm doing right now the most productive thing I can do?"

I've seen people spend all their time getting organized and getting ready for a persuasion situation that never comes about. To them, getting organized itself has become the game. Sometimes people overvalue the organizing stage because they may be so afraid of facing rejection or failure that they hide from seeing the public. In most cases, though, making organizing the end rather than the means happens simply because the salesperson does not appreciate the difference between productivity and putting too much emphasis on getting organized.

To many salespeople, time planning revolves around just buying a time planner and filling in the squares. That's of course necessary. But it's just a small part of the big picture. Time planning actually starts with goals. Why? Because that's the only way you can tell what the most productive thing possible at every given moment really is.

Take a look at five areas: family, health, finances, your spirit, and hobbies.

When you're turned on and motivated and feeling good, you persuade better. If you let yourself become just a sales machine with no time for anything else, you'll burn out. You'll also probably create problems in your personal relationships. Your health most likely will suffer as well. Besides all that, you'll have no fun, slip into feeling sorry for yourself, and your career will go down the drain.

Sometimes the most productive thing you can do may be to meet your spouse for lunch; thank him or her for supporting your goals and putting up with your long hours. Or go see your child in a school event and enjoy their childhood. Or take a physical workout to help ensure (and insure) your good health and high energy. Or plant roses if planting roses invigorates you.

To be successful, you need to be a finely tuned machine that can function over the long haul and face deadlines, rejection, the public, and your competition. You also must be able to meet your company's expectations and all the other demands put on you as a professional salesperson and problem-solver. You must keep yourself tuned and in balance — physically and psychologically — and this balance starts with goals and productivity.

Assume that your goals and priorities are in line. You know what you want and how you want to get there. Your goals are all in writing and your priorities are set. Your daily time planning should start at night before you go to bed. Go through your time planner and lay out the day to come. Get a handle on your top six priorities, as well as who you will see or call, for the next day. Then add any personal areas you need to cover the next day. Writing down the next day's top six priorities shouldn't take more than 10 to 15 minutes maximum if you do it in a nice, quiet spot. Once you do it, forget it and go to bed.

The next day, the most productive thing possible may be a 20-minute workout at 6:00 AM . . . or breakfast with the family . . . or working in the garden . . . or any of 1,000 other things that may be important to you and part of your goals and priorities. It goes the same way through the entire day. You have many choices. Only you know if what you are doing is the most productive thing in relation to the goals and aspirations you want to achieve.

People grow up being told what to do for as much as the first 20 years of their lives — at home, and then at school, and then at a job. It's not surprising that people lack a certain amount of self-discipline when they go into a career such as selling, which leaves people almost entirely to their own resources.

I'd like to have a dollar for every time I've heard a salesperson say, *I went into sales so I could be my own boss* or *I went into sales so no one would tell me what to do* or *I went into sales for more free time.* All those reasons are great. But the people who hold those reasons had better develop a strong degree of self-discipline for doing what needs to be done. If they don't, they'll soon be back at a job where someone's telling them what to do.

Discover your tomorrow

To get started with an effective time-management method, don't try to plan for every minute of the day. It's too easy to be inaccurate when you forecast time for task completion.

Instead, start by planning just 75 percent of your total work time to allow for interruptions, delays, and unexpected emergencies. As your workday planning improves, you can increase to planning 90 percent of your day. If you plan for 100 percent, you won't leave room for the unexpected, and you'll just frustrate yourself when you cannot accomplish your designated tasks.

So remain flexible. Not much is black and white in selling; there are also gray areas. By staying flexible, you can maintain your equilibrium and move on to greater things. Don't lock yourself into a time-management program so rigid that you don't have time for anything else.

Winners always plan their time. To increase your productivity and your income, you must plan your time, like a professional. Professional salespeople are very conscious of the value of their customers' time, as well as their own. All sales professionals must make daily decisions on priorities. Some are major; some are minor; but all are factors in the management of time. Every professional salesperson needs a systematic approach to setting priorities.

Over the years, I've noticed that successful people who run large companies and build fortunes don't spend much more time working than anyone else. The difference with them is that they get more productivity out of each hour of every day. They don't try to do too much at once and, because they don't, they are more productive at accomplishing each day's six most important things to do.

Where to plan

Obviously you'll need a planning device of some sort. There are many good ones available from companies such as Day-Timer, Franklin, Day Runner, TimeDesign, and Filofax to name a few. Some are even customized to the specific needs of salespeople with forms for travel itineraries, charting activity and productivity, meeting notes, expense reports, and so on. Take some time to find one you think you'll be comfortable using. If you're not comfortable, you won't use it and you'll be defeating your purpose of planning.

When it's time to plan, set aside 15 minutes at your desk or with your briefcase, if that's where you keep all of your pertinent information. Take a few moments to review all unfinished business and plan how and when you'll get it done. I strongly recommend that planning be done where business is done. If you wait until you get home, you won't have that phone number or other detail you need to record and you'll only half-plan. If that means you sit in your car to plan, so be it. You may need triggers to remember everything you need to plan and those triggers will be most available to you at your place of business.

When to plan

On the first day of every month, sit down with your planning notebook and write down everything you want to accomplish that month. Be realistic.

First, write down any family or social events that you're committed to attend. Then write down any important dates: family, friend, and client birthdays, your wedding anniversary, if it's this month. Also write down any special events, such as your child's school play or spouse's company picnic.

The next things to note are all the company meetings you must attend for the month. Then add any projects you're working on, their estimated completion dates, and reminders to follow up on them. If you're working on a large project, break it down into smaller pieces that you can accomplish each week. Taking large projects a week at a time helps you see your progress, and the one big project won't seem so oppressive.

In daily time planning, keep track of all activities as you go. Don't wait until 4:00 PM to try to remember what you did at 9:30 AM. Be truthful. Don't play around with numbers or fake anything just so you can check it off.

Don't overwhelm yourself with writing down every detail of your workday. You're not trying to write a book. Trying to capture too much detail goes back to our discussion earlier in the chapter about spending so much time preparing that you never get to work. Just note the key events and any information you simply wouldn't want to forget.

20 questions to ask yourself when you analyze your daily time planner

1. Did I accomplish all six of my high-priority items?
2. Did I reach or surpass my goals for today?
3. Did I invest as much time as I planned in persuading others?
4. Did I contact every prospect that I put on my list for today? If not, why not? What prevented me from getting to that prospect?
5. How much time did I spend prospecting for new clients?
6. How much time did I waste chatting with coworkers or clients?
7. What is the most productive thing I did today?
8. What is the least productive thing I did today?
9. Of the things I consider a waste of time, could I have avoided or eliminated any of them?
10. How much time did I spend doing something that will profit me? Can I devote more time here?
11. Was today a productive day for me? for my company?
12. Did I take care of all the paperwork I needed to take care of today?
13. How many of today's activities have helped me achieve my goals?
14. How much time today did I allot to my family? Did I spend this time with them? Was it quality time, or was I just at the same place at the same time?
15. What can I do to improve the quality of the time I devote to my family?
16. Did I plan for, and take some time to work on, my emotional or physical health?
17. If I could live today over, what would I change?
18. What did I do today that I feel really good about?
19. Did I send thank you notes to the people I dealt with today?
20. What or who wasted the greatest amount of my time?

Ten Common Time Traps

I think we can all agree that there are people out there who have raised time wasting to an art form. They have mastered the ability to fall into every time trap they encounter. However, they are not the people who get things done, help the most people, earn the biggest incomes in selling. If you want to get more *yes* in your life, learn to avoid these ten common time traps.

Desperately seeking what shouldn't be lost

A sure way to waste valuable time is to keep looking for something you desperately need because you were careless when you "put it away." This is the single biggest time-waster for everyone. How many hours have you wasted looking for the scrap of paper you wrote an important phone number on or for the folder with all the referrals that your new client gave you? How about your sunglasses or your car keys? Ring any bells? Those few minutes here and there can really add up.

Failure to do the job right the first time

Because of the demands salespeople place on themselves, they tend to rush through their paperwork and their planning of presentations without carefully checking or rechecking details.

Get out of that habit. There's a saying that goes, *If you don't have time to do it right the first time, how will you find time to do it again?* Consider how much less time it takes to do something right the first time than to go back and do it over. Don't risk angering others with costly delays or mistakes caused by carelessly written paperwork. Champions double-check everything for accuracy and clarity.

Procrastination

Procrastination and so-called call reluctance can kill your career. Don't feel alone on this one; everyone procrastinates. Everyone puts things off until they create a have-to situation.

Most people procrastinate because of fear. They fear making a mistake, so instead they do nothing. The trouble with doing nothing, though, is this: doing nothing can only produce nothing. Mistakes can and will happen. Champions accept their mistakes and learn from their experiences.

If a client phones to report a problem with the product or service she acquired from a salesperson, what do most salespeople do? They put off the challenge until tomorrow. By then, though, when they do call to apologize and solve the problem, the client may be furious and vowing never to do business with the salesperson's company again.

Always call an angry client immediately. The longer you wait, the more the situation worsens. Perhaps you've heard the saying that *A professional is someone who does things even when they don't want to.* How true. But you need discipline to do the things you don't want to do. To be truly successful, you must overcome procrastination before it leads to immobilization, the biggest killer of all careers.

Words to live by: *Do it now!*

Unnecessary or unnecessarily long phone calls

A real challenge for many businesspeople. The telephone can be your greatest ally or greatest enemy. Here are some ideas to help you deal with wasted time on the phone:

- Set aside specific time each day to take and make phone calls.
- Set a time limit for your calls.
- Write down your objective for the phone call and focus on it.
- Have all your materials and information within reach before you pick up the phone.
- Put a specific time limit on all calls.
- Find polite but effective exit lines to help you get off the phone without interrupting the other person or abruptly ending the conversation. For example, try saying, *Barbara, just one more thing before I hang up. . .* Such a statement lets the person know that you're coming to the end of the phone call.
- Let all your customers know exactly when you're available for them to call you.
- If you do business with people who chatter and won't let you off the phone, whenever they call, tell them you're in the middle of something extremely urgent and that you will call them back. Then, call them just before the time they leave for the day. You'll be surprised how brief conversations with such people can become.
- If you spend great amounts of time on the phone, or if you're in telemarketing, a high-quality headset will be a valuable investment for you.

Identifying a purpose for every call as soon as possible and focusing on that purpose should serve you well. If you think of the phone as a business tool, not unlike your computer and calculator, that thinking will help you form new habits for using it that should keep you out of this trap.

Unnecessary or unnecessarily long meetings

Attending too many nonproductive meetings can also be a major time-waster.

If you're in management and you think you waste a great deal of your time in meetings, maybe you should reevaluate how often you need to meet with your people and what you need to accomplish when you do get together. Is a daily or weekly meeting really necessary? Or can more effective communications within the company eliminate the need for such meetings? Don't hold a $1,000 meeting to solve a $50 problem.

Many people have found that holding meetings standing up is highly productive. When people don't settle into comfortable chairs for the duration, they finish their business much more quickly. I once attended a meeting to determine when the best time for another meeting would be. See what I mean?

Client lunches that last for two or more hours

As with the phone, you need to develop ways to let the client know that you've finished your business for today and that you must move on.

For example, when you sit down for lunch at noon with a notorious "friendly afternoon waster," you can say something to the effect of *This works out great. I don't have another commitment until 1:30, so I have plenty of time to talk.* Or, you could say, *Pound it down, Frank, I'm outta here in 30 minutes!* but somehow I just don't think it would be quite as effective.

Negative thinking

Negative thoughts that produce negative talk are another big waste of time for everyone. If you dwell on life's negatives, what do you think you can accomplish? I'm positive (ahem) that you will accomplish very little. Push negative thoughts from your mind. No one ever became a success in selling who was a negative thinker.

Instead of focusing on things you don't like, think about the positive things you can do. And by all means surround yourself with positive thinkers. Their positive energy will rub off on you.

Driving time

Most people in professional selling spend a lot of time in their cars driving from appointment to appointment. The average salesperson drives 25,000 miles a year for his or her job. That works out to about 500 hours a year, or about 16 weeks — your basic college semester.

How can you make the best use of this time? Hundreds of educational programs are available on cassette. Publishing companies record books on cassette because people don't always have time to read a book. You can use this driving time to listen to programs on sales training, motivation, self-esteem, financial planning, small business strategies, foreign languages, classic literature, history, as well as a growing number of how-to programs.

Unconfirmed appointments

It amazes me how many people do not confirm appointments before they leave the office or their previous customer. Why would anyone not confirm an appointment? The old standby: fear. Some salespeople fear that, if they call, the person might say, *Never mind.* Such salespeople would rather drive all the way to their customer's office and have the receptionist tell them that their customer got called out of town for the day.

A quick phone call before you leave not only can save you valuable selling time; it also tells the prospect that you're a professional with something valuable to say.

If you handle it properly, your brief call to confirm could keep your appointment from being the one that gets canceled if your customer needs to change his or her decision-making schedule. When you call to confirm an appointment, do it this way:

> *Hi, Jim, I've spent so much time preparing for our meeting, and I just thought I'd call to let you know that I'll be there right at 2:00. I think you'll be excited about what I have to show you.*

Never say, *I'm just calling to confirm.* By letting the decision-maker know how much time and effort you've put into preparing for this meeting, they'll feel guilty about canceling and be more likely to find a way to keep the appointment. If for some reason you can't get to the person you have the appointment with, tell the person taking the message that you're on your way and you'll be on time. Ask that the message-taker convey that message to the customer you're meeting with. And another benefit: Even if the decision-maker does have to cancel, you have them on the phone to immediately schedule another appointment.

Always take the time to confirm your appointments. The time you save will be well worth the time you invest. The time you save frees up your time to prospect for new business or to take care of something else on your list.

Television

In my experience with high-achievers, almost to a person they tell you that they do not waste time watching television. TV watching is probably the single least-productive activity in the American lifestyle. I'm not going to preach to you about the mindlessness of most of what's on TV these days, but I will say this: TV should be used properly. Some examples of how to use your TV are

1. Displaying your sales trophies
2. Shelving your books and tapes related to selling
3. Watching selling skills videos

What part of the word *No* can't you say?

Many of us just can't say *No* when people want a chunk of our time. But it's better that you say *No* to someone, and get the job done, than it is to say *Yes* and not get the job done.

Sometimes you're not even the most capable person to do the job. Professionals recognize their limitations. And when they bump into their limitations, they delegate requests for work that's outside their scope to colleagues who are more capable and more likely to complete the job efficiently.

If you explain the fact that there are others better suited to getting the job done right properly, with warmth and care, the people who ask you for favors will appreciate your honesty and your ability to refer them to someone trustworthy to do the job. As you become more successful, your time becomes more valuable, making it all the more important for you to learn when (and how) to say *no.*

Solo Time

Granted, you should always allow part of your day to work with people, support your coworkers, or help the company problem-solve. But it's also important to allow yourself some solo time, both at work and in your personal life. Solo time is time for whatever *you* need to do. It can be your time for emotional and physical health in your private life, as well as your most productive work time.

During your solo work time, if someone asks, *Do you have a minute?* just answer, *Not right now. Can it wait until 11?* By that time, most people who were looking for your help will have solved the problem themselves, or they will have realized that their problem wasn't all that important, anyway.

Some tips for handling interruptions:

- Rearrange your office so that your desk is out of the line of sight from people who walk down the hallway.
- Remove extra chairs from your office if possible. Position any necessary chairs as far away from your desk as possible.
- Place a large clock where you and any visitors can clearly see it.
- Don't look up when someone walks into your office.

  This habit is hard to get into, but if you appear to be extremely busy and the potential interruption is nothing serious, most people will simply walk away. This advice may sound cold, but if you can't get your work done,

> your inefficiency will cause your customers to receive less service, and it will cause you to earn a lower income.
>
> Beware: Every company has people who just like to walk around and visit.

To get started on minimizing this challenge, keep an Interruption Log just for one day. In it record

- Who is interrupting you
- What time they came and left
- How much time you wasted
- What you can do about it

If it turns out to be the same person all the time or the same type of challenge, taking a bit of time to train them or institute a new procedure can save you a lot of time in the long run.

When an occasional crisis comes up, deal with it quickly, and then go right back to your original schedule. You don't have to become antisocial around the office, but you may be surprised at how much more efficient you can be when you start taking back stray minutes here and there. Because time flies and you never hear the rustle of its gossamer wings.

High-Tech Time Savers

The rapid advancement of technology is the salesperson's friend. In the past few years, many new time-saving products have enabled salespeople to become more and more efficient.

Back in my selling days, I had to write down and keep track of an incredible amount of information. Who could have imagined back then that in 25 years we would have computers so lightweight that you can easily carry them from place to place? And who could have imagined that computers would be so small that they fit comfortably on your lap, giving you instant access to all your files and information?

Back then, who could have imagined that if you needed to get in touch with someone while you were on an airplane at 37,000 feet that you could just pick up the phone and call them? Who could have imagined that you could get a letter from Los Angeles to New York in under two minutes via a fax machine?

The high-tech revolution has accelerated the pace of all aspects of our lives. And, especially for salespeople, those changes are for the better.

The outside salesperson's best friend

If you invest in nothing else for your success, get a car phone or portable phone.

I can't imagine anyone in outside sales who wouldn't benefit greatly from these important time-savers. If you don't own one now, get one. It will more than pay for itself in the greater income you will earn because of the improved service you can give your customers.

Better yet, get a mobile phone that you can keep with you at all times. With a mobile phone, your office can always reach you if a customer has a challenge or if a prospect you've been working with calls to say that she's ready to do business with you.

Another important tool for many of today's outside salespeople is a portable fax machine. If you need vital paperwork while you're in the field, you can own no better piece of equipment than a portable fax.

Some suggestions for high-tech tools

One thing to remember about mobile phones is to use proper business etiquette. Never take a mobile phone that's turned on into a presentation unless both you and the customer are waiting for an important call about that particular meeting. If your phone rings in the middle of the presentation and you stop to take the call, you in effect tell that person that they aren't as important as whoever is calling. Not good. The same goes for beepers; put them on *vibrate* or turn them off when you're with a prospect.

When you use a fax machine, always use a cover sheet that lists all your business numbers. Then, after you fax your fax, take a minute to call the recipient and make sure that they received it. Be sure to tell them how many pages you sent. Many companies, even though they have hundreds of employees, nevertheless have only one fax machine. In such circumstances, it's easy for your fax to get misplaced. It could even get batched in with another fax that came in previously and given to the wrong person — who may not realize they have it until much later.

Even in small offices, a fax can get buried under other papers. So take a moment to call. Doing so shows the prospect that you're a caring professional.

P.S. Stay on Top of Your Paperwork

If you dread doing the paperwork, don't leave it for the end of the day if you can help it. If something unexpected should come up, you won't get to your paperwork, and the next day you'll just have twice as much to do. This buildup of paperwork in turn causes you even more anxiety because now you *really* have a big task ahead of you.

Do your paperwork in the first hour, if at all possible, when you're fresh. Once it's done, you're free to concentrate on the more productive parts of your day.

I've now spent — or I mean *invested* — a lot of time in this chapter teaching you to make every hour count. Review this material from time to time. Auditing your time is not just a one-time event. You should practice periodical 2- to 3-day time audits at least every 90 days just to keep yourself on track.

The best advice I can leave you with in this chapter about managing your time is to live by these words:

I must do the most productive thing possible at every given moment!

Part VI
The Part of Tens

The 5th Wave By Rich Tennant

PROVING THAT BIGGER ISN'T ALWAYS BEST, A CONTRACT TO BUILD A COMPUTERIZED SONAR TRACKING SYSTEM FOR THE U.S. NAVY IS AWARDED TO TROOP 708 OF THE BAYONNE, NEW JERSEY EAGLE SCOUTS.

In this part...

These short chapters are packed with quick ideas about selling and persuading that can be read anytime you have a few minutes.

Chapter 18

The Ten Biggest Sales Mistakes Everyone Makes

Let's face it, everyone makes mistakes in life. It's only normal to expect to make some when you're trying something new. Our goal in this chapter is to share with you the ten most common mistakes others who have gone before you into the selling world have made so the start of your journey might be a bit more successful.

Mistake #1: Not really understanding selling

In most cases, the only contact a business has with the outside world is through its salespeople — *and the only reason to have salespeople is to have them sell a product or service.*

This observation may seem elementary, but if you walk into most small businesses in the world today you may find it difficult to find someone who can tell you their current style of selling and how they are analyzing it for improvement. They may even have trouble describing their ideal customer to you. It's impossible to know too much about why customers do and don't buy your product or service and gaining that knowledge is a function of selling.

Professional sales training doesn't involve tips for becoming pushy or aggressive. Any sales trainer who would teach persuaders to become pushy and aggressive would have to be classified as incompetent. *Professional* salespeople or persuaders are low-key, service-oriented, and relationship-builders.

Mistake #2: Expecting things to get better by themselves

It is bad business to have incompetent or untrained people serving customers. You may as well toss your advertising dollars to the wind if your people aren't prepared to sell and service them when they contact your business.

The same goes for individuals. If you aren't satisfied with your personal rate of persuasion, or volume of sales, you must realize that there are ways you can improve. To admit that and *not* take any steps to correct the situation is simply foolish.

Sales skills are not a gift of birth. They are learned skills that anyone can master with a little study and work. Start watching others in persuasion situations wherever you go. Ask yourself why some persuaders are good and why some are bad. You will find that it's much easier to say why they are bad. When they are bad, it is usually painfully obvious that they are incompetent, that they don't know what they're talking about, or that they're just messing up in general.

But when salespeople are well-trained *and* highly skilled, things seem to move forward so smoothly that it's almost impossible to spot anything happening. That's why I tend to think that these people are just naturals. They may be naturally comfortable talking with others, however, the actual skill of persuading others must be learned.

If you just stop using the destructive things you are saying and doing that are killing your sales, your success ratio will actually go up. You can *choose* to learn selling skills.

Mistake #3: Talking too much, not listening enough

Most people think that in order to persuade you have to be a real good talker. A typical "real good talker" thinks that he or she can tell the customer enough about the product and they will automatically buy. The truth is just the opposite.

When it comes to good salespeople, I will take an interested introvert over an interesting extrovert every time. A good salesperson is just like a great detective: he asks questions, makes notes, and listens intently to the customers' spoken words, as well as to their body language.

In most cases, you will find that people who want to talk too much want to control the conversation and are more likely to be aggressive and pushy. *Professional* sales training involves more questioning techniques and intent listening techniques. It's not talking, but *knowing the proper questions to ask* that leads to a consummation of a sale. A salesperson who has been trained to ask questions leads the buyer down the path to the sale. They do not push them down that path.

When you're talking, you're only learning what you already know.

Mistake #4: Using words that kill sales

In any presentation you make, your words paint a picture. A few wrong word pictures can ruin the entire portrait you're trying to paint.

How many presentations do you suppose are made daily throughout the world in an effort to win approval, but which don't succeed just because of the sales-killing pictures that the presenter's words paint? By using the wrong words, salespeople create negative pictures in the minds of the people they strive to serve — giving them more reasons not to go ahead than to get involved.

Mistake #5: Not knowing when to close the sale

Most customers who leave a place of business without owning a product or service are shrugged off by untrained salespeople as being "just lookers" or "be-backs" or any number of other euphemisms that hide the basic fact that the salesperson did not sell the customers. A *professional* salesperson, however, refers to such customers as what they are: *lost sales.*

You ask for their decision when you recognize their buying signs. *Buying signs* are things such as asking more questions or using language that shows an attitude of ownership, such as, *Yessir, that Van Gogh original certainly will enhance our living room.* The key here is that the customer has used the word *will* instead of something more hesitant such as *might* or *would.*

Buying signs also include asking for more details, wanting to see the instructions for how to operate your product, and asking financing questions. When you see such signs, *Yes* is right around the corner.

Mistake #6: Not knowing how to close the sale

In many cases, all you have to do is ask.

If a customer asks, *Do you have it in red?* and you say, *I believe I do have a red one,* what do you gain? Nothing.

Why not ask this instead:

> *If I have the red one, do you want to take it with you today, or shall I ship it?*

Or this:

> *Let me check on our color selection. By the way, would you like it giftwrapped?*

In other words, you should ask a question that moves them into a position of having to make an ownership decision.

Mistake #7: Lack of sincerity

If you're trying to persuade someone else to adopt your point of view, to own your product, or to start an account with your service, you must first build a belief in them that you are talking with them for their benefit, not yours.

You have to get the dollar signs out of your eyes. Never let greed get in your way of doing what's right. If you don't sincerely believe that what you have to offer is good for the other party, yet you still try to convince them to own, one of two things will happen:

1. They'll recognize your insincerity, not get involved with you, and tell at least 11 other people how terrible their experience with you was, thus ruining your reputation.
2. If you do persuade them and what you're selling is not good for them, you are nothing more than a con artist and, hopefully, they'll take every measure possible to see that you are punished as one.

First and foremost in *professionally* selling or persuading others must be your sincere desire to serve others and help them get involved in something that's truly beneficial for them.

Mistake #8: Not paying enough attention to details

When you wing it on your presentation, skim over details, and ignore important cues from others, you also skim over big potential wins for yourself. Lost or misplaced orders, letters with typographical errors, and missed appointments or delivery dates all ruin your credibility with others. They take away from the high level of competence *professionals* strive so hard to display. If they don't have the impression that you are doing your best for them, they'll find someone who will — maybe even someone else in your own office. Ooh, that would hurt, wouldn't it?

Mistake #9: Letting yourself slump

If you could chart your daily activities, productivity, and winning presentations on a graph, what would it look like?

Are you a bull in the first week of every month and a bear in the last? Most people have patterns to their selling cycles and efforts. If you can watch your cycles carefully, you'll see a slump coming long before it hits and be able to correct the errors of your ways to even out your numbers of successes. Getting out of a slump takes a lot out of you, both mentally and physically. Why put yourself through hard times when you can keep on an even keel instead?

Mistake #10: Not keeping in touch

Most people who switch from your product, service, or idea to another do so because you are being apathetic and someone else is paying them more attention. Someone else is keeping in contact on a regular basis. Someone else is making them feel important.

When all it takes is a few contacts by phone or mail to keep people doing business with you, why would you ever get so lazy as to let them go?

All you need to do is schedule two or three quick phone calls to say, *Diane, this is Tom from ABC Company. I'm just calling to see if you're still enjoying the increased productivity and cost savings with your new fax machine. If all is well, I won't keep you. I just wanted to touch base with you and thank you once again for your business.* It takes about 12 seconds to say these words. Isn't a 12 second investment worth it if it keeps a customer?

Chapter 19

Ten Ways to Close a Sale Nearly Every Time

Once you attain a certain level of professionalism, you'll find that you're selling more. This is a culmination of a lot of things. You're learning how to find the best people to sell to. You're qualifying them quickly and smoothly. You recognize buying signs and, most importantly, you enjoy all of it. Here's how you get started on your rise to that fun level of professionalism.

1. Prepare yourself

Prepare yourself both mentally and physically for the challenge of persuading others. Dress appropriately. Give yourself an attitude check. Clear your mind of everything but what's necessary for the presentation. Review any notes or information that could be vital to the contact within a few hours of meeting with the people. Doing your homework will help you pass the test every time.

2. Make a good first impression

There aren't too many winning stories out there about people who overcame bad first impressions to go on and land a major account or persuade a Most Important Person to their way of thinking. Going in confident and handling the initial rapport-setting stage properly goes a long way toward winning.

3. Determine quickly if you really can help them

By asking a few simple questions, you can determine quickly if the person you're meeting with is right for your offering. By doing this, you maximize your efforts by continuing presentations only with someone who can make a decision. Making a quick determination also shows the other person the courtesy of not wanting to waste their time with detailed information that's of no benefit to them.

4. Give every presentation 110%

Never sell a prospect short. In doing so, you show a lack of respect for them which will eventually become clear to them; when it does, you'll probably lose whatever you just gained with them. Don't take shortcuts. Drop a step and you may lose a sale.

By giving every presentation as if it's the most important thing in your life at that moment, you show the decision-makers that you are sincere about their needs and that they are important to you. Generally, people will be whatever you expect them to be, so expect them to be vital to your overall success in life and treat them with the proper amount of respect.

5. Address concerns completely

If and when you hear a concern raised about something, don't ever glide over it. Let it stop you momentarily. Think about what was said and what you may have said or done to trigger the comment. Then carefully and thoughtfully address the concern with the decision-maker.

6. Confirm everything

Miscommunication costs each of us loads of money, time, and effort every year. Missed appointments, flights, or phone calls can destroy in minutes what may have taken months to build. Inattention to details, wrong orders, and wrong people handling important tasks takes its toll as well. Taking just a few seconds to confirm (and reconfirm) everything will bring you more success.

7. Ask for the decision

You have nothing to lose by asking a prospect for a decision. If they're not ready to make a decision and that's what you learn from asking, great. But if they are ready and you don't ask, you lose everything. If you truly believe in the good of what you're doing, you should have no challenge asking the other party to commit their time, effort, or money to your cause or for your product or service. Hesitation here is an indication of doubt. You should never be the one having doubts when you're in the persuader's seat.

8. Tell them about others

Few people want to be guinea pigs. They don't want to be the first to try something. They want to know that others have preceded them. By sharing experiences you've had with others just like them — others who bought your product, use your service, or are committed to the same project — you give them permission to be like those others and invest in what you're selling. They'll recognize the landscape and understand that they're not going into uncharted waters. Overcoming their little fears will take you far in convincing or persuading people, especially if you can use examples of people they know.

9. Work at it constantly

The most successful people in the world rarely take time off from what they do that makes them successful. I'm not saying that you should become a workaholic, but you can certainly think about new strategies, new ideas, and new people to contact even when you're lying on a beach in the Bahamas for a well-deserved rest. By living and breathing what you believe in the most, the best new ideas will be drawn to you. You'll constantly have your success antenna up and tuning in to the best information for you.

10. Be a product of the product

If you believe in what you're doing, then you must personally be a part of it. If you're selling Fords, you don't want to be seen driving a Chevy. If you sell home security systems, you'd better have one on your home. If you market freelance graphic design, your business cards had better be creative. If you can talk personally about your own experiences with your product, service, or idea, you'll win over a lot more people than if you can't.

Chapter 20

Ten Ways to Master the Art of Selling

If all you want to do is discover how the masters of sales accomplish what they accomplish, or to admire the top professionals for their incredible achievements, you would be able to do that by reading this book. But if you want to achieve that master's status in sales yourself, then you have to do more than a one-time read-through of this book. *Selling For Dummies* is a reference tool for people like you — people who want to learn the basic techniques of sales and to establish a strong foundation of good habits on which to build great careers.

So don't save *Selling For Dummies* a space on the top shelf of your bookcase with all the other dust-collectors. Keep it within easy reach so that when you need to refer back to one of its pearls of wisdom or encouragement, you won't have far to go.

In this chapter, you have ten choice bits of selling wisdom to return to over the years. Use this chapter as your road map to mastering the art of selling, as your ten easy steps to becoming a Champion in all your future selling situations.

Step #1: Adopt an attitude of learning.

Before you enter into any new experience, make sure you bring an attitude of positive anticipation and enthusiasm. What you learn in this book will be directly proportionate to the time you spend studying and practicing the techniques and suggestions offered in its pages. As a result of what you learn, your income will build right along with the maturity of your knowledge in sales.

If you desire to be a master of persuasion and selling, remember that all masters were first excellent students. In addition to that general advice, I can give you three specific hints to make your learning experience more productive:

- **Discover your best learning environment.**

  Figure out where and how you can most effectively focus on learning. For some, sitting in the family room with the family as they watch Monday night football may be the appropriate place, while others require silence and isolation to best comprehend what they read. Whatever your personal needs, if you plan to study, memorize, and adopt the sales techniques in this book, you need to make the most of the time you set aside for that purpose.

- **Study at a pace that fits you.**

  Pace of study is another learning variable. Some people learn better when they read little bits of information and give themselves a chance to internalize what they've learned. Others like to take big clumps of information at one sitting so they can see the bigger picture and understand the full concept of what is being presented.

- **Limit your interruptions.**

  Set up a regular time to study and let your family and friends know that you will be unavailable during this time. This may be a good time to let your answering machine screen your calls, as well as a good time to turn off your pager.

  If your concentration skills are anywhere near average, you need 8 to 10 minutes after being interrupted to regain the concentration level you were at before the interruption. That's why it's so hard to stay in the study mode when people interrupt you. It's better to have 30 minutes of uninterrupted reading and studying than to patch together four or five interrupted periods to equal an hour of study time.

  If you can't hide out for a long period of time, cut your time or break it into two sessions in order to maximize your learning.

By analyzing your optimum learning patterns and working with them, your attitude about the material being studied will be positive. You'll be more relaxed and definitely learn at a faster pace.

Step #2: Have realistic expectations of your learning.

After reading this book and continuing to study sales, you should be able to use common sales techniques in unique ways. I'm not trying to turn out uniform little sales clones by having everyone who reads this book say the same words and practice the same methods at the expense of their own individuality.

If you take from this book ideas you had not thought of before and combine them with the sales experience you already have, you will lend to the selling situation a flavor all your own. Realize that you need to *adapt* some of this material in order to create a genuine presentation and communicate naturally with the customer.

Another factor in having realistic expectations for your learning is to be patient with yourself. Don't expect to be a winner 100 percent of the time. On the other hand, be honest with yourself and recognize times when inadequate knowledge or an inaccurate application of new selling techniques has kept you from giving your best performance.

Know your limitations, but don't be bound by them. Do what you know you should do, do it the best way you know how, and stay on the lookout for ways to improve your selling skills.

Step #3: Keep an open mind, and welcome change.

It's only natural to want to return to your cocoon when things get tough, especially if you've experienced some success through your old methods. Nobody ever said that change would be easy (did they?). Think what those poor little caterpillars have to go through to become butterfies. If you have a difficult time with change, adopting some of the techniques in this book will require a supreme effort on your part. Most of the time, it's harder to change your old selling habits than it is to learn new ones.

One thing you can do to better accommodate change is to *select only a few things to change at first.* No matter how much you need to work on, you'll be too distracted and fragmented if you try to change everything at once. I'd compare changing all of your selling skills at once to going on a diet, starting an exercise program, and giving up smoking at the same time. Not an easy thing to do. For best results, choose two things to change that would significantly increase your sales, and work on those aspects of your performance until they become normal parts of your routine. When that happens, choose two more new selling skills to learn or change.

During this period of change or improvement, you'll go through the normal feelings of anxiety and confusion. Sometimes your presentation may be awkward or rough around the edges. Think of yourself as a diamond in the rough. As soon as you get some polish and put yourself in the proper setting, you'll outshine them all.

As you become a more effective salesperson, you'll find yourself applying what you've learned to your personal relationships and decisions. But there's lagtime between the practice and the perfection, so allow yourself and others time to adjust to the new and improved version of you.

For example, if your goal requires you to work many more hours than you've ever worked, share this with your family and friends and ask them to help you to be your most productive self. Recognize that they may have as much difficulty adjusting to you and your changes as you yourself will have.

Suppose that your new sales responsibilities require you to be up and working by 8:00 AM Now suppose that you're used to eating breakfast with your family at 8:00 AM What to do? Make some adjustments and let your family participate in your new life. You could begin your day much earlier and take a much-deserved 8:00 AM break for a family breakfast — even if you have to participate via telephone.

If you stay openminded and flexible, you'll be able to welcome the changes necessary for a successful career in sales.

Step #4: Rehearse, perform, and critique your new skills.

After you internalize some of your new selling techniques, it's time to practice them. At first, it's a good idea to go over them by yourself until you feel confident enough to practice them in front of your family, friends, or peers who can give you some important pointers.

If the advice comes from people you respect, listen! On the other hand, if you get unsolicited advice from people you don't respect, don't let them share in your learning experience: their responses may damage your delicate psyche.

When you've rehearsed so much that the words are permanently etched on your brain, it's time for your opening night performance.

This is a scary time — to take new selling skills and concepts and perform them in front of strangers who may recognize your twitching eye and sweaty palms as lack of polish. Give yourself permission to be a rookie, but be sure to follow the Rookie Rules — and remember, rookies can become MVPs.

1. Give yourself many, many opportunities to perfect your new selling techniques.
2. When you look back, feed the positive — celebrate all the things you did right.
3. Hold on to your rookie enthusiasm even when you become a polished sales professional.

The last part of this step is to honestly critique your performance of your new skills. At this point it is important that you look with a critical but fair eye. This part comes only after you have performed your new skills for an extended period of time and are able to see measurable increases in your sales. You need to have a tool by which to measure your success.

For example, if you've been in sales for a while but haven't been able to reach the level of success you'd hoped for, you may want to jot down your sales ratios and compare the old with the new. Seeing positive results gives you something tangible to encourage a continued pattern of improvement.

If a specific stumbling block keeps inhibiting your sales growth, ask another sales professional whom you respect for some advice. Sometimes it even helps to take such a person along on a presentation or to tape a meeting and critique it together.

In fact, you may be surprised to review a taped presentation and discover all the things you could have done differently. Critiquing a taped presentation gives you some distance from the excitement and anxiety of the initial meeting and enables you to look at your performance more objectively. Some tapes hold great entertainment value. You'll be amazed at how many things you don't remember and how many things you'd swear you never did or said — it's a real eye-opener.

Step #5: Personalize your new sales skills.

When you memorize concepts and specific words — and sometimes you must memorize word for word — look for ways to make the words you memorize reflect your personality. Practice *how* you will say them. Think about *how* you will carry yourself — how you will stand or sit when you utter those words. Use your sense of humor, use your previous knowledge, use your natural speech and mannerisms to make your new selling skills sound spontaneous.

The worst thing you can do is memorize phrases and then shut off your personality and resort to a robot imitation whenever you get desperate. The thing to remember as you sell is to be genuine and personable. Being yourself is almost impossible to do if you haven't made the concepts you've learned uniquely yours by wrapping them in your own words and actions. The last thing you want your clients to feel is that they are being given a canned presentation.

Step #6: Be disciplined.

This is probably the best advice anyone can give you.

If you crave the financial and personal freedom that a successful sales career can provide, you have to be willing to go the extra mile. If that means working on a Friday night when all your friends are at an office party, then so be it! If that means getting up hours earlier each morning until you learn your new skills, then that's what you must do! If that means no more two-hour lunches or lazy afternoons for a while, then make the sacrifice!

Be a self-disciplined self-starter, and eventually you'll reap rewards.

One of the greatest pitfalls of great success in a short period of time is a failure to *continue* to hustle. There's a tendency to want to rest on your laurels when you know you're good. Slowing down after achieving success quickly is a dangerous mistake. Just because you taste some success, that doesn't mean that you can stop hustling and fall back into the same old methods that crippled your sales career.

Stay on your feet and run the race to the finish. Don't allow yourself the luxury of self-doubts or overconfidence. They are production-killers. The real trick is to remain balanced during your successes. Don't let increased sales go to your head or repeated rejection beat you down. Although it can be almost impossible at times, always strive to keep your activities and attitudes *balanced.*

Step #7: Evaluate the results of learning.

It's hard to accurately evaluate the results you're getting with your newly learned selling skills if you don't know what your sales results were before you changed. Sure, you'll have a hunch about how things are going, but often these feelings are not to be trusted.

For example, when you're discouraged, you tend to see your accomplishments unfavorably. During such times, your successes diminish, and it's easy to feed the negative until it grows into an unconquerable monster. On the other hand, on days when you're overly optimistic, you may conveniently blame a bungled presentation or the lack of knowledge on the customer and fail to take the necessary steps for *self*-improvement.

When you evaluate the results of your learning, avoid comparing your progress to someone else's. Even if the salesperson has received the same training and has read the same books as you, everyone learns differently. Some learn more quickly than others yet can't retain the information for long. Others learn slowly and give the appearance of having fallen behind, when actually they've internalized the information and will receive longer-lasting rewards for their efforts.

Another aspect of learning the sales techniques presented in this book is that you will find yourself taking these skills and applying them to your personal relationships and family decisions. And why not? When you see how many rewards can come from using them in your business life, why not practice the same ideas in your personal life, too? Your realizations will only spur on greater achievements in both.

Step #8: Monitor and adjust.

This step goes farther than just thinking about what you did right and what you need to improve.

When I say *monitor* your performance, I mean that you should keep a success journal. By recording specific instances and details of when you successfully used new selling techniques, you not only immediately reinforce the benefits to your career; maybe more important, when you need encouragement you also can review your journal and relive a positive selling experience. Do it. You'll be surprised at what a great motivational tool a success journal can be.

When you review your success journal, compare what you did right in a given situation to what you did when you did not get the sale. When you make such a comparison, the reasons for not getting the sale should become obvious to you.

By comparing an unsuccessful experience to a successful one, you see what you left out or skimmed over and why you failed to convince the customer of the benefits of your offering.

When such negatives occur, you need to adjust your presentation or sales techniques. And the only way you can accurately adjust is to write down your achievements and recognize a good model for a successful sale. After you have contemplated what you need to do to improve your selling, the next step is to *just do it.*

If you're going to play the *If only* game, then be a finisher. It's okay to ponder what could have been: *If only I had asked more questions* or *If only I had been able to answer the client's objections with more skill.* The trouble with playing *If only,* though, is that many times you're defeated before you finish.

After you wonder about all the *If onlys,* you must envision yourself as that master of sales and then act on your visions. *If only* is a game of recognizing areas that need improvement. Once you recognize those areas, it's time to take action and turn your *If only* into *Because I:*

> *Because I asked more questions, I closed the sale.*
>
> *Because I successfully answered the client's objections, they were able to benefit by owning my offering.*

By monitoring and adjusting your new selling skills, you continue to increase your sales ratios. Be diligent and persistent in your self-evaluation, though. Don't just look at your sales once a year and make bold promises about how you'll do things differently at some unspecified future date. Be meticulous in your search for excellence and specific in your plans for improvement.

How effective can a statement like *Next year I want to do a bigger volume of business* really be? Wouldn't it be much clearer and productive to say this:

> *Beginning January 1, I will spend two hours more a day prospecting and increase my face-to-face selling by 20 percent. In the process, I will increase my sales volume by 5 percent.*

The second statement gives you a more distinct monthly, weekly, and daily activity schedule to follow in order for you to improve.

Step #9: Find a way to learn from every selling situation.

You'll be surprised at how many unexpected selling situations you notice when you keep your eyes and ears open. You'll soon see in almost every situation an opportunity for someone to sell. Not only will you be alert to the selling situation, but you'll also start to critique the selling skills used in situations that surround you on a daily basis. When you witness a good job of selling, make a note of it in your success journal. When you get sold by a master, jot down the superior job they did in selling you their offering. Make specific notes of things they did that especially impressed or influenced you.

To observe all this selling going on around you, you have to stop, listen, and take time to reflect on the situation. If you are not a party to the sale, it's of course easier to be an observer. Not being a party to the sale gives you the distance to recognize some of the familiar selling techniques being used. But that distance also enables you to observe the expressions and actions by the other party as a result of these selling methods being used. It's a great learning experience.

Sometimes you see a salesperson use a common technique with a personal twist — and you realize that the strategy you previously thought would not work for you most certainly will if you give it *your* own personal twist. Creativity is the name of the game in many selling situations. Don't let yourself become trapped into one single mode of thinking or one way of looking at things. If you can be flexible, almost anything is feasible.

And if you're one who learns by experience, isn't it better to learn from others' mistakes than from your own? Their loss becomes your gain. The experience you observe doesn't always have to be positive in order to have a positive effect on your selling career. Sometimes the negative lessons provide a stronger impact than those that look smooth and effortless.

So find a way to learn in every selling situation. When your kids try to sell you on the idea of an overnighter at a friend's home, observe their selling techniques. When your spouse sells you on a new but unnecessary gadget, pay attention and you may learn a lesson that will make you far more money than you just spent on the superfluous gadget. When your neighbors do not succeed in selling you on the idea of sharing the costs of a joint-property fence, see if you can tell where they lost you.

Create a learning experience from each selling situation you see, no matter how unorthodox it is.

Step #10: Make a commitment to master the art of selling.

Think of every technique you learn in this book as one link in the chain of your success in sales. If you have a weak chain, then you may need to review a chapter or two to build, say, your presentation or prospecting skills. If you don't go back and make the weak link stronger, your career chain will never carry the weight it needs to carry to haul you up to top-producer status.

When you find yourself in the fortunate position of top dog, champion salesperson, you'll probably get asked to teach some of what you know to others. The class you teach could be a training class for newcomers to your office. It could be a back-to-the-basics program for seasoned salespeople who have allowed their focus to blur. It could be as simple as letting your children know what gets results and what doesn't.

If you don't already know it, you'll relearn one *big* lesson every time you teach: when you teach, you learn. By teaching your techniques to others, you clarify your own skills and reinforce your knowledge of what makes an effective salesperson. Teachers are students, too. If you can remain flexible — sometimes the teacher, sometimes the student — the ability to learn in diverse situations will constantly present itself and you'll be there to learn from the experience.

If you've read all of *Selling For Dummies* and you're not quite sure what you've learned, go back and read certain sections and take notes on whatever captures your interest. By all means, pick up selling tips as you go back through the book. But also make sure that you turn this book into the reference book it's supposed to be. That way, you'll take full advantage of this book's ability to constantly remind you of its lessons on selling. And remember to use its lessons in your personal life as well as in your new selling career. More often than not, you'll get more of what you want if you practice the lessons you find in the pages of this book. Sounds good, doesn't it?

This business of getting what you want cannot be a totally selfish act, though. Your selling success increases at a significant pace when your attention to serve your clients and satisfy their needs is number one on your list. Even though you want to make more profit and more sales, remember that you're most apt to accomplish these goals only when you put your customers first.

When your clients know that you are not concerned with being the star, but that you are putting their needs before your own, they will forgive some awkwardness or lack of product knowledge. When they know your integrity and honesty, most customers go the extra mile with you to make your meetings mutually beneficial. People are the key to your sales success.

At the risk of sounding repetitious, let me say that again:

> *The key to your sales success is people.*

Treat that business resource known as the customer with much sensitivity and unflagging respect. Remember that fundamental principle—*the key to your sales success is people*—and, before you know it, all the techniques you've learned will naturally improve your ability to sell with the best of the best.

Chapter 21

Ten Steps to Professionalism

A professional is a person who has dedicated himself or herself to a career, regardless of the field. It's the opposite of an amateur. Professionals also make more money — could there be a relationship behind that fact? You bet. In selling situations, and in life, how you present yourself plays a big role in how people think of you and how much attention people are going to pay to what you say. A dedicated professional commands more respect than a casual amateur. Always.

Step #1: Start with your attitude

Are you a professional? If so, why not let everyone know it. If you're still thinking like an amateur — "no big deal," "I don't need to talk to five more people today, you handle it" — maybe that's why you're not as sucessful as you would like to be.

Step #2: Personal appearance

Are you really satisfied with your appearance? Grooming is important, good clothing is a must, and how about your health? Shape up your body, and it will shape up your attitude. Look like a professional, like you're taking what you do seriously.

How you appear to others does impact how you are treated, sad as it is to say. At the same time, don't make this mistake yourself — you never know when the bum in the T-shirt and shorts might be the biggest client or sale of your lifetime.

Step #3: Business appearance

Your customers and clients relate financial success with competence. Even banks do. You know that most banks won't lend money to people who need it but fall all over themselves to throw it at the guys who have more than they can count. So take a look at how your business presents itself to the public: Do you have an office, even a rented office as part of a suite? If you work out of your home, make arrangements to hold meetings in leased conference rooms instead of your living room. If people see your home or your car — do they communicate financial success?

Step #4. Organization

Customers relate being organized to being competent. Organization is recognized as being on time, having a neat desk, being ready with the answers, and diligent follow-up. All these things tell people that you are a person worthy of their confidence and the confidence of their friends. Saying, *Uh, I don't know where that is, I'll have to find it and call you back to give you those numbers,*wins you no points whatsoever. The impression you've just left is that you'll be counted on to lose important stuff.

Step #5. Talk like a pro

Avoid shop talk. A.k.a. jargon or slang. No, you don't sound like you know what you're talking about when you use all acronyms and strange, arcane terms — you're excluding the customer or client. Some people think that using all kinds of fancy terms means that they're experts. A real expert can explain a complex, technological process in plain English. So ask questions. Choose your words carefully. And plan your presentation from the prospect's point of view.

Step #6. Stay in tune

Traditional sales is a changing profession. You can see what has changed and use it as your cue on how to act when you are selling or persuading.

The pushy, obnoxious sterotypes are gone. The less competent are disappearing. People demand excellence and reward that excellence with referral after referral. Devote a regular part of your week to learning new skills and sharpening existing ones.

Step #7. Respect your fellow salespeople

They have the same challenges as you do. They deserve the same credit and recognition when successful, the same help and encouragement when faltering. Everyone wins when the team gets stronger.

Step #8. Remember your family and friends

They want a high-quality relationship, too. Plan time for family and social needs. This will assure you their understanding and support when business takes you away evenings and weekends.

Step #9. See the people

There are literally thousands of people in your area who need and deserve the professional services that you can provide. Make them aware of what you do. Be vocal about your abilities and qualifications. If you don't take it to them, they may not get what they really need.

Step #10. Integrity keeps you there

An opportunity to take unfair advantage of someone arises almost every day in whatever job you do. A professional knows that a dissatisfied customer today will cost him several possible transactions in the future. A professional knows how important selling with the facts is. Stretching the truth, omitting information, and avoiding present problems by stalling or blaming someone else is for the bush leaguer. Sell with the facts, and you only have to sell them once.

Chapter 22

Ten Characteristics of a Professional Persuader

In analyzing people who are most successful at persuading, convincing or selling others on their ideas, products, or services, there are ten characteristics that appear to be common among them. Read through this list of ten and see how many apply to you now. If you don't find these characteristics in your current bag of traits, consider adopting them in order to hear more *yeses* in your life.

1. You have a burning desire to prove something to someone.

You have a strong reason for wanting to succeed. My reason was to prove to myself to my parents. I quit college after 90 days knowing that formal education wasn't for me. My parents had high hopes for me and were quite disappointed, resigning themselves to accept my decision. My dad told me, "Your mother and I will always love you, even though you'll never amount to anything." That was my first motivational talk and it kindled my desire to become the best.

2. You are interested introverts, rather than interesting extroverts.

You are truly interested in other people and in making those people's lives better for knowing you. You have learned how to draw others out, making them feel important and getting to know them well enough to determine how you can help.

3. You radiate confidence and strength in your walk, talk, and overall presence.

You have good posture. You wear your clothing well. You use positive body language cues to let others read your competence level.

4. You balance ego drive and the need for success with warm and sincere empathy for the people you serve.

Your sincere interest in the happiness of the people you come in contact with creates bonds of trust and openness that allow you to serve not only your prospects well but the friends, relatives, and acquaintances that are referred to you.

5. You are highly goal-oriented.

Your goals are set and in writing. You know exactly what you're striving for and when you expect to accomplish it. Knowing how your future will look helps you keep focused on doing what is productive today.

6. You do what you plan to do in writing daily.

Having goals set allows you to plan your time most effectively to take steps toward achieving those goals. You rely on proven systems for planning your time and have learned effective time management strategies.

7. You live in the present moment and keep your enthusiasm through crises.

You know the past can't be changed and the future cannot be controlled so you live for today, doing the best you can to make each day a day of accomplishment and fulfillment.

8. You keep yourself in a positive shell and avoid jealousy, gossip, anger, or negative thinking.

You do not allow negativity to steal your energy or tempt you to stray from your chosen course.

9. You love people and use money instead of loving money and using people.

You understand the old adage that you have to spend money to make money and that persuasion is a people business. You invest wisely in things for the good of the people you serve.

10. You invest monthly in the greatest investment on earth, your mind.

Congratulations, I know you have this trait simply because you're reading this page. Set a goal to be a life-long learner. You'll never have a dull moment and you'll achieve tremendous success in whatever you set your mind to studying!

Chapter 23

Ten Advanced Closes

When you're ready to move ahead in your selling strategies, here are some additional closing stories that have proven successful for myself and others in sales.

The Wish-Ida Close

When you know what you're offering is truly good for the other party and they have agreed, but just don't seem to want to make a decision, the Wish-Ida closing story is perfect. It's lighthearted, yet makes a valid point.

We are all members of the 'Wish-Ida' club. Wish Ida bought real estate in Arizona 15 years ago. Wish Ida invested in some stock 20 years ago so I'd be rich today. Wish Ida grabbed a chance to gain an exclusive advantage and so on. Wouldn't it be great to get rid of at least one Wish Ida by saying yes to something you really want?

The Business Productivity Close

When marketing products or services to businesses, their main concern is always going to be the bottom line and whether or not it makes or saves them money. If your product does not clearly fall into one of those categories, the Business Productivity Close helps them view the decision from a different perspective — that of happier employees.

What I am offering is not just a product/service. It's a boost in employee morale. Haven't you noticed that anything new increases job interest and excitement? Excitement increases morale. Morale increases productivity and what is productivity worth?

The Best Things in Life Close

Everyone wants to have the best things in life. Everyone wants to believe that he or she has made some of the best decisions when considering major purchases or investments. This close gets the prospects' minds off the money objection and onto the enjoyment of benefits, which is what ownership is really all about.

Isn't it true that the only time you have ever really benefited from anything in your life has been when you said Yes instead of No? You said yes to your marriage. (Optional: and I can see how happy you are.) You said yes to your job, your home, your car — all the things that I'm sure you enjoy.

You see, when you say yes to me, it's not really me you are saying yes to, but all the benefits that we offer, and those are the things you really want for your family, don't you agree?

The "No" Close

When you've given your best presentation and they still say *no*, you have little to lose by saying these words and putting your shoes on their feet. *Note*: These words must be spoken with sincerity and empathy for their situation.

Mr. and Mrs. Johnson, there are many salespeople in the world and they all have opportunities they're confident are good for you. And they have persuasive reasons for you to invest with them, haven't they? You, of course, can say no to any or all of them, can't you? You see, as a professional with __________, my experience has taught me an overwhelming truth. No one can say no to me. All they can say no to is themselves and their future _______. Tell me, how can I accept this kind of no?

In fact, if you were me, would you let Mr. and Mrs. Johnson say no to anything so critical to their ___________?

The Lost Sale Close

If you've done everything and they still don't go ahead. Admit defeat. Pack up your visual aids and prepare to head for the door. Then, use the Lost Sale close like a good little Columbo fan. More often than not, it reopens conversation enough that they'll give you something to grasp onto to tell you if they might say *yes*.

Pardon me, Mr. Johnson, before I leave may I apologize for not doing my job today. You see, if I had not been inept I would have said the things necessary to convince you of the value of my product. Because I didn't, you and your company will not be enjoying the benefits of our product and service and, believe me, I am truly sorry. Mr. Johnson, I believe in my product and earn a living helping people own it. So that I don't make the same mistake again, will you please tell me what I did wrong?

The My-Dear-Old-Mother Close

I would never teach you to do anything that's untrue, so the next time you talk to your mother or grandmother or someone else's mother, ask them if they've ever been in a situation in which silence means consent. If they have, ask them to say those words to you. Now you can honestly use that line as a close. If they haven't heard of such a situation, simply ask if they believe it could happen.

This technique can be your salvation when you find yourself involved in a series of silences as you roll from close to close with the same prospect.

If you have a clever way to break tension, pressure turns into humor. Explosive laughter sometimes. Lots of people can handle pressure, but laughter will pop them wide open.

So when the pressure has been on for several seconds after your last close and it's getting heavy in the room, suddenly grin from ear to ear and say, *My dear old mother once said, 'Silence means consent.' Was she right?*

The Law of Ten Close

This close works especially well for intangibles such as financial services, insurance, or education. It's also useful for large ticket items such as real estate, stocks — items that appreciate in value. If the person is not totally a Wish-ida person, there will be something in their lives that has appreciated in value.

Mr. Johnson, I've found over the years that a good test of the value of something is to determine whether or not it will stand the test of 10-times. For example, you may have invested in a home, car, clothes, jewelry, or something that gave you great pleasure. But, after you owned it for awhile could you answer this question positively?

'Would I now be willing to pay ten times more for it than I did?' In other words, has it given you that much pleasure, increased mental attitude, or income?

If you paid for some advice that greatly improved your health, it was probably worth more than you paid for it. If you received some information that allowed you to have a life-changing experience, increase in income or self image, it was worth more than you paid for it. There are a lot of things in our lives that I think we would have paid 10 times more for considering what they've done for us.

Mr. Johnson, step with me into the future. Ten years from now, will today's investment be worth more or less to you than you'll be investing in it today?

The Buyer's Remorse Close

When people are making major decisions, you can expect them to have second thoughts about things once the decision is made. That's why so many contractual agreements for large ticket items have a 72-hour clause which allows buyers to change their minds. Champions understand this and learn how to address the issue before they leave a new client with these words:

John, Mary, I feel good about the decision you have made tonight to get involved with ______________. I can tell you're both excited and somewhat relieved.

From time to time, I have had people just like you who were so positive about the decision they had made until they shared it with a friend or relative. The well-meaning friends or relatives, not understanding all the facts and maybe even being a little envious, would discourage them from their decision for one reason or another. John, Mary, please don't let this happen to you. In fact, if you think you might change your mind, please, tell me now.

The "It's Not in the Budget" Close

Business people say *it's not in the budget* as a standard line to get rid of average salespeople. The reason is that it works with average salespeople. Professionals are businesspeople themselves and understand the value of having and managing a budget. They also know that the budget is little more than a tool and not carved in stone. If there is enough value in the product or service most companies will find a way to loosen up that budget or take steps to own it. These words will often cause the business owner to give you the real reason they aren't going ahead with your product or service so you can continue your selling cycle in the appropriate manner.

I can understand that, Jim. That's why I contacted you in the first place. I'm fully aware of the fact that every well-managed business controls the flow of its money with a carefully planned budget. The budget is a necessary tool for every company to give direction to their goals. However, the tool itself doesn't dictate how the company is run. It must be flexible. You, as the controller of that budget retain for yourself the right to flex that budget in the best interest of the company's financial present and competitive future, don't you? What we have been examining here today is a system which will allow your company an immediate and continuing competitive edge. Tell me, under these conditions, will your budget flex or will it dictate your actions?

The "Take It Away" Close

There are people who will not want to make a decision on ownership simply because they feel they can make this decision at any time. That may be the case unless you're working on a special offer or limited quantity of product. It's human nature not to want to be thought of as not good enough for something. As a child, if you knew you could play ball, but someone told you might not be good enough for the team, you all of a sudden wanted to be on the team more than ever. By subtly inferring that you'd have to see if they qualify before they could own the product anyway, some people will try awfully hard to get it. This works especially well on products which involve financing or insurance which requires they meet a certain health standard.

1. Use Similar Situation Close from Chapter 10.

   Never state that they can't do it. Be subtle.

2. Use your company or bank credit application.

   Keep saying, "Let's just jot down some of the needed details to see if it's even feasible."

   The bigger the personal ego, the greater the effectiveness of properly applied negative selling.

Appendix

Recommended Reading

These are some books that I have either read or written that I believe are useful to anyone wanting a balanced and successful life. Each area of your life affects the other. If you are physically, emotionally, or spiritually out of balance, your career and financial lives will be, too.

I've included books on selling careers, selling real estate, and sales management for anyone who wants more information on selling in the traditional sense.

Physical

Bailey, Covert. *The Fit or Fat Target Diet.* Boston, MA: Houghton Mifflin, 1984.

Diamond, Harvey. *Fit for Life.* New York: Warner Books, 1985.

McDougall, Dr. John A. *The McDougall Program.* New York: Penguin Group, 1990.

Mollen, Dr. Art. *The Mollen Method.* Emmaus, PA: Rodale Press, 1986.

Emotional

Carnegie, Dale. *How to Win Friends and Influence People.* New York: Simon & Schuster, 1936. New York: Pocket Books, 1981.

Fronk, Ron L. *Creating a Lifestyle You Can Live With.* Springdale, PA: Whitaker House, 1988.

Hopkins, Tom. *The Official Guide to Success.* Scottsdale, AZ: Tom Hopkins International, Inc., 1982. New York: Warner Books, 1983.

Mandino, Og. *The Greatest Salesman in the World.* Hollywood, FL: Frederick Fell Publishers, 1968.

Mayer, Jeffrey J. *Time Management For Dummies*, Foster City, CA: IDG Books Worldwide, 1995.

Waitley, Denis. *Seeds of Greatness.* New York: Pocket Books, 1984.

Financial

Clason, George S. *The Richest Man in Babylon.* New York: Penguin Books, 1926.

Dolan, Ken and Daria. *Straight Talk on Money.* New York: Berkeley Publishing, 1993.

———. *The $mart Money Family Financial Planner.* New York: Berkeley Publishing, 1992.

Tobias, Andrew. *The Only Investment Guide You Will Still Ever Need.* New York: Bantam Books, 1987.

Tyson, Eric. *Mutual Funds For Dummies.* Foster City, CA: IDG Books Worldwide, 1995.

———. *Personal Finance For Dummies.* Foster City, CA: IDG Books Worldwide, 1995.

Tyson, Eric and David J. Silverman. *Taxes For Dummies.* Foster City, CA: IDG Books Worldwide, 1995.

Spiritual/Relationships

The Bible.

Bright, Bill. *Promises.* San Bernardino, CA: Here's Life Publishers, Inc., 1983.

———. *Transferable Concepts for Powerful Living.* San Bernardino, CA: Here's Life Publishers, Inc., 1985.

Dobson, James C. *Love for a Lifetime.* Portland, OR: Multonomah Press, 1987.

McDowell, Josh. *More Than a Carpenter.* Wheaton, IL: Tyndale House Publishers, 1982.

Smith, Chuck. *Effective Prayer Life.* Costa Mesa, CA: The Word for Today Publishers, 1980.

Selling Career, General

Hopkins, Tom. *How to Master the Art of Selling.* Scottsdale, AZ: Tom Hopkins International, Inc., 1980. New York: Warner Books, 1982.

———. *Low Profile Selling.* Scottsdale, Tom Hopkins International, Inc., 1994.

———. *Tom Hopkins' Guide To Greatness in Sales.* Scottsdale, AZ: Tom Hopkins International, Inc. 1993. New York: Warner Books, 1993.

McKay, Harvey. *Swim with the Sharks.* New York: Wm. Morrow & Co., Inc., 1988.

Mortell, Arthur. *World Class Selling.* Chicago, IL: Dearborn Financial Publishing, Inc., 1991.

Rohn, Jim. *Seven Strategies for Wealth and Happiness.* Rocklin, CA: Prima Publishing & Communications, 1986.

Smith, Homer B. *Selling Through Negotiation.* New York: American Management Assn., 1988.

Walther, George R. *Power Talking.* New York: G.P. Putnam and Sons, 1991.

Ziglar, Zig. *Secrets of Closing the Sale.* Old Tappan, NJ: Fleming H. Revell Company, 1984.

———. *See You at the Top.* Dallas, TX: We Believe, Inc., 1975.

Selling Career, Real Estate

Hopkins, Tom. *How to Master the Art of Listing Real Estate.* Scottsdale, AZ: Tom Hopkins International, Inc., 1983.

———. *How to Master the Art of Selling Real Estate.* Scottsdale, AZ: Tom Hopkins International, Inc., 1986.

Kennedy, Danielle. *How to List and Sell Real Estate in the 90s.* Englewood Cliffs, New Jersey: Prentice Hall, 1990.

Sales Management

Blanchard, Kenneth and Spencer Johnson. *One Minute Manager.* New York: Berkeley Publishing, 1985.

Fenton, John. *The A to Z of Sales Management.* New York: AMACOM, 1981.

Stumm, David Arthur. *The New Sales Manager's Survival Guide.* New York: AMACOM, 1985.

Wickman, Floyd. *Successful Strategies for Sales Managers.* High Point, NC: Executive Press, 1987.

Index

A

• B •

• C •

• D •

• E •

• F •

• K •

• L •

• M •

• Q •

• R •

• T •

• W •

• Y •

12/20/94

The fun & easy way to learn about computers and more!

SUPER STAR

Windows 3.1 For Dummies,™ 2nd Edition
by Andy Rathbone

ISBN: 1-56884-182-5
$16.95 USA/$22.95 Canada

SUPER STAR

MORE Windows For Dummies™
by Andy Rathbone

ISBN: 1-56884-048-9
$19.95 USA/$26.95 Canada

SUPER STAR

DOS For Dummies,® 2nd Edition
by Dan Gookin

ISBN: 1-878058-75-4
$16.95 USA/$21.95 Canada

The Internet For Dummies™ 2nd Edition
by John R. Levine & Carol Baroudi

ISBN: 1-56884-222-8
$19.99 USA/$26.99 Canada

Personal Finance For Dummies™
by Eric Tyson

ISBN: 1-56884-150-7
$16.95 USA/$21.95 Canada

PCs For Dummies,™ 2nd Edition
by Dan Gookin & Andy Rathbone

ISBN: 1-56884-078-0
$16.95 USA/$21.95 Canada

SUPER STAR

Macs For Dummies,® 2nd Edition
by David Pogue

ISBN: 1-56884-051-9
$19.95 USA/$26.95 Canada

Here's a complete listing of IDG's *...For Dummies* Titles

Title	Author	ISBN	Price
DATABASE			
Access 2 For Dummies™	by Scott Palmer	1-56884-090-X	$19.95 USA/$26.95 Canada
Access Programming For Dummies™	by Rob Krumm	1-56884-091-8	$19.95 USA/$26.95 Canada
Approach 3 For Windows For Dummies™	by Doug Lowe	1-56884-233-3	$19.99 USA/$26.99 Canada
dBASE For DOS For Dummies™	by Scott Palmer & Michael Stabler	1-56884-188-4	$19.95 USA/$26.95 Canada
dBASE For Windows For Dummies™	by Scott Palmer	1-56884-179-5	$19.95 USA/$26.95 Canada
dBASE 5 For Windows Programming For Dummies™	by Ted Coombs & Jason Coombs	1-56884-215-5	$19.99 USA/$26.99 Canada
FoxPro 2.6 For Windows For Dummies™	by John Kaufeld	1-56884-187-6	$19.95 USA/$26.95 Canada
Paradox 5 For Windows For Dummies™	by John Kaufeld	1-56884-185-X	$19.95 USA/$26.95 Canada
DESKTOP PUBLISHING / ILLUSTRATION / GRAPHICS			
CorelDRAW! 5 For Dummies™	by Deke McClelland	1-56884-157-4	$19.95 USA/$26.95 Canada
CorelDRAW! For Dummies™	by Deke McClelland	1-56884-042-X	$19.95 USA/$26.95 Canada
Harvard Graphics 2 For Windows For Dummies™	by Roger C. Parker	1-56884-092-6	$19.95 USA/$26.95 Canada
PageMaker 5 For Macs For Dummies™	by Galen Gruman	1-56884-178-7	$19.95 USA/$26.95 Canada
PageMaker 5 For Windows For Dummies™	by Deke McClelland & Galen Gruman	1-56884-160-4	$19.95 USA/$26.95 Canada
QuarkXPress 3.3 For Dummies™	by Galen Gruman & Barbara Assadi	1-56884-217-1	$19.99 USA/$26.99 Canada
FINANCE / PERSONAL FINANCE / TEST TAKING REFERENCE			
QuickBooks 3 For Dummies™	by Stephen L. Nelson	1-56884-227-9	$19.99 USA/$26.99 Canada
Quicken 8 For DOS For Dummies™, 2nd Edition	by Stephen L. Nelson	1-56884-210-4	$19.95 USA/$26.95 Canada
Quicken 5 For Macs For Dummies™	by Stephen L. Nelson	1-56884-211-2	$19.95 USA/$26.95 Canada
Quicken 4 For Windows For Dummies™, 2nd Edition	by Stephen L. Nelson	1-56884-209-0	$19.95 USA/$26.95 Canada
The SAT I For Dummies™	by Suzee Vlk	1-56884-213-9	$14.99 USA/$20.99 Canada
GROUPWARE / INTEGRATED			
Lotus Notes 3/3.1 For Dummies™	by Paul Freeland & Stephen Londergan	1-56884-212-0	$19.95 USA/$26.95 Canada
Microsoft Office 4 For Windows For Dummies™	by Roger C. Parker	1-56884-183-3	$19.95 USA/$26.95 Canada
Microsoft Works 3 For Windows For Dummies™	by David C. Kay	1-56884-214-7	$19.99 USA/$26.99 Canada

FOR MORE INFORMATION OR TO ORDER, PLEASE CALL ▸ 800. 762. 2974

For volume discounts & special orders please call Tony Real, Special Sales, at 415. 655. 3048

DUMMIES PRESS

Title	Author	ISBN	Price
INTERNET / COMMUNICATIONS / NETWORKING			12/20/94
CompuServe For Dummies™	by Wallace Wang	1-56884-181-7	$19.95 USA/$26.95 Canada
Modems For Dummies™, 2nd Edition	by Tina Rathbone	1-56884-223-6	$19.99 USA/$26.99 Canada
Modems For Dummies™	by Tina Rathbone	1-56884-001-2	$19.95 USA/$26.95 Canada
MORE Internet For Dummies™	by John R. Levine & Margaret Levine Young	1-56884-164-7	$19.95 USA/$26.95 Canada
NetWare For Dummies™	by Ed Tittel & Deni Connor	1-56884-003-9	$19.95 USA/$26.95 Canada
Networking For Dummies™	by Doug Lowe	1-56884-079-9	$19.95 USA/$26.95 Canada
ProComm Plus 2 For Windows For Dummies™	by Wallace Wang	1-56884-219-8	$19.99 USA/$26.99 Canada
The Internet For Dummies™, 2nd Edition	by John R. Levine & Carol Baroudi	1-56884-222-8	$19.99 USA/$26.99 Canada
The Internet For Macs For Dummies™	by Charles Seiter	1-56884-184-1	$19.95 USA/$26.95 Canada
MACINTOSH			
Macs For Dummies®	by David Pogue	1-56884-173-6	$19.95 USA/$26.95 Canada
Macintosh System 7.5 For Dummies™	by Bob LeVitus	1-56884-197-3	$19.95 USA/$26.95 Canada
MORE Macs For Dummies™	by David Pogue	1-56884-087-X	$19.95 USA/$26.95 Canada
PageMaker 5 For Macs For Dummies™	by Galen Gruman	1-56884-178-7	$19.95 USA/$26.95 Canada
QuarkXPress 3.3 For Dummies™	by Galen Gruman & Barbara Assadi	1-56884-217-1	$19.99 USA/$26.99 Canada
Upgrading and Fixing Macs For Dummies™	by Kearney Rietmann & Frank Higgins	1-56884-189-2	$19.95 USA/$26.95 Canada
MULTIMEDIA			
Multimedia & CD-ROMs For Dummies™, Interactive Multimedia Value Pack	by Andy Rathbone	1-56884-225-2	$29.95 USA/$39.95 Canada
Multimedia & CD-ROMs For Dummies™	by Andy Rathbone	1-56884-089-6	$19.95 USA/$26.95 Canada
OPERATING SYSTEMS / DOS			
MORE DOS For Dummies™	by Dan Gookin	1-56884-046-2	$19.95 USA/$26.95 Canada
S.O.S. For DOS™	by Katherine Murray	1-56884-043-8	$12.95 USA/$16.95 Canada
OS/2 For Dummies™	by Andy Rathbone	1-878058-76-2	$19.95 USA/$26.95 Canada
UNIX			
UNIX For Dummies™	by John R. Levine & Margaret Levine Young	1-878058-58-4	$19.95 USA/$26.95 Canada
WINDOWS			
S.O.S. For Windows™	by Katherine Murray	1-56884-045-4	$12.95 USA/$16.95 Canada
MORE Windows 3.1 For Dummies™, 3rd Edition	by Andy Rathbone	1-56884-240-6	$19.99 USA/$26.99 Canada
PCs / HARDWARE			
Illustrated Computer Dictionary For Dummies™	by Dan Gookin, Wally Wang, & Chris Van Buren	1-56884-004-7	$12.95 USA/$16.95 Canada
Upgrading and Fixing PCs For Dummies™	by Andy Rathbone	1-56884-002-0	$19.95 USA/$26.95 Canada
PRESENTATION / AUTOCAD			
AutoCAD For Dummies™	by Bud Smith	1-56884-191-4	$19.95 USA/$26.95 Canada
PowerPoint 4 For Windows For Dummies™	by Doug Lowe	1-56884-161-2	$16.95 USA/$22.95 Canada
PROGRAMMING			
Borland C++ For Dummies™	by Michael Hyman	1-56884-162-0	$19.95 USA/$26.95 Canada
"Borland's New Language Product" For Dummies™	by Neil Rubenking	1-56884-200-7	$19.95 USA/$26.95 Canada
C For Dummies™	by Dan Gookin	1-878058-78-9	$19.95 USA/$26.95 Canada
C++ For Dummies™	by Stephen R. Davis	1-56884-163-9	$19.95 USA/$26.95 Canada
Mac Programming For Dummies™	by Dan Parks Sydow	1-56884-173-6	$19.95 USA/$26.95 Canada
QBasic Programming For Dummies™	by Douglas Hergert	1-56884-093-4	$19.95 USA/$26.95 Canada
Visual Basic "X" For Dummies™, 2nd Edition	by Wallace Wang	1-56884-230-9	$19.99 USA/$26.99 Canada
Visual Basic 3 For Dummies™	by Wallace Wang	1-56884-076-4	$19.95 USA/$26.95 Canada
SPREADSHEET			
1-2-3 For Dummies™	by Greg Harvey	1-878058-60-6	$16.95 USA/$21.95 Canada
1-2-3 For Windows 5 For Dummies™, 2nd Edition	by John Walkenbach	1-56884-216-3	$16.95 USA/$21.95 Canada
1-2-3 For Windows For Dummies™	by John Walkenbach	1-56884-052-7	$16.95 USA/$21.95 Canada
Excel 5 For Macs For Dummies™	by Greg Harvey	1-56884-186-8	$19.95 USA/$26.95 Canada
Excel For Dummies™, 2nd Edition	by Greg Harvey	1-56884-050-0	$16.95 USA/$21.95 Canada
MORE Excel 5 For Windows For Dummies™	by Greg Harvey	1-56884-207-4	$19.95 USA/$26.95 Canada
Quattro Pro 6 For Windows For Dummies™	by John Walkenbach	1-56884-174-4	$19.95 USA/$26.95 Canada
Quattro Pro For DOS For Dummies™	by John Walkenbach	1-56884-023-3	$16.95 USA/$21.95 Canada
UTILITIES / VCRs & CAMCORDERS			
Norton Utilities 8 For Dummies™	by Beth Slick	1-56884-166-3	$19.95 USA/$26.95 Canada
VCRs & Camcorders For Dummies™	by Andy Rathbone & Gordon McComb	1-56884-229-5	$14.99 USA/$20.99 Canada
WORD PROCESSING			
Ami Pro For Dummies™	by Jim Meade	1-56884-049-7	$19.95 USA/$26.95 Canada
MORE Word For Windows 6 For Dummies™	by Doug Lowe	1-56884-165-5	$19.95 USA/$26.95 Canada
MORE WordPerfect 6 For Windows For Dummies™	by Margaret Levine Young & David C. Kay	1-56884-206-6	$19.95 USA/$26.95 Canada
MORE WordPerfect 6 For DOS For Dummies™	by Wallace Wang, edited by Dan Gookin	1-56884-047-0	$19.95 USA/$26.95 Canada
S.O.S. For WordPerfect™	by Katherine Murray	1-56884-053-5	$12.95 USA/$16.95 Canada
Word 6 For Macs For Dummies™	by Dan Gookin	1-56884-190-6	$19.95 USA/$26.95 Canada
Word For Windows 6 For Dummies™	by Dan Gookin	1-56884-075-6	$16.95 USA/$21.95 Canada
Word For Windows For Dummies™	by Dan Gookin	1-878058-86-X	$16.95 USA/$21.95 Canada
WordPerfect 6 For Dummies™	by Dan Gookin	1-878058-77-0	$16.95 USA/$21.95 Canada
WordPerfect For Dummies™	by Dan Gookin	1-878058-52-5	$16.95 USA/$21.95 Canada
WordPerfect For Windows For Dummies™	by Margaret Levine Young & David C. Kay	1-56884-032-2	$16.95 USA/$21.95 Canada

1/26/95

Fun, Fast, & Cheap!

CorelDRAW! 5 For Dummies™ Quick Reference
by Raymond E. Werner

ISBN: 1-56884-952-4
$9.99 USA/$12.99 Canada

Windows "X" For Dummies™ Quick Reference, 3rd Edition
by Greg Harvey

ISBN: 1-56884-964-8
$9.99 USA/$12.99 Canada

Word For Windows 6 For Dummies™ Quick Reference
by George Lynch

ISBN: 1-56884-095-0
$8.95 USA/$12.95 Canada

WordPerfect For DOS For Dummies™ Quick Reference
by Greg Harvey

ISBN: 1-56884-009-8
$8.95 USA/$11.95 Canada

Title	Author	ISBN	Price
DATABASE			
Access 2 For Dummies™ Quick Reference	by Stuart A. Stuple	1-56884-167-1	$8.95 USA/$11.95 Canada
dBASE 5 For DOS For Dummies™ Quick Reference	by Barry Sosinsky	1-56884-954-0	$9.99 USA/$12.99 Canada
dBASE 5 For Windows For Dummies™ Quick Reference	by Stuart J. Stuple	1-56884-953-2	$9.99 USA/$12.99 Canada
Paradox 5 For Windows For Dummies™ Quick Reference	by Scott Palmer	1-56884-960-5	$9.99 USA/$12.99 Canada
DESKTOP PUBLISHING / ILLUSTRATION/GRAPHICS			
Harvard Graphics 3 For Windows For Dummies™ Quick Reference	by Raymond E. Werner	1-56884-962-1	$9.99 USA/$12.99 Canada
FINANCE / PERSONAL FINANCE			
Quicken 4 For Windows For Dummies™ Quick Reference	by Stephen L. Nelson	1-56884-950-8	$9.95 USA/$12.95 Canada
GROUPWARE / INTEGRATED			
Microsoft Office 4 For Windows For Dummies™ Quick Reference	by Doug Lowe	1-56884-958-3	$9.99 USA/$12.99 Canada
Microsoft Works For Windows 3 For Dummies™ Quick Reference	by Michael Partington	1-56884-959-1	$9.99 USA/$12.99 Canada
INTERNET / COMMUNICATIONS / NETWORKING			
The Internet For Dummies™ Quick Reference	by John R. Levine	1-56884-168-X	$8.95 USA/$11.95 Canada
MACINTOSH			
Macintosh System 7.5 For Dummies™ Quick Reference	by Stuart J. Stuple	1-56884-956-7	$9.99 USA/$12.99 Canada
OPERATING SYSTEMS / DOS			
DOS For Dummies® Quick Reference	by Greg Harvey	1-56884-007-1	$8.95 USA/$11.95 Canada
UNIX			
UNIX For Dummies™ Quick Reference	by Margaret Levine Young & John R. Levine	1-56884-094-2	$8.95 USA/$11.95 Canada
WINDOWS			
Windows 3.1 For Dummies™ Quick Reference, 2nd Edition	by Greg Harvey	1-56884-951-6	$8.95 USA/$11.95 Canada
PRESENTATION / AUTOCAD			
AutoCAD For Dummies™ Quick Reference	by Ellen Finkelstein	1-56884-198-1	$9.95 USA/$12.95 Canada
SPREADSHEET			
1-2-3 For Dummies™ Quick Reference	by John Walkenbach	1-56884-027-6	$8.95 USA/$11.95 Canada
1-2-3 For Windows 5 For Dummies™ Quick Reference	by John Walkenbach	1-56884-957-5	$9.95 USA/$12.95 Canada
Excel For Windows For Dummies™ Quick Reference, 2nd Edition	by John Walkenbach	1-56884-096-9	$8.95 USA/$11.95 Canada
Quattro Pro 6 For Windows For Dummies™ Quick Reference	by Stuart A. Stuple	1-56884-172-8	$9.95 USA/$12.95 Canada
WORD PROCESSING			
Word For Windows 6 For Dummies™ Quick Reference	by George Lynch	1-56884-095-0	$8.95 USA/$11.95 Canada
WordPerfect For Windows For Dummies™ Quick Reference	by Greg Harvey	1-56884-039-X	$8.95 USA/$11.95 Canada

FOR MORE INFORMATION OR TO ORDER, PLEASE CALL ▸ 800. 762. 2974

For volume discounts & special orders please call Tony Real, Special Sales, at 415. 655. 3048

12/20/94

Windows 3.1 SECRETS™
by Brian Livingston

ISBN: 1-878058-43-6
$39.95 USA/$52.95 Canada

Includes Software.

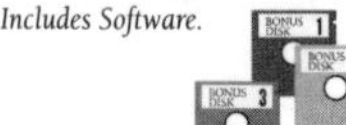

MORE Windows 3.1 SECRETS™
by Brian Livingston

ISBN: 1-56884-019-5
$39.95 USA/$52.95 Canada

Includes Software.

Windows GIZMOS™
by Brian Livingston & Margie Livingston

ISBN: 1-878058-66-5
$39.95 USA/$52.95 Canada

Includes Software.

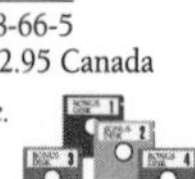

Windows 3.1 Connectivity SECRETS™
by Runnoe Connally, David Rorabaugh, & Sheldon Hall

ISBN: 1-56884-030-6
$49.95 USA/$64.95 Canada

Includes Software.

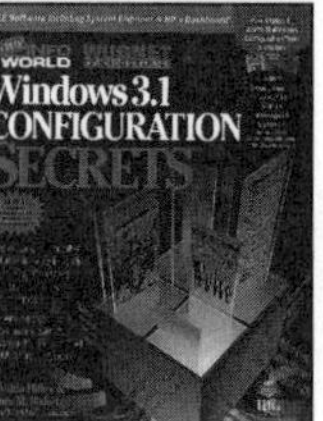

Windows 3.1 Configuration SECRETS™
by Valda Hilley & James Blakely

ISBN: 1-56884-026-8
$49.95 USA/$64.95 Canada

Includes Software.

Internet SECRETS™
by John R. Levine & Carol Baroudi

ISBN: 1-56884-452-2
$39.99 USA/$54.99 Canada

Includes Software.
Available: January 1995

Internet GIZMOS™ For Windows
by Joel Diamond, Howard Sobel, & Valda Hilley

ISBN: 1-56884-451-4
$39.99 USA/$54.99 Canada

Includes Software.
Available: December 1994

Network Security SECRETS™
by David Stang & Sylvia Moon

ISBN: 1-56884-021-7
Int'l. ISBN: 1-56884-151-5
$49.95 USA/$64.95 Canada

Includes Software.

PC SECRETS™
by Caroline M. Halliday

ISBN: 1-878058-49-5
$39.95 USA/$52.95 Canada

Includes Software.

WordPerfect 6 SECRETS™
by Roger C. Parker & David A. Holzgang

ISBN: 1-56884-040-3
$39.95 USA/$52.95 Canada

Includes Software.

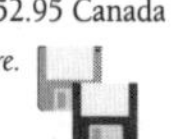

DOS 6 SECRETS™
by Robert D. Ainsbury

ISBN: 1-878058-70-3
$39.95 USA/$52.95 Canada

Includes Software.

Paradox 4 Power Programming SECRETS,™ 2nd Edition
by Gregory B. Salcedo & Martin W. Rudy

ISBN: 1-878058-54-1
$44.95 USA/$59.95 Canada

Includes Software.

Paradox For Windows "X" Power Programming SECRETS™
by Gregory B. Salcedo & Martin W. Rudy

ISBN: 1-56884-085-3
$44.95 USA/$59.95 Canada

Includes Software.

IX
FINALIST
Ninth Annual Computer Press Awards 1993

Hard Disk SECRETS™
by John M. Goodman, Ph.D.

ISBN: 1-878058-64-9
$39.95 USA/$52.95 Canada

Includes Software.

WordPerfect 6 For Windows Tips & Techniques Revealed
by David A. Holzgang & Roger C. Parker

ISBN: 1-56884-202-3
$39.95 USA/$52.95 Canada

Includes Software.

Excel 5 For Windows Power Programming Techniques
by John Walkenbach

ISBN: 1-56884-303-8
$39.95 USA/$52.95 Canada

Includes Software.
Available: November 1994

FOR MORE INFORMATION OR TO ORDER, PLEASE CALL 800 762 2974

For volume discounts & special orders please call Tony Real, Special Sales, at 415. 655. 3048

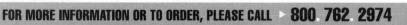

12/20/94

MACWORLD BOOKS

12/20/94

"An essential guide for anyone managing Mac networks."

Reese Jones, CEO, Farallon Computing, on Macworld Networking Handbook

Demystify the Mac!

Macworld books are built like your Macintosh – Powerful, Easy, Fun, and at a Great Value!

"I sell Macs and will recommend this book to my customers. Best computer book I have ever owned."

John Schultz, McLean, VA, on Macworld Macintosh SECRETS

Macworld System 7.5 Bible, 3rd Edition
by Lon Poole
ISBN: 1-56884-098-5
$29.95 USA/$39.95 Canada

Macworld Mac & Power Mac SECRETS,™ 2nd Edition
by David Pogue & Joseph Schorr
ISBN: 1-56884-175-2
$39.95 USA/$54.95 Canada
Includes 3 disks chock full of software.

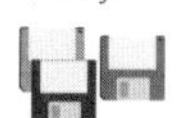

Macworld Complete Mac Handbook + Interactive CD, 3rd Edition
by Jim Heid
ISBN: 1-56884-192-2
$39.95 USA/$54.95 Canada
Includes an interactive CD-ROM.

Macworld Ultimate Mac CD-ROM
by Jim Heid
ISBN: 1-56884-477-8
$19.99 USA/$26.99 Canada
CD-ROM includes version 2.0 of QuickTime, and over 65 MB of the best shareware, freeware, fonts, sounds, and more!

Macworld Networking Bible, 2nd Edition
by Dave Kosiur & Joel M. Snyder
ISBN: 1-56884-194-9
$29.95 USA/$39.95 Canada

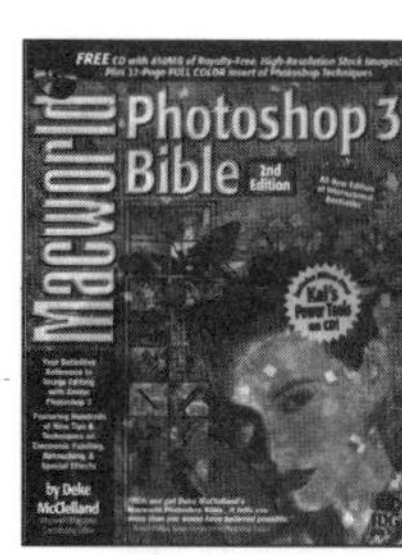

Macworld Photoshop 3 Bible, 2nd Edition
by Deke McClelland
ISBN: 1-56884-158-2
$39.95 USA/$54.95 Canada
Includes stunning CD-ROM with add-ons, digitized photos, new filters from Kai's Power Tools, and more.

Macworld Photoshop 2.5 Bible
by Deke McClelland
ISBN: 1-56884-022-5
$29.95 USA/$39.95 Canada

Macworld FreeHand 4 Bible
by Deke McClelland
ISBN: 1-56884-170-1
$29.95 USA/$39.95 Canada

Macworld Illustrator 5.0/5.5 Bible
by Ted Alspach
ISBN: 1-56884-097-7
$39.95 USA/$54.95 Canada
Includes CD-ROM with QuickTime tutorials.

FOR MORE INFORMATION OR TO ORDER, PLEASE CALL ▸ 800. 762. 2974

For volume discounts & special orders please call Tony Real, Special Sales, at 415. 655. 3048

MACWORLD BOOKS

12/20/94

"*Macworld Complete Mac Handbook Plus CD* covered everything I could think of and more!"

Peter Tsakiris, New York, NY

"Thanks for the best computer book I've ever read — *Photoshop 2.5 Bible*. Best $30 I ever spent. I *love* the detailed index...Yours blows them all out of the water. This is a great book. We must enlighten the masses!"

Kevin Lisankie, Chicago, Illinois

"*Macworld Guide to ClarisWorks 2* is the easiest computer book to read that I have ever found!"

Steven Hanson, Lutz, FL

Macworld QuarkXPress 3.2/3.3 Bible
by Barbara Assadi & Galen Gruman

ISBN: 1-878058-85-1
$39.95 USA/$52.95 Canada

Includes disk with QuarkXPress XTensions and scripts.

Macworld PageMaker 5 Bible
by Craig Danuloff

ISBN: 1-878058-84-3
$39.95 USA/$52.95 Canada

Includes 2 disks with Pagemaker utilities, clip art, and more.

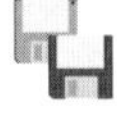

Macworld FileMaker Pro 2.0/2.1 Bible
by Steven A. Schwartz

ISBN: 1-56884-201-5
$34.95 USA/$46.95 Canada

Includes disk with ready-to-run databases.

Macworld Word 6 Companion, 2nd Edition
by Jim Heid

ISBN: 1-56884-082-9
$24.95 USA/$34.95 Canada

Macworld Guide To Microsoft Word 5/5.1
by Jim Heid

ISBN: 1-878058-39-8
$22.95 USA/$29.95 Canada

Macworld ClarisWorks 2.0/2.1 Companion, 2nd Edition
by Steven A. Schwartz

ISBN: 1-56884-180-9
$24.95 USA/$34.95 Canada

Macworld Guide To Microsoft Works 3
by Barrie Sosinsky

ISBN: 1-878058-42-8
$22.95 USA/$29.95 Canada

Macworld Excel 5 Companion, 2nd Edition
by Chris Van Buren & David Maguiness

ISBN: 1-56884-081-0
$24.95 USA/$34.95 Canada

Macworld Guide To Microsoft Excel 4
by David Maguiness

ISBN: 1-878058-40-1
$22.95 USA/$29.95 Canada

FOR MORE INFORMATION OR TO ORDER, PLEASE CALL ▸ 800. 762. 2974

For volume discounts & special orders please call Tony Real, Special Sales, at 415. 655. 3048

12/20/94

Type & Learn Windows Programming USING WinScope™
by Tom Swan

ISBN: 1-56884-071-3
$34.95 USA/$44.95 Canada
Software included.

Type & Learn C™
by Tom Swan

ISBN: 1-56884-073-X
$34.95 USA/$44.95 Canada
Software included.

Heavy Metal™ Visual C++ Programming
by Steve Holzner

ISBN: 1-56884-196-5
$39.95 USA/$54.95 Canada
Software included.

Heavy Metal™ OLE 2.0 Programming
by Steve Holzner

ISBN: 1-56884-301-1
$39.95 USA/$54.95 Canada
Software included.

The Type & Learn Programming Series is the complete starter kit for first-time programmers.

The Type & Learn Programming Series features books bundled with bestselling special edition products from leading companies like Borland International and The Periscope Company. New programmers get a cutting edge book, a proven, effective teaching method, *and* the critical software needed in order to start programming right away.

Bend the rules to your advantage with the Heavy Metal Series and take your programs from professional to legendary!

The Heavy Metal Series is the programmer's vehicle to learning precision programming techniques. These books, geared especially for the intermediate to advanced programmer, teach how to delve deep into programs to reclaim the power lost when they stick to conventional programming techniques.

Detour: The Truth About the Information Superhighway
by Michael Sullivan-Trainor

ISBN: 1-56884-307-0
$22.99 USA/$32.99 Canada

Lotus Notes Application Development Handbook
by Erica Kerwien

ISBN: 1-56884-308-9
$39.99 USA/$54.99 Canada
Covers versions 3.01 and 3.1. Software included.

The UNIX-Haters Handbook
by Simson Garfinkel, Daniel Weise & Steven Strassmann

ISBN: 1-56884-203-1
$16.95 USA/$22.95 Canada

Macworld Ultimate Mac Programming: How to Write High-Performance Code
by Dave Mark

ISBN: 1-56884-195-7
$39.95 USA/$54.95 Canada
Software included.

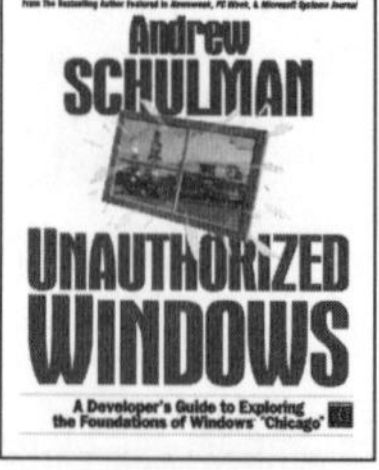

Unauthorized Windows 95: A Developer's Guide to Exploring the Foundations of Windows 95
by Andrew Schulman

ISBN: 1-56884-169-8
$29.99 USA/$39.99 Canada

Unauthorized Windows 95: Developer's Resource Kit
by Andrew Schulman

ISBN: 1-56884-305-4
$39.99 USA/$54.99 Canada
Includes Software.

FOR MORE INFORMATION OR TO ORDER, PLEASE CALL ▸ 800. 762. 2974

For volume discounts & special orders please call Tony Real, Special Sales, at 415. 655. 3048

ORDER FORM

12/20/94

Order Center: **(800) 762-2974** *(8 a.m.–6 p.m., EST, weekdays)*

Quantity	ISBN	Title	Price	Total

Shipping & Handling Charges

	Description	First book	Each additional book	Total
Domestic	Normal	$4.50	$1.50	$
	Two Day Air	$8.50	$2.50	$
	Overnight	$18.00	$3.00	$
International	Surface	$8.00	$8.00	$
	Airmail	$16.00	$16.00	$
	DHL Air	$17.00	$17.00	$

*For large quantities call for shipping & handling charges.
**Prices are subject to change without notice.

Ship to:

Name __________

Company __________

Address __________

City/State/Zip __________

Daytime Phone __________

Payment: □ Check to IDG Books (US Funds Only)
□ VISA □ MasterCard □ American Express

Card # __________ Expires __________

Signature __________

Subtotal __________

CA residents add applicable sales tax __________

IN, MA, and MD residents add 5% sales tax __________

IL residents add 6.25% sales tax __________

RI residents add 7% sales tax __________

TX residents add 8.25% sales tax __________

Shipping __________

Total __________

Please send this order form to:

IDG Books Worldwide
7260 Shadeland Station, Suite 100
Indianapolis, IN 46256

Allow up to 3 weeks for delivery.
Thank you!